Law, State and Religion in Bosnia and Herzegovina

This book explores relations between state, religion, and law in Bosnia and Herzegovina.

Historically, multi-religiousness has been a constant feature of the Bosnian polity, from its creation in the 12th century until modern times. Since the middle of the 19th century, Catholics have tended to self-identify as Croats, Orthodox Christians as Serbs, and Muslims as Bosniaks. Moreover, in a region that has undergone significant recent transformation, from the communist to the liberal political system, Bosnia and Herzegovina represents a very interesting case for the study of the relationship between state and religion. This book includes a short overview of historical aspects of these relations and a detailed analysis of the existing constitutional and legal framework on freedom of religion and relations between the state and religious communities. It assesses the actual implementation in practice, including the relevant national courts' case law. The work covers both the developments of new legal standards, while also identifying the main obstacles in their implementation.

At a time when the region is again the subject of much interest, this book will be essential reading for those working in the areas of Law and Religion, Constitutional Law and Transitional Justice.

Nedim Begović is an associate professor and Vice Dean for Quality Assurance at the Faculty of Islamic Studies, University of Sarajevo, where he teaches courses on Religion and Law, Islamic Law, and Research Methodology. As Fulbright Researcher, he spent academic year 2011/12 at the John Marshall Law School in Chicago, the United States where he conducted research on religious freedom in the case law of the European Court of Human Rights.

Emir Kovačević is a lawyer in Sarajevo, Bosnia and Herzegovina, where he has been running his law office since 1999. As a legal representative of the Islamic Community in Bosnia and Herzegovina, he actively participated in the work of the Interreligious Council of Bosnia and Herzegovina from 1999 to 2019. Since 2016, he has been a member of the OSCE/ODIHR Panel of Experts on Freedom of Religion or Belief.

ICLARS Series on Law and Religion

Series Editors:
Silvio Ferrari, University of Milan, Italy; Russell Sandberg, Cardiff University, UK; Pieter Coertzen, University of Stellenbosch, South Africa; W. Cole Durham, Jr., Brigham Young University, USA; and Tahir Mahmood, Amity International University, India

The *ICLARS Series on Law and Religion* is a new series designed to provide a forum for the rapidly expanding field of research in law and religion. The series is published in association with the International Consortium for Law and Religion Studies, an international network of scholars and experts of law and religion founded in 2007 with the aim of providing a place where information, data and opinions can easily be exchanged among members and made available to the broader scientific community. The series aims to become a primary source for students and scholars while presenting authors with a valuable means to reach a wide and growing readership.

Other titles in this series:

The Internal Law of Religions
Introduction to a Comparative Discipline
Burkhard Josef Berkmann
Translated by David E. Orton

Legal Code of Religious Minority Rights
Sources in International and European Law
Daniele Ferrari

Law, Religion, and Freedom
Conceptualizing a Common Right
Edited by W. Cole Durham, Jr., Javier Martínez-Torrón, and Donlu Thayer

Dignity and International Human Rights Law
An Introduction to the Punta del Este Declaration on Human Dignity for Everyone Everywhere
Ewelina U. Ochab and Brett Scharffs

Law, State and Religion in Bosnia and Herzegovina
Nedim Begović and Emir Kovačević

For more information about this series, please visit: www.routledge.com/ICLARS-Series-on-Law-and-Religion/book-series/ICLARS

Law, State and Religion in Bosnia and Herzegovina

Nedim Begović and Emir Kovačević

Routledge
Taylor & Francis Group
LONDON AND NEW YORK

First published 2022
by Routledge
2 Park Square, Milton Park, Abingdon, Oxon OX14 4RN

and by Routledge
605 Third Avenue, New York, NY 10158

Routledge is an imprint of the Taylor & Francis Group, an informa business

British Library Cataloguing-in-Publication Data
A catalogue record for this book is available from the British Library

Library of Congress Cataloging-in-Publication Data
Names: Begović, Nedim, author. | Kovačević, Emir, 1961– author.
Title: Law, state and religion in Bosnia and Herzegovina / Nedim Begović, Emir Kovačević.
Description: Abingdon, Oxon ; New York : Routledge, 2021. | Series: ICLARS | Includes bibliographical references and index.
Identifiers: LCCN 2021033891 (print) | LCCN 2021033892 (ebook) | ISBN 9780367218874 (hardback) | ISBN 9781032171302 (paperback) | ISBN 9780429266683 (ebook)
Subjects: LCSH: Religion and state—Bosnia and Herzegovina. | Freedom of religion—Bosnia and Herzegovina,
Classification: LCC KJK8269 . B44 2021 (print) | LCC KJK8269 (ebook) | DDC 342.4974208/52—dc23
LC record available at https://lccn.loc.gov/2021033891
LC ebook record available at https://lccn.loc.gov/2021033892

ISBN: 978-0-367-21887-4 (hbk)
ISBN: 978-1-032-17130-2 (pbk)
ISBN: 978-0-429-26668-3 (ebk)

DOI: 10.4324/9780429266683

Typeset in Galliard
by Apex CoVantage, LLC

Contents

Detailed contents

Abbreviations

AFBiH	Armed Forces of Bosnia and Herzegovina
BAM	Convertible mark
BAHS	Basic Agreement between the Holy See and Bosnia and Herzegovina
BASOC	Basic Agreement between Bosnia and Herzegovina and the Serb Orthodox Church
BDBiH	Brčko District of Bosnia and Herzegovina
BHTV-1	Public Radio and Television Service of Bosnia and Herzegovina
BiH	Bosnia and Herzegovina
CC	Catholic Church
CMBiH	Council of Ministers of Bosnia and Herzegovina
DBAIC	Draft Basic Agreement between Bosnia and Herzegovina and the Islamic Community in Bosnia and Herzegovina
ECHR	European Convention on Human Rights
ECtHR	European Court of Human Rights
EU	European Union
FBiH	Federation of Bosnia and Herzegovina
FMCS	Federal Ministry of Culture and Sports
HDZ	Croatian Democratic Union
HJPC	High Judicial and Prosecutorial Council of BiH
HRCBiH	Human Rights Chamber for Bosnia and Herzegovina
IC	Islamic Community in Bosnia and Herzegovina
ICCPR	The International Covenant on Civil and Political Rights
ICESCR	International Covenant on Economic, Social and Cultural Rights
ICTY	International Criminal Tribunal for the Former Yugoslavia
IOHR	Institution of Ombudsman for Human Rights of Bosnia and Herzegovina
IRC	Interreligious Council in Bosnia and Herzegovina
JC	Jewish community of Bosnia and Herzegovina
LFR	Law on Freedom of Religion and the Legal Status of Churches and Religious Communities in Bosnia and Herzegovina
MCA	Ministry of Civil Affairs of Bosnia and Herzegovina
MDBiH	Ministry of Defense of Bosnia and Herzegovina
MHRR	Ministry of Human Rights and Refugees of Bosnia and Herzegovina

MICT	International Residual Mechanism for Criminal Tribunals
MJ	Ministry of Justice of Bosnia and Herzegovina
MP	Member of parliament
NGO	Non-govermental organization
ODIHR	Office for Democratic Institutions and Human Rights
OSCE	Organization for Security and Cooperation in Europe
PABiH	Parliamentary Assembly of Bosnia and Herzegovina
PBiH	Presidency of Bosnia and Herzegovina
RS	Republic of Srpska
RTRS	Radio-Television of the Republic of Srpska
SDA	Party of Democratic Action
SDP	Social Democratic Party
SDS	Serb Democratic Party
SIPA	State Investigation and Protection Agency
SKJ	League of Communists of Yugoslavia
SNSD	Alliance of Independent Social Democrats
SOC	Serb Orthodox Church
SRBiH	Socialist Republic of Bosnia and Herzegovina
UN	United Nations
UNHRC	UN Human Rights Committee
U.S.	United States
VAT	Value Added Tax

Legislation

Primary legislation

Agreement Between BiH and the Holy See on the Pastoral Care of Catholic Believers, Members of the AFBiH, *Official Gazette of BiH – International Agreements*, 8/10;

Agreement on the Establishment, Organization and Manner of Functioning of the Military Muftiate in the Ministry of Defense and the Armed Forces of BiH, 11 September 2007;

Agreement on the Establishment, Organization and Manner of Functioning of the Orthodox Pastoral Care in the Ministry of Defense and the Armed Forces of BiH, 11 September 2007;

Agreement on the Establishment, Organization and Manner of Functioning of the Catholic Pastoral Care in the Ministry of Defense and the Armed Forces of BiH, 11 September 2007;

Agreement on the Pastoral Care of Catholic Believers, Members of the Armed Forces of Bosnia and Herzegovina, accessed 26 April 2021;

Basic Law on Marriage–Consolidated text, *Official Gazette of the SFRY* (Socialist Federal Republic of Yugoslavia), 12/65;

Basic Agreement between Bosnia and Herzegovina and the Serb Orthodox Church, *Official Gazette of BiH – International Agreements*, 6/08;

Basic Agreement between the Holy See and Bosnia and Herzegovina, *Official Gazette of BiH – International Agreements*, 10/07;

Bračna pravila Srpske pravoslavne crkve (BP), 2nd ed. (Beograd: The Holy Synod of Bishops, 1994);

Codex Iuris Canonici Fontium Annotatione Auctus – Zakonik kanonskog prava s izvorima (Zagreb: Glas koncila, 1996);

Constitution of Bosnia and Herzegovina, accessed 16 January 2021, www.ccbh.ba/public/down/USTAV_BOSNE_I_HERCEGOVINE_engl.pdf;

Constituton of the Federal People's Republic of Yugoslavia, accessed 20 April 2020, file:///C:/Users/Nedim/Downloads/aj_10_02_10_txt_ustav1946.pdf;

Constitution of the Federation of Bosnia and Herzegovina, *Official Gazette of FBiH*, 1/94, 13/97, 16/02, 22/02, 52/02, 63/03, 9/04, 20/04, 33/04, 71/05, 72/05, 88/08;

Constitution of the Islamic Community in Bosnia and Herzegovina, accessed 7 February 2021, www.islamskazajednica.ba/images/stories/Ustavi/Ustav_IZ-e_precisceni_tekst_2014.pdf;

Constitution of the Republic of Srpska, *Official Gazette of the RS*, 21/92, 28/94, 8/96, 13/96, 15/96, 16/96, 21/96, 21/02, 26/02, 30/02, 31/02, 69/02, 31/03, 98/03, 115/05, 117/05;

Criminal Code of the Brčko District of Bosnia and Herzegovina, *Official Gazette of the BDBiH*, 19/20;

Criminal Code of the Federation of Bosnia and Herzegovina, *Official Gazette of the FBiH*, 36/03, 21/04, 69/04, 18/05, 42/10, 42/11, 59/14, 76/14, 46/16, 75/17;

Criminal Code of the Republic of Srpska, *Official Gazette of the RS*, 64/17, 104/18, 15/21;

Declaration on the Elimination of All Forms of Intolerance and of Discrimination Based on Religion or Belief, www.ohchr.org/en/professionalinterest/pages/religionorbelief.aspx;

European Convention on Human Rights (ECHR), www.echr.coe.int/Pages/home.aspx?p=basictexts&c;

European Prison Rules, https://rm.coe.int/european-prison-rules-978-92-871–5982–3/16806ab9ae;

Family Law of the Federation of Bosnia and Herzegovina, *Official Gazette of the FBiH*, 35/05, 31/14;

Family Law of the Brčko District of Bosnia and Herzegovina, *Official Gazette of the BD BiH*, 23/2007;

Family Law of the Republic of Srpska, *Official Gazette of RS*, 54/2002, 41/2008, 63/2014, 56/2019;

Family Law of the Socialist Republic of Bosnia and Herzegovina, *Official Gazette of the SR BiH*, 21/79, 42/89;

General Framework Agreement for Peace in Bosnia and Herzegovina, www.osce.org/files/f/documents/e/0/126173.pdf;

International Covenant on Civil and Political Rights, www.ohchr.org/en/professionalinterest/pages/ccpr.aspx;

Labour Law of the Brčko District of Bosnia and Herzegovina, *Official Gazette of the BD BiH*, 34/19;

Labour Law of the Federation of Bosnia and Herzegovina, *Official Gazette of the FBiH*, 26/16, 89/18;

Labour Law of the Republic of Srpska, *Official Gazette of the RS*, 1/16;

Law on Cemeteries and Funeral Services of the Republic of Srpska, *Official Gazette of the RS*, 31/13, 6/14;

Law on Civil Service in the Federation of Bosnia and Herzegovina, *Official Gazette of the FBiH*, 29/03, 23/04, 39/04, 54/04, 67/05, 8/06, 77/06, 34/10, 45/10, 4/12, 99/15, 9/17;

Law on Civil Service in the Institutions of Bosnia and Herzegovina, *Official Gazette of BiH*, 19/02, 35/03, 4/04, 17/04, 26/04, 37/04, 48/05, 2/06, 32/07, 43/09, 10/08, 40/12;

Law on Civil Service in the Public Administration Bodies of the Brčko District of Bosnia and Herzegovina, *Official Gazette of the BDBiH*, 9/14;

Law on Civil Service in the Republic of Srpska, *Official Gazette of the RS*, 118/2008, 117/2011, 37/2012, 57/2016;

Law on Courts in the Brčko District of Bosnia and Herzegovina – consolidated text, *Official Gazette of the BDBiH*, 18/20;

Law on Courts in the Federation of Bosnia and Herzegovina, *Official Gazette of the FBiH*, 38/05, 22/06, 63/10, 72/10, 13/07, 7/13, 52/14;

Law on Courts in the Republic of Srpska, *Official Gazette of the RS*, 37/12, 14/14, 44/15, 39/16, 100/17;

Law on Freedom of Religion and the Legal Status of Churches and Religious communities, *Official Gazette of BiH*, 5/04;

Law on Churches and Religious Communities, *Official Gazette of Republic of Serbia*, 36/2006;

Law on Defense of Bosnia and Herzegovina, *Official Gazette of BiH*, 88/05;

Law on Execution of Criminal Sanctions in the Federation of Bosnia and Herzegovina, *Official Gazette of the FBiH*, 44/98, 42/99, 12/09;

Law on Execution of Criminal and Misdemeanor Sanctions of the Republic of Srpska, *Official Gazette of the RS*, 63/18;

Law on Health Care of the Republic of Srpska, *Official Gazette of the RS*, 106/09, 44/15;

Law on Health Care of the Federation of Bosnia and Herzegovina, *Official Gazette of the FBiH*, 46/10;

Law on Higher Education of the Canton Sarajevo, *Official Gazette of Canton Sarajevo*, 33/17;

Law on Holidays of the Republic of Bosnia and Herzegovina, *Official Gazette of the Republic of Bosnia and Herzegovina* 2/92, 13/94;

Law on Holidays of the Republic of Srpska, *Official Gazette of the RS*, 43/07;

Law on Labour in the Institutions of Bosnia and Herzegovina, *Official Gazette of BiH*, 26/04, 7/05, 48/05, 50/08, 60/10, 32/13, 93/17;

Law on Police and Internal Affairs, *Official Gazette of the RS*, 57/16, 110/16, 58/19, 82/19;

Law on Police Officers of Bosnia and Herzegovina, *Official Gazette of BiH*, 27/04, 63/04, 5/06, 58/06, 15/08, 50/08, 63/08, 35/09, 7/12;

Law on Police Officers of the Brčko District of Bosnia and Herzegovina, *Official Gazette of the BD BiH*, 41/07, 04/08, 36/09, 60/10, 37/14, 13/16, 14/19;

Law on Police Officers of the Federation of Bosnia and Herzegovina, *Official Gazette of the FBiH*, 27/05, 70/08;

Law on Prohibition of Discrimination, *Official Gazette of BiH*, 59/09, 66/16;

Law on Property, Inheritance and Gift Tax, *Official Gazette of Zenica-Doboj Canton*, 9/09, 13/11;

Law on Property, Inheritance and Gift Tax, *Official Gazette of Tuzla Canton*, 14/09, 3/10, 4/10, 8/14, 13/19, 8/20;

Law on Protection and Welfare of Animals of Bosnia and Herzegovina, *Official Gazette of BiH*, 25/09, 9/18;

Law on Public Order of the Republic of Srpska, *Official Gazette of the Republic of Srpska*, no. 11/15;

Law on Public Prosecutor's Offices of the Republic of Srpska, *Official Gazette of the RS*, 69/16;

Law on Rights, Obligations and Responsibilities of Patients of the Federation of Bosnia and Herzegovina, *Official Gazette of the FBiH*, 40/10;

Law on Service in the Armed Forces of Bosnia and Herzegovina, *Official Gazette of BiH*, 88/05, 53/07;

Law on the Court of Bosnia and Herzegovina, *Official Gazette of BiH*, 49/09, 74/09, 97/09;

Law on the Federal Prosecutor's Office of the Federation of Bosnia and Herzegovina, *Official Gazette of the FBiH*, 19/03;

Law on the Legal Status of Religious Communities in Croatia, *Official Gazette of Republic of Croatia*, 83/02, 73/12;

Law on the Legal Status of Religious Communities in the Socialist Republic of Bosnia and Herzegovina, *Official Gazette of the SRBiH*, 36/76;

Law on the Human Rights Ombudsman of Bosnia and Herzegovina, *Official Gazette of BiH*, 19/02, 35/04, 32/06;

Law on the Procedure for Concluding and Executing International Agreements, *Official Gazette of BiH*, 29/00;

Law on the Prosecutor's Office of Bosnia and Herzegovina – consolidated text, *Official Gazette of BiH*, 49/09;

Law on Value Added Tax of Bosnia and Herzegovina, *Official Gazette of BiH*, 9/2005, 35/2005, 100/2008, 33/2017;

Real Estate Tax Act, *Official Gazette of the RS*, 91/15;

Real Estate Sales Tax, *Official Gazette of Zenica – Doboj Canton*, 6/09, 6/13, 6/18, 12/20;

Real Estate Sales Tax, *Official Gazette of the Tuzla Canton*, 5/21 – consolidated text;

Real Estate Sales Tax and Inheritance and Gift Tax Act, *Official Gazette of the Canton Sarajevo*, 28/18;

Tax Act, *Official Gazette of the Herzegovina-Neretva Canton*, 2/09, 3/09;

Tax Act, *Official Gazette of the Herzegovina-Neretva Canton*, 2/09, 3/09;

Statute of the BD BiH – Consolidated Text, *Official Gazette of the BDBiH*, 2/10;

European Union – Treaty of Amsterdam, accessed 28 September 2021, https://europa.eu/european-union/sites/default/files/docs/body/treaty_of_amsterdam_en.pdf;

Universal Declaration on Human Rights, www.un.org/en/about-us/universal-declaration-of-human-rights.

Secondary legislation

Decision on Determining Non-working Days in the Brčko District of BiH for the Period April 2019–January 2020, no. 01–02–573/19 of 10 April 2019;

Decision on Strategic Goals of the Serb People in Bosnia and Herzegovina, *Official Gazette of the RS*, 22/93;

Rulebook on the Organization and Manner of Operation of the Religious Service in the Ministry of Defense of Bosnia and Herzegovina and in the Armed Forces of Bosnia and Herzegovina, no. 06–38–5133/07, 12 November 2007;

Rulebook on Nutrition in the Armed Forces of Bosnia and Herzegovina in Peace, no. 11-02-3-2923/15, 3 August 2015;

Report on the Work of the Parliamentary Military Commissioner of Bosnia and Herzegovina for 2013, 2 February 2014;

Rulebook on Amendments to the Rulebook on Wearing Uniforms, no. 17-07-02-1161-7/06, 30 January 2017;

Instructions on the Implementation of the Law on Freedom of Religion and the Legal Status of Churches and Religious Communities in BiH, *Official Gazette of BiH*, 28/19;

Rulebook on the Establishment and Management of Single Register of Churches and Religious Communities, Their Associations and Organizational Forms in Bosnia and Herzegovina, *Official Gazette of Bosnia and Herzegovina*, 46/04;

Rules of the Constitutional Court of Bosnia and Herzegovina, *Official Gazette of BiH*, 94/14.

Cases

Constitutional Court of Bosnia and Herzegovina

Case no. U 5/98 IV, 18–19 August, 2000
Case no. U 62/01, 5–6 April 2002
Case no. AP 913/04, 20 December 2005
Case no. U 4/04, 31 March 2006
Case no. AP 286/06, 29 September 2007
Case no. U 19/14, 24 September 2014
Case no. U 3/13, 26 November 2015
Case no. U 8/17 of 30 November 2017
Case no. AP 2190/13, 9 July 2015
Case no. AP 3947/12, 9 July 2015
Case no. AP 2575/13, 26 October 2016
Case no. AP 4583/14, 15 June 2017

Human Rights Chamber for Bosnia and Herzegovina

Islamic Community in Bosnia and Herzegovina v. the Republika Srpska, Case no. CH/96/29, 11 June 1999;
Human Rights Chamber for BiH, Case no. CH/02/9628, 9 May 2003;
Islamic Community in Bosnia and Herzegovina (Mrkonjić Grad) v. the Republika Srpska, CH/01/7701, 22 December 2003.

Institution of Ombudsman for Human Rights of Bosnia and Herzegovina

Recommendation no. Ž-BR-04–26/17, 31 May 2017;
Recommendation no. 238/18, 23 October 2018.

Lower courts of Bosnia and Herzegovina

E. P. v. the Judgement of the Cantonal Court in Bihać, no. Gž-796/00 of 5 April 2001;

Municipal Court in Livno, Case no. 68 0 P 017561 11 P, 7 December 2011;
Cantonal Court in Bihać, no. 17 0 Rs 030553 12 RSŽ, 6 February 2012;
Cantonal Court in Livno, Case no. 68 0 P 017561 12 Gž, 24 January 2013;
Supreme Court of the Federation of Bosnia and Herzegovina, Case no. 68 O P 017561 17 Rev 2, 11 July 2017;
Basic Court in Kotor Varoš, Case no. 73 0 Pr 025108 17 Pr 2, 23 November 2017;
District Court in Banja Luka, Case no. 73 0 Pr 025108 17 Pžp 2, 28 February 2018;
Municipal Court in Sarajevo, Case no. 65 0 P 733856 18 P, 9 January 2020.

European Court/Commission of Human Rights (Council of Europe)

Agga v. Greece (no. 2), no. 50776/99 and 52912/99, 17 October 2002;
Alujer Fernández and Caballero García v. Spain (dec.), no. 53072/99, ECHR 2001-VI;
Darby v. Sweden, 23 October 1990, Series A no. 187;
Eweida and Others v. the United Kingdom, nos. 48420/10 and 3 others, ECHR 2013;
Fernàndez Martínez v. Spain [GC], no. 56030/07, ECHR 2014;
Hamidović v. Bosnia and Herzegovina, no. 57792/15, 5 December 2017;
Hasan and Chaush v. Bulgaria [GC], no. 30985/96, § 78, ECHR 2000-XI;
Jehovah's Witnesses of Moscow and Others v. Russia, no. 302/02, 10 June 2010;
Kimlya and Others v. Russia, nos. 76836/01 and 32782/03, § 100, ECHR 2009;
Kokkinakis v. Greece, 25 May 1993, Series A no. 260-A;
Lautsi and Others v. Italy [GC], no. 30814/06, § 70, ECHR 2011;
Magyar Keresztény Mennonita Egyház and Others v. Hungary, no. 70945/11 and 8 others, ECHR 2014;
Masaev v. Moldova, no. 6303/05, 12 May 2009;
Metropolitan Church of Bessarabia and Others v. Moldova, no. 45701/99, ECHR 2001-XII;
Orlović and Others v. Bosnia and Herzegovina, no. 16332/18, 1 October 2019;
Otto-Preminger-Institut v. Austria, 20 September 1994, Series A no. 295-A;
Refah Partisi (the Welfare Party) and Others v. Turkey [GC], nos. 41340/98 and 3 others, ECHR 2003-II;
Roman Catholic Archdiocese of Vrhbosna v. Bosnia and Herzegovina, no. 40694/13, 5 June 2018;
Sejdić and Finci v. Bosnia and Herzegovina [GC], nos. 27996/06 and 34836/06, ECHR 2009;
Savez crkava "Riječ života" and Others v. Croatia, no. 7798/08, § 91–93, 9 December 2010;
Sindicatul "Păstorul cel Bun" v. Romania [GC], no. 2330/09, §163–165, ECHR 2013;

Supreme Holy Council of the Muslim Community v. Bulgaria, no. 39023/97, § 93–96, 16 December 2004;
Şerif v. Greece, no. 38178/97, ECHR 1999-IX;
Wasmuth v. Germany, no. 12884/03, 17 February 2011.

International Criminal Tribunal for the Former Yugoslavia

Trial Judgement Summary for Ratko Mladić, Case No. IT-09–92-T, The Hague, 22 November 2017.

International Residual Mechanism for Criminal Tribunals

Case no. MICT-13–55-A, 20 March 2019;
Case no. MICT-13–56-A, 8 June 2021;
Case no. IT-04–74-A, 29 November 2017.

International Court of Justice

Case Concerning Application of the Convention on the Prevention and Punishment of the Crime of Genocide (*Bosnia and Herzegovina v. Serbia and Montenegro*), 26 February 2007.

Introduction

The collapse of the communist system and the political changes that took place in the late 1980s and early 1990s brought about a religious resurgence and return of religion into the public sphere across the countries of Eastern Europe. These societal and political developments found their legal expression in major changes of national laws governing religion-state relations in the region.[1] These laws showed two, somewhat opposite trends. On the one hand, the adoption of liberal standards of the right to freedom of religion or belief has created an environment for the "democratization" of the religious sphere by the accession of new religious participants. On the other hand, the new legislation gave "traditional" religions a privileged status by providing them with protective mechanisms in the newly established "free market of religious ideas".[2] The latter trend led A. Sarkissian to argue that traditional or prevailing churches were in fact re-established in the Orthodox countries of the former communist bloc.[3] However, other authors have noted that the constant balancing between the demands for equality and human rights, on the one hand, and history and tradition, on the other, is in no way specific to Eastern European countries, i.e. that similar patterns are easily recognizable in Western European countries.[4]

Bosnia and Herzegovina (hereafter referred to as BiH or Bosnia) here comes as no exception to these general trends in the region. Nevertheless, the analysis of its post-communist setup of relations between the state and religion should not

1 Silvio Ferrari and W. Cole Durham, Jr., eds., *Law and Religion in Post-Communist Europe* (Leuven: Peeters, 2003), 5.

2 W. Cole Durham, Jr., Natalie J. Peterson and Elizabeth A. Sewell, "Introduction: A Comparative Analysis of Religious Associations Laws in Post-Communist Europe," in *Laws on Religion and the State in Post-Communist Europe*, eds. W. Cole Durham, Jr. and Silvio Ferrari (Leuven: Peeters, 2004), VII–XLIII.

3 Anni Sarkissian, "Religious Reestablishment in Post-Communist Polities," *Journal of Church and State* 51, no. 3 (2009): 472–501.

4 Silvio Ferrari, "Conclusion," in *Law and Religion in Post-Communist Europe*, eds. Silvio Ferrari and W. Cole Durham, Jr. (Leuven: Peeters, 2003), 421; Siniša Zrinščak, "Church, State and Society in Post-communist Europe," in *Religion and the State: A Comparative Sociology*, eds. Jack Barbalet, Adam Possamai and Bryan S. Turner (London and New York: Athem Press, 2011), 158.

DOI: 10.4324/9780429266683-1

overlook certain peculiarities of its history, demography, and the post-war constitutional restructuring. To understand the complex image of the state-religion relations in present-day BiH, it is necessary to take into account several important facts that will be discussed in more detail in the historical and sociological overview that forms part of this introduction. First, a pronounced multi-ethnic and multi-religious character distinguishes BiH from most other countries of Eastern Europe that have one prevailing confession. Second, throughout its history, a number of different systems of state-religion relations have been represented in the country, from the regime of official or state religion to the secular model, which under communist rule implied a hostile attitude of the state towards religion. Third, the transition to a democratic political system and the revitalization of religion occurred in BiH, as in the rest of the former federal Yugoslavia, in symbiosis with the reaffirmation of ethnic identity, which in the case of Bosniaks, Serbs and Croats is crucially determined by belonging to one of the three major religions, Islam, Orthodoxy, and Catholicism, respectively. Fourth, the Dayton Peace Agreement ended the devastating war of the early 1990s and established a very complex constitutional system in BiH in which, despite a single state law on religious communities, there is a noticeable asymmetry in the *de facto* position of the prevailing religion at the entity level.

In the existing scholarly literature on the state-religion systems that are in force in the post-communist countries of Eastern Europe, very little or no attention has been paid to the respective developments in BiH. The two pioneering volumes on law and religion in post-communist Europe, edited by S. Ferrari and W. Cole Durham, Jr., were prepared before the new legislation on religion was in place in BiH.[5] Even later published works on the topic did not include analyses on religion and state in post-communist and post-war BiH.[6] The same is true of volumes of wider comparative scope, such as works of W. C. Durham and B. G. Scharffs, J. Temperman, or N. Doe.[7] In fact, a brief look at the Bosnian constitutional provisions affecting religion was taken in Temperman's work, but an analysis of sub-constitutional laws and judicial doctrine was lacking.[8] Doe's comparative description of national religion laws in Europe, which includes countries in both Western and Eastern Europe, does not contain references to BiH or any other former Yugoslav republics other than Slovenia. One possible exception is the literature of authors who applied the concept of "governance of religion" as an

5 Ferrari and Durham, eds., *Law and Religion in Post-Communist Europe*; W. Cole Durham, Jr. and Silvio Ferrari, eds., *Laws on Religion and the State in Post-Communist Europe* (Leuven: Peeters, 2004).

6 See e.g. Greg Simons and David Westerlund, eds., *Religion, Politics and Nation-Building in Post-Communist Countries* (London and New York: Routledge, 2015).

7 W. Cole Durham Jr. and Brett G. Scharffs, *Law and Religion: National, International, and Comparative Perspectives* (New York: Aspen Publishers, 2010); Jeroen Temperman, *State-Religion Relationships and Human Rights Law: Towards a Right to Religiously Neutral Governance* (Leiden and Boston: Martinus Nijhoff Publishers, 2010); Norman Doe, *Law and Religion in Europe: A Comparative Introduction* (Oxford: Oxford University Press, 2011).

8 Temperman, *State-Religion Relationships and Human Rights Law*, 103–104.

analytical tool in their studies on the accommodation of Islam in post-communist countries.[9] However, these works, by focusing on Muslim communities, do not provide a complete picture of the relationships between the state and religious communities in BiH.

To fill the gap in the academic literature, this book explores the dynamics of the relationship between law, state, and religion in post-communist/post-war Bosnia in order to answer the following main questions: what are the new legal solutions that have allowed both states and religious communities to adapt to liberal democratic standards of religious freedom? Are the approaches of legislation and courts in defining the relationship between the state and religion closer to the principle of strict government neutrality or, alternatively, do they provide more room for cooperation between the state and religion? And, what are the main unresolved issues regarding the protection of religious freedoms and the consolidation of relations between the state and the main religious communities in the country?

The main focus of this book is constitutional norms on religious matters, their detailed exposition in the 2004 Law on Freedom of Religion as a special law (*lex specialis*) in this field, and the decisions of the Constitutional Court of BiH that are important for resolving dilemmas regarding the scope and limits of religious freedom and the appropriate relationship between the state and religious communities. The next layer of our analysis consists of bilateral protocols agreed between the state and religious communities, as well as relevant bylaws that further elaborate specific issues. In addition, the subject of our interest are other laws governing the exercise or limitations of religious rights in a variety of important areas, such as labour, civil service, judiciary, healthcare, taxation, marriage, and so forth, the materials of the Institution of the Human Rights Ombudsman of BiH, international reports on BiH that include sections on issues of religious freedom, and data collected from various levels of government under the laws on the right to access information of public importance. The book describes, analyses and, where necessary, evaluates domestic normative solutions in the light of international standards on religious freedom, in particular the case law of the European Court of Human Rights.

Based on this analysis, this book argues that BiH has made significant progress in the post-communist and post-war period in expanding the scope of religious freedom and advancing the institutional mechanisms for its protection. A new, robust framework for regulating freedom of religion and state-religion relations has been introduced, the backbone of which is the 2004 state law on religions. It is worth mentioning that this law, unlike the similar acts in a number of contemporary Eastern European countries, has not been amended or challenged in terms of its compatibility with constitutional norms. The law provides for a range

9 Arolda Elbasani, "Governing Islam in Plural Societies: Religious Freedom, State Neutrality and Traditional Heritage," *Journal of Balkan and Near Eastern Studies* 19, no. 1 (2017): 4–18; Ahmet Alibašić and Nedim Begović, "Reframing the Relations Between State and Religion in Post-War Bosnia: Learning to Be Free!" *Journal of Balkan and Near Eastern Studies* 19, no. 1 (2017): 19–34; Egdūnas Račius, *Islam in Post-Communist Eastern Europe: Between Churchification and Securitization* (Leiden and Boston: Brill, 2020).

of individual and collective religious rights, while also ensuring state authorities' neutrality towards the various religious communities as well as their equal treatment. However, it does not prevent state cooperation with these communities on issues of common concern that has been formalized through their bilateral agreements. Accordingly, this book further argues that BiH, after almost five decades of tight state control over religions, has opted for a "cooperationist system" (also called "hybrid") of state-religion relations which, in addition to the functional separation of state and religious authorities, recognizes the important societal role and contribution of religious communities.

However, both the principle of state neutrality and the functioning of a cooperationist system have been challenged in a variety of ways, especially at the level of practical politics. In particular, the structuring of the state into entities with ethnic/religious majorities has made it possible to *de facto* favour the dominant religious community. This trend is particularly noticeable in the Republic of Srpska, where the Serb Orthodox Church (SOC) is privileged in various matters, including state funding, presentation of church symbols and iconography in public institutions, and the inclusion of church rites in public holiday celebrations. In fact, the said practices appear to be a continuation of the factual implementation of the entity constitution's provision envisaging a cooperation between the state and the SOC "in all areas",[10] which the Constitutional Court of BiH has declared contrary to the principle of separation of state and religion. At the state level, the functioning of the cooperationist system has been challenged by the politicization of the issue of concluding a bilateral protocol between BiH and the Islamic Community (IC), as well as the weak implementation of already agreed protocols with the Catholic Church (CC) and the SOC. The purpose of these protocols is not only to strengthen religious autonomy and facilitate the cooperation of sacred and profane authorities, but also to consolidate the authority of traditional religious communities in the era of liberalization of standards of religious freedom.

It is important to note that the subject of this book has not been comprehensively treated even in the South Slavic-speaking area. Therefore, the book represents the first systematic monograph on the relationships between the state and religious communities in BiH in the period from the 1990s onwards. Still, several books, edited volumes, and journal articles deserve to mentioned because of their relevance to our research. In 2007, A. Alibašić edited the collection of papers dedicated to the role of religion in the secular state from Jewish, Christian, and Islamic perspectives with focus on the South-Eastern Europe.[11] Then, in 2011, F. Karčić gave a concise treatment of historical and contemporary aspects

10 Art. 28, para. 4, Constitution of the RS, *Official Gazette of the RS*, 21/92 – consolidated text, 28/94, 8/96, 13/96, 15/96, 16/96, 21/96, 21/02, 26/02, 30/02, 31/02, 69/02, 31/03, 98/03, 115/05, 117/05.

11 Ahmet Alibašić, ed., *Religija i sekularna država: Uloga i značaj religije u sekularnom društvu iz muslimanske, kršćanske i jevrejske perspektive sa fokusom na Jugoistočnu Evropu* [Religion and the Secular State: The Role and Significance of Religion in Secular Society from a Muslim, Christian and Jewish Perspective with a Focus on Southeast Europe] (Sarajevo: Konrad Adenauer Foundation – Representation in BiH, European Abrahamic Forum, and Interreligious Institute in BiH, 2007).

of state-religion relations in BiH in his propaedeutic work on religion and law. The following year, N. Ademović edited a volume that included articles dealing with issues of secularism, religious pluralism, religious symbols, financial relations between the state and religious communities, and religious education in public schools in BiH.[12] Eventually, in 2015, a collection of papers, edited by E. Šarčević and D. Bojić, dealt with the topics of return of religion in the public sphere and the relationships between the state and religious communities in the three countries of the region, BiH, Serbia, and Croatia, respectively, from the political, sociological, legal, and philosophical perspectives.[13] In addition, the topic of religious education in public schools in BiH has been covered to a significant extent.[14]

While a history of the state-religion relations in BiH is beyond the scope of this book, a general acquaintance with the main events in the past is crucial to understand more properly the contemporary developments.[15] Throughout its centuries of history, Bosnia has always been a religiously heterogeneous polity where the influence of the three great civilizations intertwined: the Roman Catholic, the Byzantine-Orthodox, and the Islamic.[16] The country's religious landscape which in the medieval period was composed by the Bosnian *Krstjanis'*,[17] the Catholic and the Orthodox later became even more diversified. With the Ottoman conquest in the mid-15th century, the Bosnian Church gradually disintegrated and Islam made significant gains. Soon after, groups of Sephardic Jews who were expelled from the Iberian Peninsula settled in the country. The Austro-Hungarian occupation of 1878 also brought some small groups of Protestants to the country. The following communist regime, 1945–1990, favoured the creation of a new stratum of atheists, which has apparently receded since the 1990 regime changes. Since the mid-19th century, different religious identities have

12 Nedim Ademović, ed., *Doktrinarni i praktični aspekti odnosa između države, crkava/vjerskih zajednica i pojedinca* [*Doctrinal and Practical Aspects of the Relationship between the State, Churches/Religious Communities and the Individual*] (Sarajevo: European Academy for Applied Research and Education in BiH, 2012).

13 Edin Šarčević and Drago Bojić, eds., *Sekularnost i religija: BiH i regija* [Secularity and Religion. BiH and Region] (Sarajevo: Fondacija Centar za javno pravo, 2015).

14 See e.g. Charles J. Russo, "Religion and Education in Bosnia: Integration Not Segregation?" *BYU Law Review*, no. 3 (2000): 945–966; Ahmet Alibašić, "Religious Education in Public Schools in Bosnia and Herzegovina: Towards a Model Supporting Coexistence and Mutual Understanding," accessed 3 June 2021, file:///C:/Users/Nedim/Downloads/Religious_Education_in_Bosnian_Public_Sc.pdf.; Zorica Kuburić and Christian Moe, *Religion and Pluralism in Education: Comparative Approaches in the Western Balkans* (Novi Sad: CEIR and Kotor Network, 2006).

15 This historical overview is partially based on: Alibašić and Begović, "Reframing the Relations Between State and Religion in Post-War Bosnia: Learning to Be Free!" 20–22; Nedim Begović, "Freedom of Religion or Belief: Bosnian Muslim Engagement with a Fundamental Human Right," *Context – Journal of Interdisciplinary Studies* 7, no. 1 (2020): 65–72.

16 The name "Bosnia and Herzegovina" originated from the time of the Austro-Hungarian occupation in 1878. However, even before that, the territory of Herzegovina was an integral part of the Bosnian state. See Mustafa Imamović, *Historija Bošnjaka* [History of Bosniaks] (Sarajevo: Bošnjačka zajednica kulture, 1997), 11.

17 For more details on Bosnian Church see Noel Malcolm, *Bosna: Kratka povijest* [Bosnia: A Short History] (Sarajevo: Buybook, 2011), 83–108.

tended to overlap with ethnicities – Orthodox Christians commonly self-identify as Serbs, Catholics as Croats and Muslims as Bosniaks.[18] Today's Bosnian society is characterized by a high degree of declared religiosity and trust in religious communities. According to a recent Pew Research Center survey, BiH is the 6th most religious of 34 European countries.[19] Another study found that religious communities enjoyed the greatest trust of Bosnian citizens among all civil society organizations with increasing rates from 2009 to 2017.[20]

Along with the shift of political regimes under which Bosnia has survived as a separate administrative unit for most of its history,[21] the balance of power between major religions and the ways of ordering relations between the state and religious communities changed repeatedly. During the medieval period, Bosnia was an independent or semi-independent country (1180–1463) and periods of peaceful coexistence between the various religious groups alternated with campaigns of papal inquisition aimed at purging the country of "heretics" and establish the dominance of Catholicism.[22] Under the Ottoman reign, Bosnia was integrated within a cosmopolitan empire that united very varied religious and ethnic constituents. Since Islam was the religion of the ruling dynasty, it had the greatest social and legal impact and, as such, occupied a *de facto* position of state religion. The organic unity of Islam and state under the Ottomans manifested itself, *inter alia*, in the absence of a distinct religious organization of Muslims, separated from state structures. Instead, the *ulama*, including jurisconsults (*muftis*) and judges (*qadis*), were an integral part of the Ottoman bureaucracy. In contrast, other denominations were organized into their autonomous self-governing religious communities under the Ottoman *millet* system. However, from 1856 on, a series of imperial reform decrees declared the validity of secular legal codes for all subjects, as a result of which most *millets*' autonomy was lost.[23] The *Tanzimat* reforms (1839–1856) also reduced the power of Muslim clergy and introduced a dual judicial system: one system of courts was founded on state legislation, while the other was based on religious precepts. Nevertheless, Sharia courts maintained legal authority over key personal matters of Muslim subjects.[24]

The subsequent Austro-Hungarian regime (1878–1918) signalled another important shift in religious balances within the country. Islam lost the position

18 Alibašić and Begović, "Reframing the Relations Between State and Religion in Post-War Bosnia," 20.

19 *See* Jonathan Evans and Chris Baronavski, "How Do European Countries Differ in Religious Commitment? Use Our Interactive Map to Find Out," 2018, accessed 1 May 2020, www.pewresearch.org/fact-tank/2018/12/05/how-do-european-countries-differ-in-religious-commitment/.

20 Božo Skoko and Dejan Lučka, *Povjerenje u medije i medijske slobode* [Trust in the Media and Media Freedoms] (Sarajevo: Friedrich-Ebert-Stiftung, 2017), 19–20.

21 Bosnia was an *eyalet* or *vilayet* in the Ottoman Empire, a "crown land" in the Habsburg monarchy, and a republic in the federal Yugoslavia.

22 See Malcolm, *Bosna: Kratka povijest*, 62–82.

23 The Editors of Encyclopaedia, "Millet," in *Encyclopedia Britannica*, 7 September 2010, accessed 1 June 2021, www.britannica.com/topic/millet-religious-group.

24 Alibašić and Begović, "Reframing the Relations Between State and Religion in Post-War Bosnia," 21.

of state religion, but it was recognized as one of the country's religions. This was indicated by a series of proclamations of the Austro-Hungarian authorities addressed to the "people of Bosnia and Herzegovina" and the Convention on the Regulation of the Occupation of Bosnia and Herzegovina of 1879 with guarantees of their right to manifest their religion and maintain spiritual relations with the Caliph in Istanbul.[25] Austro-Hungary was a religiously plural state, in which Catholics were nonetheless accorded informal privileges. In the new political environment, Muslims were forced to organize themselves into a religious community that was functionally separate in structure from the state, after the model the Catholic and Orthodox Churches. The Sharia courts were modernized and kept going as state bodies, while a modern school for training Sharia judges, the predecessor of the current Faculty of Islamic Studies, was established in Sarajevo.[26] After the end of the World War I, in 1918, Bosnia and Herzegovina (BiH) joined the first joint state of the Southern Slavic nations, the Kingdom of Serbs, Croats and Slovenes. It would later be renamed the Kingdom of Yugoslavia. It opted for the model of recognized religious communities, but now it was the Orthodox community that was informally privileged. Sharia courts were allowed to operate and Muslim structures preserved some of their previous institutions. Nonetheless, they strove to maintain independence, especially after the dictatorship came into power in 1929.[27] Given its short lifespan during the World War II (1941–1945), the Independent State of Croatia, which controlled the territory of BiH, did not significantly alter the balance between religious communities in the country.[28]

Major changes occurred after the end of the World War II when communist Yugoslavia was established. Similar to most other communist states, it established a regime of separation of state and religion. The communist version of a secular state distinguished itself by: (a) rapidly reducing the social and political influence of religious communities, (b) the restrictive scope of freedom to manifest religion, especially in public, (c) adopting the atheistic worldview by the Communist Party, which operated in complete symbiosis with the state apparatus, and (d) subjecting religious communities to the tight control by the state authorities. The Sharia courts were abolished in 1946, resulting in a transformation of Sharia from a system of positive law sanctioned by the state to one of religious and ethical norms adhered to by Muslims on a voluntary basis. The new atheist elite occupied the key positions in state bodies, institutions, and the state-controlled economy.[29] The autocratic rule of Josip Broz Tito and the Communist Party and the denial of the right to manifest national feelings only served to foster a degeneration of

25 Fikret Karčić, *Historija šerijatskog prava* [History of Sharia law] (Sarajevo: Fakultet islamskih nauka, 2005), 219.

26 See Fikret Karčić, *The Other European Muslims: A Bosnian Experience* (Sarajevo: Center for Advanced Studies, 2015), 153–164; Alibašić and Begović, "Reframing the Relations Between State and Religion in Post-War Bosnia," 21.

27 See Karčić, *Historija šerijatskog prava*, 229–237.

28 Alibašić and Begović, "Reframing the Relations Between State and Religion in Post-War Bosnia," 21.

29 Begović, "Freedom of Religion or Belief," 68–69.

nationalism into extremism and violence.[30] The artificial forcing of a common Yugoslav identity failed. The 1991 census showed that the population of BiH comprised 1.9 million Bosnian Muslims (43.5%), 1.4 million Serbs (31.2%), and 760,000 Croats (17.4%), so that more than 90% of the population identified with a major ethno-religious group. Only 6% saw themselves as Yugoslav.[31]

The process of democratization of the political system in the former Yugoslavia began in 1990 amid growing disagreements between republic-level leadership groups of the League of Communists of Yugoslavia (SKJ), which is what ultimately produced the final disintegration. In Bosnia and Herzegovina, the first multi-party elections were held in the autumn of 1990 and won by the new parties dominated by the interests of three major ethnic groups, namely the Party of Democratic Action (SDA), the Serb Democratic Party (SDS), and the Croat Democratic Union (HDZ). The fall of the communist system and the process of transition to a liberal democratic socio-political system were followed by violence and warfare in the first half of the 1990s. The war against BiH (1992–1995), caused by great nation-state projects of Serbia and Croatia, modified the demographic structure and created a great gap as well as mistrust among the members of the major ethnic groups in the country.[32] The first post-war census of 2013 showed a general population reduction to 3.5 million, out of which 50.7% were Muslims, 30.75% were Orthodox, and 15.19% Catholics.[33]

These processes and the involvement of the international community in the closing stages of the war and the restructuring of the state in the mid-1990s effected a redefinition of aspects of the legal system that regulates religion's standing in society and in particular the right to freedom of religion or belief and relations between state and the organized religious communities. Democratization of political and social order entailed an increase in the scope of religious freedom. This happened on a practical level even before the adoption of the new Law on Freedom of Religion and was especially evident in the return of religion to the public sphere. Confessional religious education was reintroduced into the public education system, religious programmes began to be broadcast on state radio and television, and politicians and government officials began to express their religious commitments openly.

The development of the state religion law in a democratic BiH can be divided into two stages. During the first phase, from 1990 to 2004, the 1976 communist law on religions remained formally in force, although its provisions restricting the manifestation of religion to the private sphere were *de facto* suspended.[34] Given the fact of the war, the right to freedom of religion underwent separate

30 Malcolm, *Bosna: Kratka povijest*, 16–17.

31 Agencija za statistiku Bosne i Hercegovine, "Analiza: Država Bosna i Hercegovina," [Analysis: State of Bosnia and Herzegovina] accessed 27 February 2019, www.statistika.ba/.

32 Alibašić and Begović, "Reframing the Relations Between State and Religion in Post-War Bosnia," 21.

33 Agencija za statistiku Bosne i Hercegovine, "Analiza."

34 Law on the Legal Status of Religious Communities in the Socialist Republic of Bosnia and Herzegovina, *Official Gazette of the SRBiH*, 36/76.

constitutional standardization in the Federation of Bosnia and Herzegovina (FBiH) in 1994 and the self-proclaimed Republic of Srpska (RS) in 1992.[35] Regardless of the proclaimed constitutional guarantees of religious freedom and other fundamentals rights, war atrocities and crimes against humanity, genocide, and the destruction of a large number of religious facilities were committed in the territory under the control of the Army of the RS and the Croat Defence Council.[36] Bosniaks, making up about 83% of all civilian casualties of the war, suffered the greatest losses. In total, 832 mosques, 125 Orthodox, and 65 Catholic churches were destroyed.[37] The war was brought to a close by the General Framework Agreement for Peace in Bosnia and Herzegovina, negotiated in Dayton, USA, and signed in Paris, France, on 14 December 1995. The Constitution of BiH, adopted as Annex 4 to the Dayton Agreement, included broad guarantees of the right to freedom of religion or belief, but did not deal with a model of relations between the state and religious communities.

The second stage of the development of state religion law, in which the constitutional provisions on religion were concretized, began with the adoption of the Law on Freedom of Religion and the Legal Status of Churches and Religious Communities in 2004.[38] Through their representatives in the Interreligious Council in Bosnia and Herzegovina (IRCBiH) and the Board of Legal Experts, the four traditional religious communities played an active role in drafting this law. Cole Durham, the U.S. expert on freedom of religion, also provided advice in the law-making process. The Law regulates major issues related to the standing of religion in society, including freedom of religion and religious practice, relations between the state and religion, and the legal status and the founding of churches and religious communities (hereafter in this book both are commonly referred to

35 Karčić, *Religija i pravo: Kratak uvod*, 52 58.

36 The International Criminal Tribunal for the Former Yugoslavia (ICTY) has convicted six prominent leaders of the self-proclaimed "Croat Republic of Herceg-Bosna" of committing a joint criminal enterprise aimed at creating an ethnically pure Croat entity in BiH and annexing it to the Republic of Croatia. See International Tribunal for the Prosecution of Persons Responsible for Serious Violations of International Humanitarian Law Committed in the Territory of the Former Yugoslavia since 1991, Case no. IT-04–74-A, 29 November 2017. Radovan Karadžić and Ratko Mladić, two top wartime Bosnian Serb political and military leaders, were sentenced by the International Residual Mechanism for Criminal Tribunals (IRMCT) to life in prison for genocide, crimes against humanity, and violation of the laws or customs of war. See International Residual Mechanism for Criminal Tribunals, Case no. MICT-13–55-A, Judgement of 20 March 2019, accessed 23 June 2021, www.irmct.org/sites/default/files/casedocuments/mict-13-55/appeals-chamber-judgements/en/190320-judgement-karadzic-13-55.pdf; International Residual Mechanism for Criminal Tribunals, Case no. MICT-13–56-A, Judgement of 8 June 2021, accessed 23 June 2021, www.irmct.org/sites/default/files/case_documents/210608-appeal-judgement-JUD285R0000638396-mladic-13-56-en.pdf.

37 A. Alibašić, "History of Inter-Religious Dialogue in Bosnia and Herzegovina: From Force-Feeding to Sustainability?" *Interdisciplinary Journal for Religion and Transformation in Contemporary Society* 6, no. 2 (2020): 343–364.

38 Law on Freedom of Religion and the Legal Status of Churches and Religious Communities, *Official Gazette of BiH*, 5/04.

as religious communities). Thanks to the general change of the political climate and active involvement of prominent religious communities in BiH, notable change has been achieved regarding the paradigm for religion's place in society with the creation of the new state religion law. It is no longer just a "private matter" (*res privata*) practiced in the intimacy of the home or within mosques and churches – the dominant conception of the communist era. The 2004 law emphasizes the right of believers and their communities to proclaim religious principles and values publicly.

Against this theoretical and historical background, this book seeks to explore the contemporary trends in the state religion law in BiH. The term "religion law" as one of the main concepts of this study differs from systems of "religious law", that is, the "normative systems of religious organizations and traditions", such as Jewish, Christian, or Islamic law. These terms are "increasingly used in the secondary literature in the field of law and religion, which is itself starting to be seen as involving the study of both state law on religion (international and national) and religious law".[39] While this book is focused on the analysis of state religion law, it was also necessary to explore certain aspects of religious law and its interactions with state norms, which is particularly noticeable in Chapters 6 and 9.

The book is divided into two parts, the first of which outlines the general contours of state religion law, while the second includes thematic studies that deal with more specific aspects of its implementation. The first part is comprised of three chapters. In Chapter 1, a complex, multi-layered normative framework governing freedom of religion and state-religion relations is described. This is followed in Chapter 2 by an analysis of the scope of freedom of religion and its limitations under the legislation in force and the doctrine of domestic human rights courts. Chapter 3 is dedicated to the discussion on the cooperationist system of relations between the state and religion in contemporary Bosnia and the challenges that stand in the way of its full implementation.

The second part consists of six chapters. Chapter 4 discusses the extent to which religion has been accommodated in a variety of regulatory contexts, such as military, police service, labour, healthcare, prisons, and so on. In Chapters 5 and 6, an analysis of the legal position, autonomy, property, and the finances of religious communities is developed. Chapter 8 deals with state regulations on religious holidays as well as the function of religious symbols in public space. Finally, Chapter 9 explores the interaction of state law and religious norms in the area of private law.

39 Doe, *Law and Religion in Europe*, 1.

I

State religion law

General contours

1 Freedom of religion or belief and state-religion relations

A normative framework

1 Introduction

The Dayton Peace Agreement, which ended the 1992–1995 war against Bosnia and Herzegovina (BiH or Bosnia), provided for "an extremely intricate decentralized administrative structure" aimed to accommodate the interests of the country's major ethnic groups.[1] The Agreement created a no-win situation in which all parties to the war had to accept some concessions. The territorial integrity of BiH within its internationally recognized borders was preserved and the continuity of its international legal subjectivity was confirmed, while at the same time the state was decentralized in order to compensate for the separatist aspirations of the Serb and Croat sides in the armed conflict.[2] Annex 7 of the Dayton Agreement provided that the warring parties would not only enable the return of refugees and displaced persons to their pre-war homes, but also "create in their territories the political, economic and social conditions conducive to the voluntary return and

1 Ahmet Alibašić and Nedim Begović, "Reframing the Relations Between State and Religion in Post – War Bosnia: Learning to Be Free!" *Journal of Balkan and Near Eastern Studies* 19, no. 1 (2017): 22.

2 The General Framework Agreement for Peace in BiH was negotiated in Dayton (USA) and signed in Paris (France) on 14 December 1995. The signatories to the agreement were the Republic of Bosnia and Herzegovina, the Republic of Croatia, and the Federal Republic of Yugoslavia. The Constitution of BiH was adopted as Annex 4 of the Agreement. Its Art. I, para. 3 provided that BiH "shall consist of the two Entities, the Federation of Bosnia and Herzegovina and the Republika Srpska". The Federation of Bosnia and Herzegovina (FBiH) consists of ten cantons (of which eight are dominantly Bosniak or Croat and two with mixed ethnic composition), while the Republic of Srpska (RS) is a homogenous entity. The International Arbitration Award of 1999 established the Brčko District of Bosnia and Herzegovina (BDBiH) as a separate administrative unit of local self-government, which does not belong to any entity and which is under the sovereignty of the state. See Nedim Begović, "Ustavni okvir i Zakon o slobodi vjere i pravnom položaju crkava i vjerskih zajednica u BiH," [Constitutional Framework and Law on Freedom of Religion and Legal Status of Churches and Religious Communities: Normative Projection of Bosnian-Herzegovinian Secularism] in *Sekularnost i religija: BiH i* regija, eds. Edin Šarčević and Drago Bojić (Sarajevo: Fondacija Centar za javno pravo, 2015), 72–73. The text of the Dayton Peace Agreement is available at, accessed 28 June 2021, www.osce.org/files/f/documents/e/0/126173.pdf.

DOI: 10.4324/9780429266683-3

harmonious reintegration of refugees and displaced persons".[3] However, since Annex 7 was only partially implemented,[4] the division of the country in two Entities, each dominated by one ethnic group – Serbs in the RS and Bosniaks and Croats in the FBiH – sanctioned in many ways the results of genocide and ethnic cleansing.[5] In addition, for more than two decades after the end of the war, the Dayton constitutional order proved to be an obstacle to reaching an effective consensus even on key political issues, such as meeting the preconditions and obligations on the country's path to Euro-Atlantic integrations.

Fortunately, the post-war settlement of relations between the state and religious communities, at least concerning their general contours, escaped that fate. This can be explained by „the general, even if not always fully functional, acceptance of freedom of religion and equality as the main framework" for resolving issues concerning the regulation of the religious sphere in society.[6] Both the state and religious communities are going through a gradual process of adjusting to liberal democratic principles of ordering religious rights and the organization of state-religion relations that were adopted as part of the post-war redesign of the legal architecture in BiH. As a basis for this process of adjustment, with the assistance of international actors, a very robust system of protection of the right to freedom of religion or belief, as well as other fundamental human rights, has been established.[7]

The protection of religious freedom in contemporary BiH is established at several normative levels: (a) constitutional law, (b) legislation, (c) bilateral agreements on state-religion relations, (d) bylaws and implementing agreements, and (e) a body of evolving case law. These documents are broadly framed by the text of the Dayton Agreement, which makes the European Convention on Human Rights (ECHR) an integral part of Bosnian constitution. Specifically, Art. II, para. 2 of the Constitution stipulates that the ECHR and its protocols shall directly apply

3 Arts. I-II, Annex 7, "Agreement on Refugees and Displaced Persons," accessed 16 January 2021, www.ohr.int/dayton-peace-agreement/annex-7-2/.

4 Different parameters of the 2013 Census of Population, Households and Dwellings in Bosnia and Herzegovina indicate a change in the ethnic structure of the territories of the two entities compared to 1991. Thus, e.g. there was a decrease in the number of municipalities with a Bosniak majority from 63 in 1991 to 54, while the number of municipalities with a Serb majority increased from 54 to 64 ("Analiza: Država," accessed 19 June 2019, http://statistika.ba). The dominance of one ethnic group is present in both entities, so that in the RS Serbs make up 81.51% of the population (Bosniaks 13.99%, Croats 2.41%, others 0.17%, not declare their nationality 1.25%), while in the FBiH Bosniaks make up 70.40% of the population (Croats 22.44%, Serbs 2.55%, others 0.19%, not declare their nationality 3.6%). See *Census of Population, Households and Dwellings in Bosnia and Herzegovina: Final Results* (Sarajevo: Agency for Statistics of Bosnia and Herzegovina, 2016), 54, accessed 16 January 2021, www.popis.gov.ba/popis2013/doc/RezultatiPopisa_BS.pdf.

5 On genocide and other war crimes committed in Bosnia and Herzegovina see International Court of Justice, Case Concerning Application of the Convention on the Prevention and Punishment of the Crime of Genocide (*Bosnia and Herzegovina v. Serbia and Montenegro*), Judgment of 26 February 2007, accessed 8 June 2021, www.icj-cij.org/public/files/case-related/91/091-20070226-JUD-01-00-EN.pdf.

6 Alibašić and Begović, "Reframing," 19.

7 Alibašić and Begović, "Reframing," 19–20.

to BiH and its entities; and it shall have priority over all other law.[8] Individuals and religious communities can, therefore, directly invoke ECHR provisions in domestic courts and other authorities in matters concerning religious freedom.

2 Religion and belief in the constitutional law

The complex legal framework and related international standards translate into an impressive system of individual and collective religious freedoms for all citizens of BiH.[9] Even the Preamble of the Constitution acknowledges its inspiration from the principles of

> the Universal Declaration of Human Rights; the International Covenants on Civil and Political Rights and on Economic, Social and Cultural Rights; the Declaration on the Rights of Persons Belonging to National or Ethnic, Religious and Linguistic Minorities and other human rights instruments.

Articles regulating citizenship rights assert that "No person shall be deprived of ... citizenship on any ground such as ... religion ..."[10] The specific enumeration of human rights also includes "freedom of thought, conscience and religion".[11] The next paragraph prohibits discrimination on religious grounds. Annex I enumerates no less than 15 international agreements on human rights that apply directly to BiH. The International Covenant on Civil and Political Rights (ICCPR) and the International Covenant on Economic, Social and Cultural Rights (ICESCR) place particular emphasis on religious freedoms.

Entity-level constitutions ensure yet another layer of religious freedoms applicable within their respective territory. FBiH's constitution protects "freedom of thought, conscience and belief" but also "freedom of religion, including private and public worship".[12] Similar to the BiH Constitution, the FBiH Constitution replicates that no one can be deprived of citizenship on the basis of religion.[13] It also imposes an obligation on authorities to collaborate with "any international human rights monitoring mechanisms".[14] In line with incorporation of the international standards, it further guarantees the application "of the highest level of internationally recognized rights and freedoms" within its territory.[15] Annex 1 enlists 22 international instruments on human rights that apply directly to the FBiH. Among the most relevant instruments concerning religious freedom are

8 Constitution of BiH, accessed 16 January 2021, www.ccbh.ba/public/down/USTAV_BOSNE_I_HERCEGOVINE_engl.pdf.

9 This section is mostly based on: Alibašić and Begović, "Reframing," 23–24.

10 Art. I, para. 7, Constitution of BiH.

11 Art. II, para. 3(i), Constitution of BiH.

12 Part II, Art. 2, Constitution of the FBiH, *Official Gazette of FBiH*, 1/94, 13/97, 16/02, 22/02, 52/02, 63/03, 9/04, 20/04, 33/04, 71/05, 72/05, 88/08.

13 Part II, Art. 5, Constitution of the FBiH.

14 Part II, Art. 7, Constitution of the FBiH.

15 Part II, Art. 2, Constitution of the FBiH.

the Universal Declaration of Human Rights, ICCPR, ICESCR, ECHR, and the Declaration on the Elimination of All Forms of Intolerance and of Discrimination Based on Religion or Belief.

The Constitution of RS does not fall short of guaranteeing the "protection of human freedoms and rights in accordance with international standards".[16] All citizens are further guaranteed "equal legal protection irrespective of their religion".[17] In its case, however, "freedom of religion" is perceived predominantly in terms of collective rights. Accordingly:

> Religious communities shall be equal before the law and shall be free to perform religious affairs and services. They may open religious schools and perform religious education in all schools at all levels of education; they may engage in economic and other activities, receive gifts, establish legacies and manage them, in conformity with the law.[18]

In contrast to FBiH's constitution, RS's constitution mentions specifically the connection between a particular church and ethnic group: "The Serb Orthodox Church (SOC) shall be the church of the Serb people and other people of Orthodox religion."[19] However, an additional provision on the special privileges of the SOC has been declared unconstitutional, which will be discussed in more detail in Chapter 3.

According to the RS Constitution, its provisions on freedom of religion and other guaranteed rights and freedoms are implemented in accordance with Art. 8–11 of the ECHR,[20] which means that decisions of the European Court of Human Rights (ECtHR) interpreting and applying Art. 9 of the European Convention are relevant to potential dilemmas regarding the exercise of religious freedom in the RS entity.

3 Religion and belief legislation

The constitutional guarantees of the right to freedom of religion or belief are concretized through the legislation, in particular the Law on Freedom of Religion and the Legal Status of Churches and Religious Communities in Bosnia and Herzegovina (LFR).[21] Drafted by the Interreligious Council in Bosnia and Herzegovina (IRC),[22]

16 Art. 5, Constitution of the RS, *Official Gazette of the RS*, 21/92. Amendments of Constitution of RS, *Official Gazette of the RS*, 28/94, 8/96, 13/96, 15/96, 16/96, 21/96, 21/02, 26/02, 30/02, 31/02, 69/02, 31/03, 98/03, 115/05, 117/05.

17 Art. 10, Constitution of the RS.

18 Art. 28, para. 2, Constitution of the RS.

19 Art. 28, para. 3, Constitution of the RS.

20 Art. 49, para. 5, Constitution of the RS.

21 Law on Freedom of Religion and the Legal Status of Churches and Religious Communities, *Official Gazette of BiH*, 5/04.

22 The Interreligious Council in Bosnia and Herzegovina (IRCBiH) is a non-governmental organization bringing together representatives of four traditional religious communities in BiH, i.e. the Islamic Community (IC), the Serb Orthodox Church (SOC), the Catholic

the law covers the most important aspects of state-religion relations, including freedom of religious beliefs and practices, legal status of religious communities, relations between the state and religious entities, the formation of new religious communities, and so on. The particular importance of the law lies in the fact that it regulates the most important issues concerning the state and religion in unified manner for the entire territory of the state. Therefore, all other primary and secondary legislation on religious matters, whether adopted at the state or lower levels of government, must comply with the provisions of this law.[23] Since the Constitution of BiH is not explicit on matters of the state-religion relations and that a large portion of legislative competencies and public policies is entrusted to the entities' level (in FBiH further distributed to cantonal jurisdiction), the LFR represent an important achievement in the complex political milieu of a multi-ethnic Bosnian society.

Unlike related laws of neighbouring countries, Croatia and Serbia, which are almost entirely focused on the protection and realization of the collective dimension of the right to freedom of religion,[24] Bosnian law on religions seeks to strike a balance in standardizing the protection of individual religious rights and freedoms, on the one hand, and the collective rights of churches and religious communities, on the other hand.

In addition to the LFR, at the state, entity or cantonal level, a number of other laws have been adopted that in some ways affect the freedom of religion of individuals or the position of churches and religious communities. These laws usually deal with some individual aspects of the manifestation of religion (e.g. religious marriage,[25] ritual slaughter of animals,[26] the position of religious educational institutions,[27] etc.) or the application of the right to freedom of religion in specific contexts (e.g. respect for religious or non-religious beliefs of patients

---

Church (CC), and the Jewish Community (JC). It was established in 1997 with the aim of contributing to reconciliation and rebuilding trust among the peoples of Bosnia and Herzegovina, a year and a half after the end of the war. It has implemented numerous inter-religious projects in order to achieve the mentioned goal, as well as to build civil society through inter-religious dialogue. See Interreligious Council in Bosnia and Herzegovina, "O nama," accessed 16 January 2021, https://mrv.ba/o-nama-2/.

23 Art. 2, para. 1–2, LFR.

24 Law on the Legal Status of Religious Communities in Croatia, *Official Gazette of Republic of Croatia*, 83/02, 73/12; Law on Churches and Religious Communities, *Official Gazette of Republic of Serbia*, 36/2006.

25 Art. 2, para. 3 of the Family Law of the FBiH, *Official Gazette of the FBiH*, 35/05, 31/14 (envisaging that spouses, after entering into a civil marriage, may proceed to a religious marriage ceremony).

26 "An animal may be slaughtered only if it was stunned before bleeding, unless it is a special slaughter procedure by a certain religious rite or if the animal is in agony." Art. 16, para. 1, Law on Protection and Welfare of Animals of Bosnia and Herzegovina, *Official Gazette of BiH*, 25/09, 9/18.

27 For the sake of illustration, Art. 178, para. 1 of the Law on Higher Education of the Canton Sarajevo (*Official Gazette of Canton Sarajevo*, 33/17) prescribes that the provisions of this law also apply to "theological faculties, colleges of theology and theological academies, except in those parts whose application would jeopardize the specifics of the overall social function of these institutions".

when providing health services and the right of patients to perform religious rites in hospitals,[28] etc.).

4 Agreements between the state and religious communities

Additional stratum of normative protection to religious freedom is ensured by the legally provided possibility of concluding an agreement between the state or its entities and religious communities. It represents an important novelty in relation to the earlier communist legislation on the position of religion in society. The Catholic Church (CC), that is, the Holy See, as its universal authority, was the first to approach the contractual regulation of religious issues with the state. Thus, on 19 April 2006, the Basic Agreement between the Holy See and BiH was signed with the status of an international agreement.[29] The next religious organization that concluded an agreement with the state was the SOC, on 3 December 2007. The agreement was signed on behalf of the SOC by the Serb Patriarch Pavle, and on behalf of BiH by Safet Softić, the Minister of Human Rights and Refugees, with the authorization of the Presidency of Bosnia and Herzegovina (PBiH).[30] The remaining two traditional religious organizations, the Islamic and the Jewish community, have not yet entered into agreements with the state. While the former, due to its small size, has shown no interest in concluding an agreement, the latter is awaiting the adoption of the draft agreement by the PBiH, which will be discussed in more detail in Chapter 3.

5 Institutional mechanisms for the protection of freedom of religion or belief

There are currently two types of institutional mechanisms in the legal system of BiH under which individuals, groups and religious communities may seek protection in cases where their constitutional right to freedom of religion or belief has been restricted. The first refers to the claim of the mentioned right before the competent regular courts, and the second to the initiation of proceedings before

28 Art. 30 of the Law on Rights, Obligations and Responsibilities of Patients of the FBiH (*Official Gazette of the FBiH*, 40/10) prescribes that in all circumstances of providing and using healthcare, the patient has the right to protection of his worldview, moral and religious beliefs. Art. 47 of the same law stipulates that "a patient during his stay in an inpatient health care institution, as a rule, may exercise the right to perform religious rites in the space provided for that, including the right to be equipped in the morgue in case of death, with religious rites – separately by denominations, in accordance with the spatial possibilities of the health institution".

29 Basic Agreement Between the Holy See and Bosnia and Herzegovina, *Official Gazette of BIH – International Agreements*, 10/07. The text of document was also accessed 17 January 2021, http://bibliotecanonica.net/docsab/btcabe.htm.

30 Basic Agreement Between Bosnia and Herzegovina and the Serb Orthodox Church, *Official Gazette of BiH – International Agreements*, 6/08.

the departments of state bodies or institutions for the protection of human rights. These are the Ministry of Human Rights and Refugees of BiH (MHRR), the Institution of Ombudsman for Human Rights of BiH (IOHR), and the Constitutional Court of BiH.

The organization of the judicial system in Bosnia is based, *inter alia*, on the principle of two-tier or three-tier decision-making, which ensures better protection of citizens' rights and greater consistency in the interpretation and application of the constitution and laws. Persons who consider that their right to freedom of religion or belief has been unjustifiably restricted, that is, that they have been discriminated against on the basis of religion or belief, can apply to the locally competent municipal courts in the FBiH, meaning basic courts in the RS, and their decisions can be appealed to the cantonal courts in the FBiH, that is, district courts in RS. The third line of defense of citizens' rights is the supreme courts of the entities – Supreme Court of the FBiH and Supreme Court of the RS – which judge appeals and revisions that are submitted in order to review the decisions of cantonal or district courts. In the BDBiH, the protection of the right to freedom of religion or belief is sought before the Basic and Appellate Courts.[31]

To illustrate, Jana Martina Katović, a nun and a member of the Community "Adorers of the Blood of Christ", after many years as the director of the public kindergarten in Glamoč, re-applied for the competition announced for the post in June 2008. Considering that she was the only candidate and that she met the conditions prescribed by the competition, the Board of Directors of the Kindergarten made a decision on her appointment to the said position. However, the Municipal Council of Glamoč, as the founder of the Kindergarten, refused to give its consent to her appointment without offering an official explanation. On 28 March 2011, Radovan Marković, the Mayor of Glamoč, as a guest on the state television (BHTV-1) programme, explained that there was no agreement in the Municipal Council on the appointment of J. M. Katović due to the fact that she was a nun and wore a religious uniform. J. M. Katović decided to wage a legal battle to exercise her constitutionally guaranteed right to work, arguing that she was discriminated against on the basis of religion. After the Municipal[32] and Cantonal Courts in Livno[33] ruled that the plaintiff was discriminated against on the grounds of religion, the Supreme Court of the FBiH quashed the first and second instance verdicts and rejected the allegation of discrimination. Finally, the Constitutional Court of BiH upheld the appeal of the plaintiff and found a violation of her right to a fair trial under Art. II, para. 3(e) of the Bosnian Constitution and Art. 6, para. 1 of the ECHR.[34]

31 See Nedim Hogić, *Pravosudni sistem u Bosni i Hercegovini* [Judicial System in Bosnia and Herzegovina] (Sarajevo: Foundation for the Development of Media and Civil Society "Mediacentar," 2014).

32 Municipal Court in Livno, Case no. 68 0 P 017561 11 P, 7 December 2011.

33 Cantonal Court in Livno, Case no. 68 0 P 017561 12 Gž, 24 January 2013.

34 Constitutional Court of BiH, Case no. AP 4583/14, 15 June 2017.

In addition to the courts of regular jurisdiction, there are three constitutional courts in Bosnia, at the state and two entity levels, which are considered special courts. The Constitutional Court of BiH, pursuant to Art. VI, para. 1 of the Bosnian Constitution has nine members, four of which are elected by the House of Representatives of the FBiH Parliament, two by the RS National Assembly, and the remaining three by the President of the ECtHR, after consultation with the PBiH.[35] The general condition for judges of the Constitutional Court is that they are "lawyers of high moral standing", and an additional condition for judges elected by the President of the ECtHR is that he or she is not a citizen of BiH or any neighbouring country.[36] The decisions of the Constitutional Court are final and binding,[37] and there are several competencies that may be relevant to the protection of freedom of religion.

First, the Constitutional Court has jurisdiction to decide on any dispute between two entities or between the state and one or both entities, and between the institutions of BiH, including the assessment of the conformity of any provision of entity constitutions or laws with the Constitution and the ECHR. The request for constitutional review cannot be initiated by citizens in a private capacity, but only by holders of certain political functions, namely a member of PBiH, chairman of the Council of Ministers of Bosnia and Herzegovina (CMBiH), chairman or deputy chairman of any house of the Parliamentary Assembly of Bosnia and Herzegovina (PABiH), and a quarter of the delegates of any house of the legislature of the state or entity.[38] The realization of this competence of the Constitutional Court in the domain of protection of the constitutional right to freedom of religion can be followed in case U 8/17 of 30 November 2017, where the Court decided on the request of Safet Softić, Deputy Chairman of the House of Peoples of the PABiH, to review the constitutionality of the Rulebook on uniforms for the BiH Border Police officers, which forbade wearing a beard.[39] A similar example is provided by the constitutional review of the RS Law on Cemeteries and Funeral Services in the case U 19/14 of 24 September 2014.[40]

Further, the Constitutional Court has jurisdiction to consider appeals against decisions of regular courts which the applicants consider to constitute a violation

35 The inclusion of foreign judges in the Constitutional Court of BiH can be understood as an expression of the need for a neutral element that will amortize the danger of conducting constitutional policy along ethnic lines, given that the remaining judges are elected by the entity rather than the state parliament. One can also think about the need for judges from developed democracies in Western Europe in the process of transition of the judicial system of a former socialist country. See Nedim Kulenović, *Court as a Policy-Maker? The Role and Effects of the Constitutional Court of Bosnia and Herzegovina in Democratic Transition and Consolidation* (Sarajevo: Analitika – Center for Social Research, 2016), 14–16.

36 Art. VI, para. 1. b., Constitution of BiH.

37 Art. VI, para. 4., Constitution of BiH.

38 Art. VI, para. 3. a., Constitution of BiH.

39 Constitutional Court of BiH, Case no. U 8/17, 30 November 2017.

40 Constitutional Court of BiH, Case no. U 19/14, 24 September 2014.

of human rights guaranteed by the Constitution.[41] Appeals may be filed by the parties participating in the proceedings in connection with the decision that is the subject of the appeal.[42] Finally, the Constitutional Court is empowered to issue an expert opinion, at the request of any court in BiH, on whether a law to be applied by that regular court is in conformity with the Constitution, the ECHR or the laws of BiH.[43]

The Human Rights Ombudsman of BiH (IOHR or Institution) is an independent institution established to promote good governance and the rule of law, as well as the protection of human rights and freedoms in BiH. In this regard, this institution has the task of monitoring the work of the institutions of BiH, the entities and the BDBiH.[44] The legal basis for the establishment of the Institution is contained in Annexes IV and VI of the Dayton Peace Agreement. Namely, Annex IV, which contains the Constitution of BiH, provided for the establishment of a Human Rights Commission with the aim of ensuring the implementation of internationally recognized human rights.[45] According to Annex VI, which contains the "Agreement on Human Rights", the Office of the Ombudsman together with the Human Rights Chamber of BiH forms the Commission for Human Rights of BiH whose main task was to contribute to faster and more efficient protection of human rights in post-war society.[46] Today, the Institution of Ombudsman operates on the basis of the constitutional provisions and the Law on the Ombudsman for Human Rights of BiH of 2002 and the amendments to the Law adopted in 2004 and 2006.[47] The 2009 Law on Prohibition of Discrimination in BiH expanded the powers of the Institution assigning it the role of a central institution for protection against discrimination.[48]

The Institution consists of three persons who can individually conduct inquiries and consider individual complaints or problems *ex officio*, but jointly make suggestions, recommendations and reports. Unlike the Constitutional Court of BiH, whose composition is largely determined by the entity legislatures, ombudsmen

41 Art. VI, para. 3. b., Constitution of BiH.

42 Art. 16, para. 1. b), Rules of the Constitutional Court of BiH, *Official Gazette of BiH*, 94/14 – consolidated text. In the aforementioned case no. AP 4583714 the Constitutional Court ruled on the appeal of the plaintiff against the decision of the Supreme Court of the FBiH.

43 Art. VI, para. 3. c., Constitution of BiH.

44 Art. 1, Law on the Human Rights Ombudsman of BIH, *Official Gazette of BiH*, 19/02.

45 Art. II, para. 1, Constitution of BiH.

46 Art. II, Annex 6 of the Human Rights Agreement of the General Framework Agreement for Peace in Bosnia and Herzegovina, accessed 17 January 2021, www.ohr.int/dayton-peace-agreement/annex-6/.

47 Law on the Human Rights Ombudsman of BiH, *Official Gazette of BiH*, 19/02; Law on Amendments to the Law on the Human Rights Ombudsman of BiH, *Official Gazette of BiH*, 35/04; Law on Amendments and Supplements to the Law on the Human Rights Ombudsman of BiH, *Official Gazette of BiH*, 32/06.

48 Art. 7, Law on Prohibition of Discrimination, *Official Gazette of BiH*, 59/09; Law on Amendments and Supplements to the Law on Prohibition of Discrimination, *Official Gazette of BiH*, 66/16.

are appointed by the PABiH. It is explicitly stipulated that the distribution of tasks among them must not depend on the ethnic origin of the complainant.[49] Ethnic representation is ensured by the provision according to which "ombudsmen are appointed from the three constituent peoples (Bosniak, Serb and Croat), which does not exclude the possibility of appointment from the ranks of others". Interestingly, unlike the Constitution, which quite laconically defines the conditions for judges of the Constitutional Court of BiH, the criteria for appointment to the position of Ombudsman are more strictly and in more detail regulated. In addition to the high moral reputation and citizenship of BiH, it is required that they are law graduates with "passed bar exam and at least ten years of experience in the legal profession, in which they excelled, who have proven experience in protecting human rights and freedoms".[50]

In general, the competencies of the Institution can be classified into quasi-judicial and promotional.[51] The first group of competencies includes handling individual complaints, conducting investigations and issuing recommendations. Namely, in order to carry out its mission, the Institution is authorized to consider complaints of natural and legal persons against violations of the rights guaranteed by the Constitution of BiH and international documents listed in its Annex I, and to conduct appropriate investigations checking the requested information, conducting personal interviews and reviewing the necessary records.[52] The obligation of all government bodies in BiH to cooperate with the Institution and provide it with assistance in the investigation and control of their work, is explicitly prescribed.[53] Moreover, in the field of anti-discrimination, the competencies of the Institution have been extended to the private sector, which means that it can investigate cases of discrimination committed by any legal or natural person in BiH. The second group of competencies, namely promotional, includes various activities aimed at educating and raising public awareness and preventing discrimination and human rights violations (e.g. collecting statistics on human rights violations, submitting reports on the activities of the Institution to the state and entity legislatures, conducting research, etc.).

In cases when the Institution finds through an investigation that there has been a violation of human rights by an official of a government body in BiH, it

49 Art. 3, Law on Amendments and Supplements to the Law on the Human Rights Ombudsman of BiH.

50 Art. 6, Law on Amendments and Supplements to the Law on the Human Rights Ombudsman of BiH.

51 Adrijana Hanušić, *The Ombudsman in the System of Protection Against Discrimination in BiH: Situation Analysis and Characteristic Problems* (Sarajevo: Analitika – Center for Social Research, 2012), 19.

52 Art. 2, para. 1–3 and Art. 3–4, Law on the Human Rights Ombudsman of BiH.

53 Art. 25–28, Law on the Human Rights Ombudsman of BiH. According to Art. 7, para. (6) and (7) of the Law on Prohibition of Discrimination, they have the obligation to submit the requested data and documents within 30 days from the date of receipt of the request of the Institution, i.e. to cooperate with this Institution, *inter alia*, by submitting reports on the effects of recommendations aimed at eliminating discrimination.

shall issue a recommendation to the given body on how to correct the violation of rights.[54] The case is not closed by issuing a recommendation, but there is a system for monitoring their implementation. Failure to comply with the recommendations as well as the refusal to cooperate with the Institution in terms of elimination and prevention of discrimination entails the possibility of initiating a misdemeanour proceedings and imposing relatively high fines on responsible persons in legal entities and individuals.[55] In addition to individual measures concerning specific complaints, the Institution may recommend to the authorities general measures to prevent future human rights violations, including proposals for amendments to the law. If the competent authorities do not take measures within the deadline set by the Institution, nor offer a valid explanation of the reason for not taking such measures, the Institution will point out this problem in a special or annual report.[56]

The protection of religious freedoms and non-discrimination on religious grounds have so far not been the subject of special reports by the Institution, but individual complaints are regularly pointed out in its regular annual reports. Although the statistics in the reports contain separate subcategories of cases called religious freedom/religion and discrimination based on religion,[57] complaints regarding the exercise of religious rights can be found in other sections of the report such as minorities, prisons, labour relations, education, and so on.

Below we point out three concrete examples of the use of the mechanism of the Institution by believers individually and religious communities with different final outcomes. In the first case, the recommendation was implemented but after a protracted period of time. Namely, in 2014, the Institution found a violation of the rights of the religious community of Jehovah's Witnesses, considering a complaint about the negative labelling of this group in the textbook of Orthodox religious education for the eighth grade of primary schools. The implementation of this recommendation came only at the beginning of 2017 by removing the disputed content from the textbook.[58]

54 Art. 29–31, Law on the Human Rights Ombudsman of BiH.

55 Hanušić, *Ombudsman*, 23–24.

56 Art. 32, para. 1–4, Law on the Human Rights Ombudsman of BiH.

57 In the period from 2014 to 2018, a total of 27 complaints were recorded within subcategory 04 – Religious Freedom/Religion, and five cases within this subcategory in which the Institution issued a recommendation. In the same period, a total of 13 complaints were recorded under subcategory 01–10 Discrimination on the basis of religion. The Institution's reports regularly indicate that the number of reported cases of human rights violations does not reflect their actual number in society, as this Institution has the information that many victims do not report human rights' violations due to their distrust in state institutions and fear of facing possible negative consequences. See e.g. the Institution of the Human Rights Ombudsman of Bosnia and Herzegovina, *2017 Annual Report on the Results of the Activities of the Institution of the Human Rights Ombudsman of Bosnia and Herzegovina* (Banja Luka, 2018), 105, accessed 17 January 2021, www.ombudsmen.gov.ba/documents/obmudsmen_doc2018030810344228eng.pdf.

58 Human Rights Ombudsman, *2017 Annual Report*, 88.

In the second case, the responsible institutions did not inform the Institution about the implementation of a recommendation and its effects. Namely, the Institution issued a recommendation to both the Ministry of Education and Culture of the RS and Elementary School "Branko Ćopić" in Banja Luka to take the necessary measures in order not to violate the rights of students of the school, that is, not to be exposed to sanctions due to the cessation of attending confessional religious education in the fifth grade. The complaint was filed by the students' mother stating that the school administration had not issued a formal decision verifying the parents' decision that the children should stop attending religious education.[59]

In the third case, the recommendation affected the outcome of the proceedings before the competent court, which led to the exercise of the protection of the right to freedom of belief.[60] A patient of the University Clinical Center Tuzla filed a complaint with the Institution that she was denied surgery, to which she was entitled as a health insured person, because she refused to agree to a blood transfusion that violates her religious beliefs. In this regard, the Ombudsman sent a recommendation to the University Clinical Center Tuzla and the Ministry of Health of Tuzla Canton to consider the appellant's case and the possibility of satisfying her religious request. Complying with the Institution's recommendation, the Cantonal Court in Tuzla issued a judgment requiring the University Clinical Center Tuzla to provide a requested health service to the complainant without blood transfusions, thus accommodating her religious beliefs.[61]

Finally, the Institution recommended the Ministry of Finance and Treasury of BiH to consider the issue of harmonization of regulations on customs policy with the LFR regarding the payment of customs duties on imports of religious literature.[62] In this and similar cases where it is proposed to initiate changes in legislation, the Institution not only acts to eliminate a specific violation of rights, but also solves problems systematically and prevent new violations.

According to the LFR and the Law on Ministries and other Administrative Bodies of BiH, the MHRR BiH is responsible for the state's relations with religious communities. It communicates and cooperates with religious communities in order to resolve all issues concerning religious freedom and the relationships between the state and religious communities.[63]

Thus, the MHRR has the authority to receive inquiries or reports from citizens and believers individually, groups of believers, and religious communities concerning restrictions on their right to freedom of religion or belief. After

59 Human Rights Ombudsman, *2017 Annual Report*, 89, 162.

60 The Institution noted that its recommendations are increasingly used as evidence in court proceedings, which indicates the strengthening of citizens' trust in this institution (Human Rights Ombudsman, *2017 Annual Report*, 9).

61 Human Rights Ombudsman, *2017 Annual Report*, 101–102.

62 Institution of the Human Rights Ombudsman of Bosnia and Herzegovina, *2018 Annual Report on the Results of the Activities of the Institution of the Human Rights Ombudsman of Bosnia and Herzegovina* (Banja Luka, 2019), 127, 175, accessed 29 June 2021, www.ombudsmen.gov.ba/documents/obmudsmen_doc2019030109434379eng.pdf.

63 Art. 15, para. 2 and Art. 17, para. 3, Law on Freedom of Religion.

receiving and inspecting the petition, the Ministry may request from the competent authorities, state, entity, cantonal, or municipal, to undertake the activities necessary to protect the freedom of religion or belief. The competent authority is then expected to submit a report on the activities performed to the Ministry, after which the Ministry will inform the applicant about the outcome of the procedure within the prescribed deadlines.[64] However, the potential provided by this competence of the MHRR has been insufficiently used. According to the information received from the Ministry, in the period from 2014 to 2018 to which our inquiry referred, this body did not receive any reports of restrictions on the right to freedom of religion or belief.[65]

Further, the MHRR is authorized, at the request of a religious community, to give an expert opinion on the justification of the restriction of freedom of religion in public, taking into account international standards and the circumstances of the case. However, in the event that the restriction is introduced for the protection of public safety, it is envisaged that the expert opinion is issued by the CMBiH.[66] In the aforementioned period, which was the subject of our inquiry, the MHRR considered a number of requests for interpretation of the provisions of the LFR, including inquiries concerning the protection of property rights of the IC in the city of Mostar and the CC in the Municipality of Drvar.[67]

6 Conclusion

The complex and decentralized constitutional structure of BiH established by the 1995 "Dayton Constitution" has proved extremely difficult to reach a political compromise. Fortunately, the regulation of the societal religious sphere escaped that fate. The state and religious communities underwent a gradual transition to a democratic system characterized by enhanced religious freedom of both individual believers and religious collectives. The normative preconditions for this transition process are ensured by the establishment of a robust system for regulating the freedom of religion and the relations between the state and religious communities.

64 Art. 17, para. 1–2, LFR; Art. 4, Instructions on the Implementation of the Law on Freedom of Religion and Legal Status of Churches and Religious Communities in Bosnia and Herzegovina, *Official Gazette of BiH*, 28/19.

65 Ministry for Human Rights and Refugees, Information no. UP-I-05–07–7–25–3/19, 26 July 2019.

66 Art. 4, Instructions on the Implementation of the Law on Freedom of Religion.

67 Ministry for Human Rights and Refugees, Information no. UP-I-05–07–7–25–3/19, 26 July 2019.

2 Freedom of religion or belief and its limitations

1 Introduction

The two essential components that the right to freedom of religion or belief embraces are, to use the words of the United States Supreme Court, "freedom to believe" and "freedom to act".[1] In the glossary of international human rights instruments, this right includes freedom to have, change or to adopt a religion or belief of one's choice and the freedom to manifest one's religion or belief,[2] either alone or in community with others and in public or private, through worship, observance, practice, and teaching.[3] According to the case law of the ECtHR, the first part of Art. 9, para. 1 of the ECHR refers to the internal domain (*forum internum*) of religious freedom and is absolutely protected.[4] The second part of the said provision concerns the external area (*forum externum*) of religious freedom which may be subject to the restrictions necessary to protect other, equally important interests.[5] The Court's approach to the interpretation and application of Art. 9 is well established and, in the majority of religious freedom cases, consists

1 W. Cole Durham, Jr. and Brett G. Scharffs, *Law and Religion: National, International, and Comparative Perspectives* (New York: Aspen Publishers, 2010), 165.

2 On the protection of *forum externum* of the right to freedom of religion or belief in the Strasbourg doctrine see Javier Martínez Torrón, "Manifestations of Religion or Belief in the Case Law of the European Court of Human Rights," in *The European Court of Human Rights and the Freedom of Religion or Belief: The 25 Years Since Kokkinakis*, eds. Jeroen Temperman, T. Jeremy Gunn and Malcolm D. Evans (Leiden: Brill, 2019), 55–81.

3 Art. 18, Universal Declaration on Human Rights, accessed 9 May 2021, www.un.org/en/about-us/universal-declaration-of-human-rights; Art. 18, para. 1, International Covenant on Civil and Political Rights, accessed 9 March 2021, www.ohchr.org/en/professionalinterest/pages/ccpr.aspx; Art. 9, para. 1, European Convention on Human Rights (ECHR), accessed 9 March 2021, www.echr.coe.int/Pages/home.aspx?p=basictexts&c.

4 For a discussion of *forum internum* protection see Manfred Nowak and Tanja Vospernik, "Permissible Restrictions on Freedom of Religion," in *Facilitating Freedom of Religion or Belief: A Deskbook*, eds. Tore Lindholm, W. Cole Durham, Jr. and Bahia G. Tahzib-Lie (Leiden: Martinus Nijhoff Publishers, 2004), 148–150.

5 Jim Murdoch, *Protecting the Right to Freedom of Thought, Conscience and Religion Under the European Convention on Human Rights* (Strasbourg: Council of Europe, 2012), 18. On the distinction between *forum internum* and *forum externum* in the case law of the ECtHR see *Kokkinakis v. Greece*, 25 May 1993, § 31, 33, Series A no. 260-A.

DOI: 10.4324/9780429266683-4

of several common steps. The first two steps involve examining (a) whether a particular appeal falls within the scope of Art. 9 and (b) whether there has been an interference with the right to freedom of religion or belief. If the answer to these two questions is affirmative, the Court proceeds to examine the justification of the limitation by addressing the following questions: (c) is the limitation on manifestation of religion or belief "prescribed by law", (d) whether there is a "legitimate aim" for the limitation and (e) whether the limitation is "necessary in a democratic society". If the answers to the last three questions are in the negative, the Court will find a violation of the right to freedom of religion or belief.[6]

Against this background, this chapter will consider the scope of religious freedom and its limitations in the state religion law of Bosnia and Herzegovina (BiH or Bosnia). The relevant provisions of the 2004 Law on Freedom of Religion on the protection of both the internal and external aspects of freedom of religion and belief have been analysed in detail. In addition, it will be investigated how the developing case law of the domestic human rights courts – the Human Rights Chamber for BiH (HRCBiH)[7] and the Constitutional Court of BiH – has interpreted concepts such as "manifestation of religion", "prescribed by law", "legitimate aim", "necessity", and and other related terms. In what follows, we are going to prove, first, that the scope of religious freedom envisaged in the national religion law is broadly construed and, second, that the limitations of religious manifestations must not be arbitrary, that is, that they are permissible only to protect some public interests of essential importance. In addition, we argue that the domestic human rights courts generally followed the reasoning patterns of the ECtHR when considering cases of interference with the right to manifest a religion or belief.

2 The right to freedom of religious or other belief

In accordance with the case law of the ECtHR, the 2004 Law on Freedom of Religion (LFR) distinguishes between the right to (religious) belief, as an absolutely protected component of the right to freedom of religion or belief, and the right to exercise (religious) belief as a relatively protected element. This difference is visible in Art. 4, para. 1 which represents the document's central provision

6 Mark Hill and Katherine Barnes, "Limitations on Freedom of Religion and Belief in the Jurisprudence of the European Court of Human Rights," in *The European Court of Human Rights and the Freedom of Religion or Belief: The 25 Years Since Kokkinakis*, eds. Jeroen Temperman, T. Jeremy Gunn and Malcolm D. Evans (Leiden: Brill, 2019), 83.

7 The HRCBiH was established by the Human Rights Agreement contained in Annex 6 of the Dayton Peace Agreement. The Chamber's jurisdiction included consideration of allegations of violations of the rights guaranteed by the ECHR, as well as allegations of discrimination in the protection of those rights. As a judicial body composed by domestic and international judges, it played an important role in the post-war period in the field of the protection of fundamental human rights, when the regular courts were not yet ready to take on this responsibility. The Chamber's mandate ended on 31 December 2003. For more information on this judicial body see D. Yeager, "The Human Rights Chamber for Bosnia and Herzegovina: A Case Study in Transitional Justice," *International Legal Perspectives* 14 (2004): 44–53.

on the right to freedom of religion or belief as applied to the individual (and indirectly to religious communities):

> Everyone has the right to freedom of religion or belief, including the freedom to publicly profess or not a religion. Also, everyone has right *to adopt or change his or her religion*, and the freedom – individually or in community with others, in public or private – to manifest his religion or belief in any manner in worship, practice and observance, maintenance of customs and other religious activities. Everyone shall have the right to religious education, which shall be provided solely by persons appointed so to do by an official representative of his church or religious community, whether in religious institutions or in public and private pre-school institutions, primary schools and higher education which shall be regulated according to the specific regulations.[8]

The restrictive clause contained in Art. 14, para. 7 of the Law refers exclusively to the *forum externum*, that is, to the right to manifest a religious belief.

> *Freedom to manifest religion or belief* may be subject only to such limitations as are prescribed by law and in accordance with international standards when it is shown by the competent authorities to be necessary in the interests of public safety, to protect health, public morals, or for the rights and fundamental freedoms of others. Churches and religious communities shall have the right of appeal against such decisions. Prior to the decision on appeal the appellate body must request from the Ministry of Human Rights and Refugees of BiH an opinion relating to such case of limitation of the freedom to manifest religion or belief.[9]

In the context of the protection of the *forum internum* of the right to freedom of religion or belief, the LFR provides for a number of accessory provisions. First, the denigration or ridiculing of any religion is prohibited.[10] Although the broad wording of this provision may suggest the adoption of meaning of the concept of prohibition of the defamation of religion, we are of the opinion that it should be understood only in relation to the provisions prohibiting incitement to religious hatred.[11] Namely, while incitement to religious hatred is qualified as a criminal offense,[12] this is not the case with ridicule of religious beliefs and

8 Art. 4, para. 1., Law on Freedom of Religion. The text in italics refers to the *forum internum* of the right to freedom of religion or belief.

9 Art. 14, para. 7., Law on Freedom of Religion. Italics added.

10 Art. 5, para. 2, adent e), Law on Freedom of Religion.

11 Art. 4, para. 2 and Art. 5, para. 2, adent g), Law on Freedom of Religion.

12 Art. 163, Criminal Code of the Federation of Bosnia and Herzegovina (FBiH), *Official Gazette of the FBiH*, 36/03, 21/04, 69/04, 18/05, 42/10, 42/11, 59/14, 76/14, 46/16, 75/17; Art. 359, Criminal Code of the Republic of Srpska (RS), *Official Gazette of the RS*, 64/17, 104/18, 15/21; Art. 160, Criminal Code of the Brčko District of Bosnia and Herzegovina (BDBiH), *Official Gazette of the BDBiH*, 19/20 – consolidated text.

practices. Second, it is forbidden to force any person to reveal his or her religious beliefs.[13] Third, there is the negative right of the individual not to be compelled to profess a religion or belief or to participate in religious rites of any denomination.[14] However, this right does not apply to officials and employees of religious communities for whom the employer may define a code of rights and duties that is in accordance with the religious or canonical regulations of the given community.[15] Fourth, the individual must not be forced to act contrary to his or her religious conscience, for example, to take an oath contrary to his faith or belief.[16] Specifically, the priests have the right not to disclose information about a crime or misdemeanour obtained in the form of confession from their church members.[17]

The issue of protection of the *forum internum* appeared in the case law of the Constitutional Court of BiH during the consideration of cases AP 913/04 and AP 39/01. In its decision, the Court stated that Art. 9, para. 1 of the ECHR declaratively guaranteed "the right to freedom of the so-called *forum internum*, that is, the inner, spiritual world of man, which sublimates in itself the freedom of thought, conscience and especially religion".[18] The understanding of the Constitutional Court is that the *forum internum* encompasses freedoms that are absolutely protected, primarily because thoughts, opinions and beliefs, as long as they are not expressed, cannot be controlled from the outside.[19] Whether a restriction on freedom of thought is justified in the light of Art. 9, para. 2 of the ECHR can be judged only if the thoughts are expressed and provided that their content is religious in nature.[20]

3 The right to manifest religion or belief

The state religion law and the courts' case law define what constitutes manifestation of religion. The mentioned provision of Art. 4, para. 1 of the LFR encompasses four general forms of religious manifestations from Art. 9, para. 1 of the ECHR, that is, worship, teaching, practice, and observance.[21] They are further

13 Art. 6, para. 2. b), Law on Freedom of Religion.

14 Art. 6, para. 2. a), Law on Freedom of Religion.

15 Art. 6, para. 1, Art. 11, para. 3, and Art. 14, para. 6, Law on Freedom of Religion.

16 Art. 6, para. 2 c), Law on Freedom of Religion.

17 Art. 8, para. 2, Basic Agreement Between the Holy See and Bosnia and Herzegovina, *Official Gazette of BiH – International Agreements*, 6/08.

18 Constitutional Court of BiH, Case no. AP 913/04, 20 December 2005, para. 22.

19 Although it is conceivable to think of a person's inner convictions as inaccessible to other people's minds, there are still situations in which practical issues arise regarding the protection of the sphere of belief, as can be seen from the mentioned legal provisions.

20 Constitutional Court of BiH, Case no. AP 913/04, 20 December 2005, para. 22–23. See Jasmin Muratagić, "Vjerske slobode u praksi Ustavnog suda BiH: konkretizacija modela sekularnog uređenja," [Religious Freedoms in the Case Law of the Constitutional Court of BiH: Concretization of the Model of Secular Organization] in *Sekularnost i religija: BiH i regija*, eds. Edin Šarčević and Drago Bojić (Sarajevo: Foundation Public Law Centre, 2015), 116–117.

21 Art. 4 of the Basic Agreement between the Holy See and BiH guarantees the Catholic Church the freedom of "divine worship", "apostolic mission" and "teaching" (*Official Gazette of BiH – International Agreements*, 10/07).

concretized through a list of possible individual and collective manifestations of religious belief that should not be understood as final.[22] Thus, the law stipulates that everyone has the right:

1 In daily life to practise the principles of his or her religion or belief and act in accordance with them;
2 To practise religious rituals in own, leased or rented buildings or premises which, according to specific regulations, meet the requirements for gathering larger number of people, in the open spaces of the religious buildings, cemeteries and houses and estates of its believers;
3 Freely to organize public religious celebrations and other religious and religiocultural gatherings in public places in accordance with the Law on Public Assembly;
4 To establish, maintain and administer religious institutions, including institutions formed for humanitarian and educational purposes in compliance with the law;
5 To make, acquire, possess, import, export and use items and materials relating to the rituals or customs of his religion or belief in compliance with the law;
6 To establish, possess and dissolve public information services in compliance with the law;
7 To write, publish and distribute books, textbooks and handbooks and disseminate relevant publications in written or pictorial form via the press, electronic media and other forms of electronic communication in compliance with the law;
8 Freely to organize attendance at public religious celebrations, places of worship, processions, organized pilgrimages etc., both within the country and abroad.[23]

The case law of domestic human rights courts has acknowledged that the manifestation of religious beliefs and feelings includes, *inter alia*, "the display of religious symbols and clothing that expresses religious affiliation",[24] "wearing the hijab – headscarf",[25] "wearing a beard", and "special diet",[26] "the right to build a space for practicing" religion and "participation in funerals processions",[27] the burial conducted in accordance with religious regulations and practice,[28] "the constructions

22 The Constitutional Court of BiH noted "that the ways of expressing religion and belief are not given *numerus clausus* in Art. 9 of the European Convention. On the contrary, it is up to each individual to decide in what form to express one's faith or belief. See Constitutional Court of BiH, U 8/17, 30 November 2017, para. 23.

23 Art. 7, Law on Freedom of Religion.

24 Constitutional Court of BiH, Case no. AP 3947/12, 9 July 2015, para. 38.

25 Constitutional Court of BiH, Case no. AP 2190/13, 9 July 2015, para. 47.

26 Constitutional Court of BiH, Case no. U 8/17, 30 November 2017, para. 23 and 24.

27 Human Rights Chamber for Bosnia and Herzegovina, *The Islamic Community in Bosnia and Herzegovina Against the Republika Srpska*, Case no. CH/96/29, 11 June 1999, para. 182, 186.

28 Human Rights Chamber for Bosnia and Herzegovina, *The Islamic Community in Bosnia and Herzegovina (Mrkonjić Grad) against the Republika Srpska*, CH/01/7701, 22 December 2003, para. 128.

of tombstones and the entry of data on them", as well as "the arrangement and maintenance of cemeteries of religious communities",[29] In some cases, the courts have explicitly stated to which general forms of manifestation of religion the appellant's action belongs, while in most cases they have not dealt with these nuances. The former approach is visible in the HRCBiH opinion that a burial conducted in line with Islamic regulations and practice "falls within the ambit of Art. 9 insofar as it relates to freedom of religion, including, in particular, freedom to manifest religion in *practice and observance*".[30] The letter approach is illustrated by the Constitutional Court's observation that "the display of religious symbols and clothing that expresses religious affiliation is one of the most common forms of manifestation of religious feelings".[31] The right to manifest religion or belief, according to the state religion law and case law of national courts "does not represent exclusively individual right, but also contains the collective dimension".[32] Thus, the holders of this right can be individual believers, but also religious communities.[33]

The Constitutional Court has not developed its own theory on the importance of the right to freedom of religion and its manifestation, but instead mainly relies on the principles of Strasbourg jurisprudence of Art. 9 of the ECHR. The following principles seem particularly emphasized: (a) religious liberty and religious pluralism form the foundations of a democratic society, (b) freedom of religion or belief is not only essential to protect the identity of believers, but also the worldview of nonbelievers, (c) although religious freedom is primarily a matter of personal conscience, it does include freedom to manifest religion or belief, (d) in a religiously plural society, there may be a need to limit certain manifestations of religion or belief in order to reconcile the interests of opposing groups, (e) it is a positive obligation of the state to ensure the unhindered enjoyment of the right to freedom of religion, (f) the sphere of individual conscience to which religion primarily belongs differs from the sphere of "private law" which is a legitimate area of state organization, and so.[34]

Interference with the right to manifest religion is prohibited to the state and all third parties. Accordingly, criminal laws provide protection from such an interference. However, the provisions of criminal law concerning religious freedom are not harmonized at the state level and differ from one entity to another. In general, the criminal law of BiH envisages the following criminal offenses that directly or indirectly protect freedom of religion, namely violation of equality of

29 Constitutional Court of BiH, U 9/14, 24 September 2014, para. 49.

30 Human Rights Chamber for Bosnia and Herzegovina, *The Islamic Community in Bosnia and Herzegovina (Mrkonjić Grad) Against the Republika Srpska*, CH/01/7701, 22 December 2003, para. 128.

31 Constitutional Court of BiH, Case no. AP 3947/12, 9 July 2015, para. 38.

32 Constitutional Court of BiH, Case no. U 9/14, 24 September 2014, para. 45.

33 Human Rights Chamber for Bosnia and Herzegovina, *The Islamic Community in Bosnia and Herzegovina Against the Republika Srpska*, Case no. CH/96/29, 11 June 1999, para. 128.

34 See e.g. Constitutional Court of BiH, Case no. AP 2190/13, 9 July 2015, para. 42–44; Constitutional Court of BiH, Case no. AP 3947/12, 9 July 2015, para. 32–34; Constitutional Court of BiH, Case no. U 9/14, 24 September 2014, para. 41–44.

citizens,[35] obstruction or prevention of religious rites,[36] that is, denial of freedom of religion and its exercise, and denial of religious communities' right to equality and worship in public,[37] as well as provoking national, racial and religious hatred, discord, and intolerance.[38]

4 Limitations of religious manifestations

The limits on religious manifestations provided for in the 2004 Law on Freedom of Religion mirror the wording of the restrictive clauses of key international provisions on religious freedom. Accordingly,

> freedom to manifest religion or belief may be subject only to such limitations as are *prescribed by law* and in accordance with international standards when it is shown by the competent authorities to be *necessary in the interests of public safety, to protect health, public morals, or for the rights and fundamental freedoms of others.*[39]

As can be noticed, the concept of "public order" has been omitted, and elsewhere in the text of the law it has been replaced by the concept of "legal order". Thus, the provision on permissible restrictions on the activities of religious communities reads:

> Churches and religious communities must not act with their content and manner of performing religious rites and other manifestations of religion that are contrary to *the legal order*, public safety, morals or to the detriment of life and health,[40] ie. to the detriment of the rights and freedoms of others.[41]

It should be noted that the meaning of the concept of legal order differs from that of the notion of public order in international human rights instruments. There is a convincing understanding among legal commentators that the notion of public order should be interpreted narrowly in the sense of preventing public disorder and not confused with a similar legal term used in private international law, *ordre public*, which relates to the fundamental public policies of country. In addition, the use of the term legal order does not seem quite appropriate in the

35 Art. 177, Criminal Code of the FBiH, *Official Gazette of the FBiH*, 36/03, 21/04, 69/04, 18/05, 42/10, 59/14, 76/14, 75/17; Art. 139, Criminal Code of the RS, *Official Gazette of the RS*, 64/17, 104/18, 15/21; Art. 175, Criminal Code of the BDBiH, *Official Gazette of the BDBiH*, 19/20 – consolidated text.

36 Art. 378, Criminal Code of the FBiH; Art. 372, Criminal Code of the BDBiH.

37 Art. 159, Criminal Code of the RS.

38 Art. 163, Criminal Code of the FBiH; Art. 359, Criminal Code of the RS; Art. 160, Criminal Code of the BDBiH.

39 Art. 14, para. 7, Law on Freedom of Religion. Italics added.

40 The protection of life can be understood as complementary to the protection of health and rights and freedoms of others.

41 Art. 4, para. 3, Law on Freedom of Religion. Italics added.

context of the restriction of the right to manifest one's religion, as many appellants try to justify their deviation from general legal obligations by invoking their conscience or deeply held religious beliefs.[42]

In addition to the general grounds for limiting religious manifestations, the LFR stipulates some specific restrictions that can be subsumed under the protection of order, safety, and rights and freedoms of others. Thus, religious communities are prohibited from spreading hatred and prejudice towards other churches and communities when preaching the faith, as well as towards citizens without religious affiliation, and from preventing them from publicly professing their religion or belief.[43]

The reasoning of the Constitutional Court and the former HRCBiH when considering appeals on restricting the right to manifest religion generally follows the pattern established by the ECtHR. In the first stage, the courts examine whether there was an interference, that is, restriction on the rights under Art. 9 of the ECHR. If the answer to that question is in the affirmative, then the courts proceed to the second stage and examine whether three criteria for legitimate restriction were met, namely that (a) the restriction was prescribed by law, (b) introduced for the protection of legitimate aims, and (c) necessary in a democratic society, that is, that there was a reasonable relationship of proportionality between the restriction and the legitimate aim pursued. Some cases were resolved in the first stage,[44] while others were decided on the basis of an assessment of the above three limiting criteria.

In most human rights cases, the courts had no difficulty in establishing that the restriction of the right to manifest religion was prescribed by law. The courts interpret the term "law" broadly in the sense that it encompasses not only laws passed by parliament, but also lower-level regulations, as well as regulatory measures of entities with delegated powers. In one case, the appellant complained that the ban on wearing beards for police officers was not prescribed by law, but instead by a bylaw, that is, the Rulebook on wearing a uniform issued by the director of the BiH Border Police. The Constitutional Court of BiH, referring to the established Strasbourg jurisprudence, concluded that the restrictive provision was nevertheless prescribed by law, given that it was issued by the Director of the Border Police on the basis of the powers granted to him by the BiH Law on Police Officers and that the Border Police officers were familiar with the provision's content and implications.[45]

Singnificantly, in the case of *the Islamic Community v. Republika Srpska*, the HRCBiH found that the respondent party had committed such a grave violations of religious freedom[46] that an examination of the fulfilment of the criteria for the

42 See Manfred Nowak and Tanja Vospernik, "Permissible Restrictions on Freedom of Religion or Belief," in *Facilitating Freedom of Religion or Belief: A Deskbook*, eds. Tore Lindholm, W. Cole Durham, Jr. and Bahia G. Tahzib-Lie (Leiden: Martinus Nijhoff Publishers, 2004), 217–223.

43 Art. 4, para. 2, Law on Freedom of Religion.

44 See Constitutional Court of BiH, Case no. AP 2190/13, 9 July 2015.

45 Constitutional Court of BiH, U 8/17, 30 November 2017, para. 40.

46 As stated in the decision, "the Chamber could hardly find a more extreme manner in which religious beliefs could be opposed than physical violence such as the stoning of believers participating in funeral processions and provocation through unauthorised intrusion on

legality of the restriction was not necessary at all.[47] The case concerned a lawsuit filed by the Islamic Community in BiH (IC) against RS authorities for destroying 15 mosques, as well as killing, expelling, and displacing Muslims in Banja Luka during the past war. The applicant also alleged that after the entry into force of the Dayton Peace Agreement, the RS authorities "destroyed and removed the remains of the mosques and desecrated the cemeteries or allowed such things to happen, and failed to take certain measures required by the applicant to protect the rights of its members".[48] In the first place, the HRCBiH recalled that its jurisdiction was limited to reviewing human rights violations that had occurred since the signing of the Dayton Peace Agreement on 14 December 1995. It ruled that the municipal authorities of Banja Luka, by refusing to grant permission for the reconstruction of destroyed mosques, unjustifiably restricted the Muslims' right to freedom of religion, since the refusal did not serve any of the legitimate aims of Art. 9, para. 2 of the ECHR. By failing to identify and punish the perpetrators of attacks on Muslims during prayers and burials, the local authorities further violated Art. 9 of the ECHR, which imposes a positive obligation on the state to ensure the peaceful enjoyment of the right to freedom of religion.[49] Later, in a series of cases, the Chamber established the responsibility of the RS authorities for discriminating against Muslims, together with the violation of their right to freedom of religion.[50]

Regarding the criterium of legitimate aim, one can observe three different approaches of the human rights courts. First, the Constitutional Court has so far referred to some of the generally accepted grounds for restricting religious freedom,[51] but has also added some that are not explicitly mentioned in Art. 9, para. 2 of the ECHR. Therefore, in one case, the Constitutional Court invoked the protection of the dignity of a judicial institution and the secular organization of the state as the allegedly legitimate aim of restricting the right of witnesses in court proceedings to express their religious beliefs by wearing a skullcap.[52]

religious premises with the aim of interrupting worship". Human Rights Chamber for Bosnia and Herzegovina, *The Islamic Community in Bosnia and Herzegovina Against the Republika Srpska*, Case no. CH/96/29, 11 June 1999, para. 186. For more details on this case see B. Dakin, "*The Islamic Community in Bosnia and Herzegovina v. The Republika Srpska*: Human Rights in a Multi-Ethnic Bosnia," *Harvard Human Rights Journal* (2002): 245–268.

47 *The Islamic Community in Bosnia and Herzegovina Against the Republika Srpska*, Case no. CH/96/29, 11 June 1999, para. 182.

48 *The Islamic Community in Bosnia and Herzegovina Against the Republika Srpska*, Case no. CH/96/29, 11 June 1999, para. 1.

49 *The Islamic Community in Bosnia and Herzegovina Against the Republika Srpska*, Case no. CH/96/29, 11 June 1999, para. 182–188.

50 See Nedim Begović, "Ustavni okvir i Zakon o slobodi vjere i pravnom položaju crkava i vjerskih zajednica u BiH," in *Sekularnost i religija: BiH i* regija, eds. Edin Šarčević and Drago Bojić (Sarajevo: Fondacija Centar za javno pravo, 2015), 82.

51 For example, the Constitutional Court concluded that restrictions on religious freedom, consisting of the right of a local government unit to prescribe more detailed conditions for the construction and maintenance of cemeteries and the manner of burying and exhuming the dead, could be justified by legitimate aims to protect the safety, health and rights, and freedoms of others. See Constitutional Court of BiH, Case no. U 19/14, 24 September 2014, para. 53.

52 Constitutional Court of BiH, Case no. AP 3947/12, 9 July 2015, para. 43.

However, the ECtHR did not support the reasoning of the Constitutional Court in the part relating to the reference to the dignity of the court as a legitimate aim, as it is not contained in the restrictive clause of Art. 9 para. 2 of the ECHR.[53] Second, in some cases, the Constitutional Court has ruled on whether there has been a violation of the appellant's right to freedom of religion without explicitly resolving the issue of legitimate aim of the restriction.[54] Third, there were cases in which it was found that the restriction on freedom of religion did not serve any of the legitimate aims set out in Art. 9, para. 2 of the ECHR. Examples of such restrictions can be found in the Banja Luka municipal authorities' refusal to allow the reconstruction of mosques destroyed during the war[55] and the general ban on wearing beards imposed on the BiH Border Police officers.[56]

Finally, the application of the necessity test in the practice of domestic human rights courts can be monitored in the following cases. The first case concerns a complaint lodged by the IC against the RS with the HRCBiH for the seizure of land previously used by the IC as a graveyard, the construction of business premises over non-exhumed graves, and the utilization of the use of the yard of the demolished Kizlaragina Mosque in Mrkonjić Grad as a parking lot and a refuse dump. The mosque, whose complex was entered into the registry of Cultural Monuments as National Heritage in the former Yugoslavia, was destroyed during the 1992–1995 armed conflict.[57] During the on-site inspection in Mrkonjić Grad, on 12 May 2003, the Chamber found that "the construction of business premises on top of the Muslim cemetery was not provided for in the urban regulatory plan". Since the respondent Party "has failed to satisfy the principle of lawfulness contained within paragraph 2 of Art. 9", the Chamber was of the opinion that it was not necessary to consider whether the remaining requirements of this Article were met. However, even assuming that the responsible party had provided the appropriate legal documentation – the Council continued,

> the interference with the applicantís rights cannot be considered necessary and as mentioned above, the respondent Party is under a positive obligation to protect religious communities and monuments for the purposes for which they are intended. The respondent Party has singularly failed in its duty to secure the rights of the applicant in this regard. Therefore, the Chamber finds that the interference amounts to a violation of Article 9 of the ECHR.[58]

53 *Hamidović v. Bosnia and Herzegovina*, no. 57792/15, § 35, 5 December 2017.

54 See Constitutional Court of BiH, Case no. AP 2190/13, 9 July 2015, para. 56.

55 Human Rights Chamber for Bosnia and Herzegovina, *The Islamic Community in Bosnia and Herzegovina Against the Republika Srpska*, Case no. CH/96/29, 11 June 1999, para. 182.

56 Constitutional Court of BiH, U 8/17, 30 November 2017, para. 43–44.

57 The mosque was built in 1590, during the Ottoman rule in Bosnia. See Human Rights Chamber for Bosnia and Herzegovina, *The Islamic Community in Bosnia and Herzegovina (Mrkonjić Grad) Against the Republika Srpska*, Case no. CH/01/7701, 22 December 2003, para. 1, 17–18.

58 Human Rights Chamber for Bosnia and Herzegovina, *The Islamic Community in Bosnia and Herzegovina (Mrkonjić Grad) Against the Republika Srpska*, Case no. CH/01/7701, 22 December 2003, para. 128–131.

The second case concerns an appeal against the imposition of a criminal sanction on a witness in proceedings before the Court of BiH for refusing to take off his skullcap, contrary to the order of the acting judge. The Constitutional Court of BiH held that the Appellate Chamber of the Court of BiH – by reducing the originally imposed financial sanction – has satisfied the test of necessity, that is, achieved the proportionality of the restriction of the apellant's right to manifest his religion with the legitimate aims pursued.[59] Contrary to the majority of the Court, Judge Ćeman held that in this case a fair balance had not been struck between competing claims for the protection of the public interest and the rights of the individual guaranteed by the ECHR. He argued that the interference with the appellant's interference with the freedom of religion was not clearly based on the court's house rules, and that wearing a cap for religious reasons could hardly be compared with confirmed forms of contempt of court such as, for example, loud laughter in the courtroom, loud commenting on someone's testimony, or refusing to stand before a judge.[60]

In another case, the Constitutional Court was called upon to examine, *inter alia*, whether the new RS Law on Cemeteries was in line with the constitutionally guaranteed right to freedom of religion. The request for the review of the constitutionality of the mentioned law was submitted by ten Bosniak delegates in the Council of Peoples of the National Assembly of the RS. The disputed provisions of the law stipulated that municipalities can make decisions on the construction and maintenance of cemeteries, the appearance of graves and tombstones and the entry of data on them, the manner of burial and exhumation of deceased persons, as well as relocation of cemeteries under certain conditions. These provisions were of a general nature and applied to both public and cemeteries owned by religious communities. The applicants alleged that these provisions provided a basis for unjustified state interference in matters governed by the regulations and practices of religious communities regarding the burial of the deceased, construction and maintenance of tombstones, and so on. They pointed out that the impugned provisions violated the LFR, which provides for the autonomy of religious communities in managing their property, including the cemeteries owned by them. Given the suffering of Bosniaks and the genocide committed against them in the RS entity during the past war, the applicants pointed out in particular the danger that the impugned law could potentially be used to remove Muslim cemeteries as the last traces of their presence in some parts of the RS entity.[61]

After the Constitutional Court established the legality of the interference and the existence of legitimate aims (the need for spatial and urban planning and fulfilment of sanitary measures), it proceeded to assess whether the interference met the necessity test. First, the Court pointed to the neutral character of the impugned law in the sense that it applied equally to all religious communities and other legal entities providing funeral services and rejected assumptions about

59 Constitutional Court of BiH, Case no. AP 3947/12, 9 July 2015, para. 45.

60 Constitutional Court of BiH, Case no. AP 3947/12, 9 July 2015. Separate opinion of President Mirsad Ćeman on partial disagreement.

61 Constitutional Court of BiH, Case no. U 19/14, 24 September 2014, para. 1, 5–14.

possible decisions of Serb-dominated municipal authorities towards ethnic and religious minorities regarding the application of the law. If violations of constitutional rights occurred in the application of the law, this would be considered on a case-by-case basis. Second, the Court found that the balance between the public interest and the right to freedom of religion was achieved by the law's Art. 6, para. 2, according to which the scope of municipal authorities' powers to regulate the construction and maintenance of religious cemeteries and the burial of the deceased in them was limited by "respect for religious norms and customs". Third, with regard to the provisions of the law allowing the relocation of cemeteries of religious communities under certain conditions, the Court was of the opinion that they also pass the necessity test. In doing so, the Court took into account that the said provisions stipulated that the relocation of cemeteries could be carried out only if justified by urban planning to meet needs of public importance and that cemeteries of cultural and historical significance were excluded from their scope.[62]

5 Conclusion

The 2004 Law on Freedom of Religion and the case law of the domestic human rights courts make a distinction between the internal aspect (*forum internum*) of the right to freedom of religion or belief which enjoys an absolute protection and the external aspect (*forum externum*) that may be lawfully restricted to protect certain public interests. A number of accompanying provisions protecting the proclaimed freedom of religious or other belief are provided by law, such as the prohibiton of forcing the disclosure of beliefs or the participation in the rites of any denomination, and so on. On the other hand, the law protects a broad array of individual and collective religion and belief manifestations that can be subsumed under the general forms of freedom to manifest religion or belief recognized by Art. 9 of the ECHR. The prohibition of third party interference in the expression of a religion or belief is particularly emphasized by the criminal sanctions prescribed for its violation, which, unfortunately, are not harmonized at the state level. In considering religious freedom claims, domestic human rights courts generally follow the methodology developed by the ECtHR in determining whether interference with the right to freedom of religion or belief constitutes a violation of Art. 9 of the ECHR.

62 Constitutional Court of BiH, Case no. U 19/14, 24 September 2014, para. 53–63.

3 Relations between the state and religious communities

1 Introduction

The 1995 Constitution of Bosnia and Herzegovina (BiH or Bosnia) does not include a clause to regulate the relationship between religion and the state, which prompted J. Temperman to conclude, in his study on comparative constitutional laws, that BiH is following "a regime of non-identification". This regime implies that the state does not declare that it is secular or establish and support a particular religion.[1]

The absence of any constitutional clause on the state's attitude towards religion has been supplemented by the doctrinal engagement of the Constitutional Court of BiH and relevant provisions of the 2004 LFR, which indicate the adoption of a model of separation *with* cooperation. This is further evidenced by the state's engagement in concluding agreements with centralized religious hierarchies which represent major groups in the country. These agreements serve to concretize constitutional and legislative guarantees of freedom of religion and to regulate the area of cooperation between the sacred and profane authorities, but also to delineate the necessary boundaries between them. In addition, they tend to consolidate the position and authority of traditional religious communities *vis-à-vis* various institutional and ideological alternatives that flourished in the era of religious freedom.

However, the process of establishing a normative framework for cooperation between the state and major religious communities in the country has not yet been completed. It has been challenged at the level of practical politics which is particularly evident in the dispute over the Draft Basic Agreement between BiH and the Islamic Community in BiH (the DBAIC). An argument can be made that the whole issue has become a subject of politicization, as well as numerous other public issues in the complex and poorly functioning political system of post-war Bosnia.

In what follows, we will first prove, through a systematic interpretation of the constitutional provisions, relevant legislation and judicial doctrine, that BiH has opted for a cooperative model of state-religion relations which is currently

1 Jeroen Temperman, *State-Religion Relationships and Human Rights Law: Towards a Right to Religiously Neutral Governance* (Leiden and Boston: Martinus Nijhoff Publishers, 2010), 103–104.

DOI: 10.4324/9780429266683-5

dominant in Europe.[2] The main features of this model are "substantial respect of individual religious freedom, guarantee of the autonomy and, in particular, the self-administration of the religious denominations, and selective collaboration of the states with the churches".[3] This "selective collaboration" is usually regulated by distinct laws on religious denominations or agreements between the state and religious communities[4] and often includes state financial aid, tax exemptions, possibility of offering confessional religious education in public schools, or other privileges. After the examination of legal texts and judicial doctrine, we will proceed to an analysis of the process of negotiating and implementation of agreements between the state and particular religious communities in BiH.

2 Separation of state and religion: the doctrine of the Constitutional Court

The Constitution of BiH does not have an expressed notion of the separation of state and religion, nor, on the other hand, is any religion (or religious community) designated as state or traditional.[5] Instead, this document guarantees freedom of religion and equality of citizens irrespective of their religious affiliation. According to Art. I b., "no person shall be deprived of Bosnia and Herzegovina or Entity citizenship on any ground such as ... religion" while Art. II, para. 4. prohibits discrimination based on religion in the enjoyment of constitutional human rights and freedoms.[6]

2 The examples of European countries with the cooperation system are Germany, Austria, and Spain.

3 Silvio Ferrari, "Conclusion: Church and State in Post Communist Europe," in *Law and Religion in Post-Communist Europe*, eds. Silvio Ferrari and W. Cole Durham, Jr. (Leuven, Paris and Dudley: Peeters, 2003), 421.

4 See Norman Doe, *Law and Religion in Europe: A Comparative Introduction* (New York: Oxford University Press, 2011), 35–38.

5 This section is partially based on: Nedim Begović, "Freedom of Religion or Belief: Bosnian Muslim Engagement with a Fundamental Human Right," *Context – Journal of Interdisciplinary Studies* 7, no. 1 (2020): 73–75.

6 However, one should not lose sight of the fact that the state Constitution reserves all positions in the Presidency of BiH (PBiH) and the House of Peoples of the Parliamentary Assembly of BiH (PABiH), as well as certain other government offices for members of the three "constituent peoples" – Bosniaks, Serbs and Croats – who are predominantly Muslim, Orthodox, or Catholics, thus establishing systematic discrimination against "others", including ethnic and, in some cases, religious minorities. In the case of *Sejdić and Finci v. Bosnia and Herzegovina*, the European Court of Human Rights (ECtHR) ruled that these provisions of Bosnian Constitution were discriminatory against the applicants, who, as members of the Roma or Jewish minorities cannot run for positions in the aforementioned state bodies. The verdict has not yet been implemented. See *Sejdić and Finci v. Bosnia and Herzegovina* [GC], nos. 27996/06 and 34836/06, ECHR 2009; U.S. Department of State – Office of International Religious Freedom, *2020 Report on International Religious Freedom: Bosnia and Herzegovina*, accessed 10 June 2021, https://ba.usembassy.gov/wp-content/uploads/sites/270/BOSNIA-AND-HERZEGOVINA-2020-INTERNATIONAL-RELIGIOUS-FREEDOM-REPORT.pdf.

Reflecting the general constitutional provisions on the equality of religions, that is, the citizens of different faith, the LFR provides for more detailed norms aimed to implement the principle outlined: (a) the state cannot assign the status of state religion to any church or religious community; (b) the state may not interfere in the affairs and internal organization of religious communities; (c) no religious community can enjoy special privileges from the state; and (d) the state may provide material assistance to religious communities but only without discrimination. Unlike the state Constitution, the LFR is clear about the separation of state and religious communities.[7]

These legal norms, taken together with the aforementioned constitutional provisions on the right to freedom of religion or belief and citizenship which is not conditioned with religious affiliation,[8] regulate three fundamental social relations in a way that corresponds to the values of the liberal democratic tradition, namely, (a) a relation between the state and religion in which the principle of separation applies, (b) a relation between the state and the individual where the principle of citizenship (but not confessional affiliation) applies, and (c) a relation between the individual and a religion (or religious community) in which the principle of freedom of religion is valid.[9]

The case law of the Constitutional Court of BiH confirmed that separation of the state and religious communities is necessary for the realization of religious freedom in the multi-religious Bosnian society. On 18 and 19 August 2000, the Constitutional Court considered a petition for review of the constitutionality of a provision of the Constitution of the Republic of Srpska (RS), which granted a privileged position to the SOC.[10] The relevant part of Art. 28 reads:

> The Serb Orthodox Church is a church of the Serb people and other peoples of the Orthodox faith.
>
> The state materially helps the Orthodox Church, cooperates with it in all areas, and especially on the preservation, cultivation and development of cultural, traditional and other spiritual values.[11]

Referring to the absence of explicit obligations under the ECHR or the Constitution of BiH on the separation of state and religion, the Constitutional Court

7 Art. 14, LFR.

8 Art. 17, Constitution of BiH.

9 See Nedim Begović, "Ustavni okvir i Zakon o slobodi vjere i pravnom položaju crkava i vjerskih zajednica u BiH," [Constitutional Framework and Law on Freedom of Religion and Legal Status of Churches and Religious Communities: Normative Projection of Bosnian-Herzegovinian Secularism] in *Sekularnost i religija: BiH i regija*, eds. Edin Šarčević and Drago Bojić (Sarajevo: Fondacija Centar za javno pravo, 2015), 84–85; Fikret Karčić, *The Other European Muslims: A Bosnian Experience* (Sarajevo: Center for Advanced Studies, 2015), 84–85.

10 Constitutional Court of BiH, Case no. U 5/98 IV, 18 August 2000.

11 Art. 28, para. 3–4, Constitution of the RS, *Official Gazette of the RS*, 21/92 – consolidated text, 28/94, 8/96, 13/96, 15/96, 16/96, 21/96, 21/02, 26/02, 30/02, 31/02, 69/02, 31/03, 98/03, 115/05, 117/05.

suggested that granting special status to the SOC in the RS does not *per se* discriminate against other religious communities. Moreover, according to the case law of the supervisory bodies of the European Convention, even the adoption of the system of state religion is not in conflict with Art. 9. of the Convention, provided that there are effective guarantees of the individual's right to freedom of religion. However, the Court referred to the ECtHR's judgment in *Otto Preminger v. Austria*,[12] according to which the state is obliged to create a public atmosphere in which free expression of religion is ensured. The Constitutional Court expressed doubt as to whether the RS could create such a "public atmosphere" given Art. 28, para. 4. The Court found that the paragraph does not have only a declaratory meaning, but also to establish the influence of one church *vis-à-vis* "public atmosphere" and the creation of a system of values and beliefs. Reviewing the practice of religious freedom in the RS at the time of the decision, the Constitutional Court came to the conclusion that the provision, in combination with discrimination on a religious and ethnic basis, had the effect of suppressing the free expression of other faiths. Accordingly, the failure of the RS authorities to ensure the right of Muslims and Catholics to manifest their religions freely justifies the conclusion that Art. 28, para. 4 of the entity constitution contravenes to the Constitution of BiH.[13]

However, paragraph 3 of this article remained an integral part of the constitutional text. The first part of this paragraph could suggest that the SOC has the status of a state/official religion, but this is precluded by the clause on the equality of religious communities that precedes it. Thus, we are confronted, as noted by S. Flere, M. Lavrič, and D. B. Djordjević, with "a constitutional *contradictio in adiecto* situation, i.e., a declaratory constitutional situation where the official precedence given to the church at issue is at variance with other provisions of the same constitution".[14] However, the spirit of this provision is very much alive, which is noticeable in the privileged position of the SOC in many areas, including government funding, public education, display of religious symbols, and so on, which will be discussed in more detail in Chapters 7 and 8.

Returning to the main course of the analysis, we should point to another landmark decision of the Constitutional Court of BiH that was even more explicit in its interpretation of the nature of relationships between religion and the state. Adopted after the 2004 LFR, the Court's decision – concerning the appeal of the Bugojno-based Parish of Saint Anthony of Padova of the Franciscan Province of Bosnia and Herzegovina regarding the estate of a deceased member of the order – referred to the state's secular organization as a common principle enshrined in Art. 14

12 *Otto-Preminger-Institut v. Austria*, 20 September 1994, Series A no. 295-A.

13 Ahmet Alibašić and Nedim Begović, "Reframing the Relations Between State and Religion in Post – War Bosnia: Learning to Be Free!" *Journal of Balkan and Near Eastern Studies* 19, no. 1 (2017): 27–28.

14 Sergej Flere, Miran Lavrič and Dragoljub B. Djordjević, "Religious References in the Constitution of European Post-Communist Countries and Ethno-Symbolism," *Journal of Church and State* 59, no. 3 (2017): 483–484.

of the law. The separation of the spheres of political and religious authority within the legislative framework of BiH has a dual character: (a) religion is separated from the state in the sense that no religion can have privileged status and religious officials can participate in the work of political institutions and so directly affect the formation of public policy, and (b) the state is separated from faith in the sense that individuals are guaranteed freedom of choice of faith, just as religious communities enjoy autonomy in self-organization, management, and operation.[15]

3 State and religion: separation with cooperation

The separation of religious communities and the state is not, however, strict or in all spheres. The paradigm of separate spheres is complemented by a concept of mutual cooperation on issues of "common interest", especially manifest in educational, cultural, and charitable work. The most important provision of the LFR that paves the way for cooperation between the state and the religions is in Art. 15, which provides for concluding agreements between religious communities and the relevant state or entity authorities, namely the Presidency of BiH (PBiH), the Council of Ministers of BiH (CMBiH) and the entity governments. Furthermore, Art. 17 provides for the MHRR of BiH "cooperat[ing] with all registered churches and religious communities or those preparing for registration and discuss[ing] all issues related to freedom of religion and the legal status of churches and religious communities". Some specific forms of cooperation are already indicated in the LFR. For example, faith-based educational, charitable, social welfare, and healthcare institutions are recognized and equal in privileges with those established by the state, which includes the possibility of state financial support. Cooperation between the state and religious communities is also envisaged in terms of organizing and conducting religious education in schools and preschool institutions. The reasons for commitment to a cooperative relationship between the state and religious communities are best set out in Art. 1 of the Basic Agreement between the Holy See and BiH (BAHS), which state that "the state and the Catholic Church, each in its proper sphere, are independent and autonomous" and obliges them "to mutual cooperation for integral human development, both spiritual and material, and for the promotion of the common good".[16] Thus, after nearly five decades of suspicion and a sometimes open hostility of the state towards religion, BiH has opted for the approach taken by most other European countries in recognizing the positive social role of religious communities.

The idea of concluding the BAHS which would create a new normative framework for the operation of the Catholic Church (CC) in accordance with the changed political and social circumstances in democratic BiH arose even before the adoption of the LFR, shortly before the first visit of Pope John Paul II to BiH in 1997. Thus, in 2002, two commissions were appointed, one state and the

15 Begović, "Ustavni okvir i Zakon o slobodi vjere," 86.

16 Art. 1, Basic Agreement between the Holy See and Bosnia and Herzegovina, *Official Gazette of BiH – International Agreements*, 10/07.

other church, with the task of preparing a draft agreement. These two commissions completed their work on 18 December 2002 by submitting a draft to the competent BiH authorities with the hope that it could be signed six months later, during Pope John Paul II's second visit to BiH. However, due to the opposition expressed by other religious communities, as well as certain political actors in the country, further activities regarding the contractual regulation of the position of the CC in BiH have been postponed. It was argued that before concluding bilateral agreements with religious communities, a new religion law should first be adopted that would set general standards for equal treatment of religious communities. Otherwise, the CC would be favoured, which would not be appropriate for a multi-religious Bosnian society.[17]

After the LFR came into force in March 2004, the CC sought to resolve the dilemmas that arose regarding the justification for concluding an agreement between the Holy See and BiH. The church argued that: (a) concluding an agreement was in the interest not only of the CC but also of BiH, as it would testify to the state's determination to break with the communist legacy and follow the experience of European democracies in ensuring a high level of religious freedom; (b) the agreement would strengthen the provisions of the LFR, guaranteeing the equality of religious communities; (c) the principle of equality of religious communities has not prevented a different treatment of the Holy See with regard to its international legal subjectivity, and (d) a number of neighbouring states have concluded similar agreements.[18]

In February 2006, a government working group presented a new draft agreement to the CMBiH, which was very similar in content to the original draft. The document was adopted by the CMBiH and the PBiH the same month, with some minor corrections. The agreement was signed in Sarajevo on 19 April 2006.[19] Immediately after that, the Office of the High Representative of the International Community in BiH pointed out to the problematic nature of its Art. 10, para. 3, which provided for the state's obligation to restitute the property of the CC which was nationalized during the communist regime, within the period of ten years. The provision was assessed as threatening to the weak economic system of the country. Following intensive negotiations with the Office and government officials in BiH during the summer of 2006, the CC withdrew from specifying a timeframe for the restitution of its property, thus removing a potential obstacle to ratification of the agreement. On 29 September 2006, the Additional Protocol

17 Pietro Parolin, "Temeljni ugovor između Svete Stolice i Bosne i Hercegovine u odnosu prema pravoslavnoj i muslimanskoj zajednici," [Basic Agreement Between the Holy See and Bosnia and Herzegovina in Relation to the Orthodox and Muslim Community] accessed 8 August 2019, www.ktabkbih.net/info.asp?id=20630; Tomo Vukšić, "Značenje Temeljnog ugovora između Svete Stolice i BiH te Dodatnog protokola na njega," [The Meaning of Basic Agreement Between the Holy See and Bosnia and Herzegovina and Additional Protocol on It] accessed 29 January 2021, www.kuvn.org/upload/file/Temeljni%20ugovor.pdf.

18 Parolin, "Temeljni ugovor."

19 On behalf of the Holy See, the Agreement was signed by Alessandro D'Erico as Apostolic Nuncio to BiH, and on behalf of BiH by Ivo Miro Jović, a Croat member of the PBiH.

to the BAHS was signed, which stipulated that the issue of restitution will be resolved by adopting a single law on restitution that will treat all nationalized property, including that of the CC.[20]

In terms of structure, the BAHS consists of a preamble and 19 articles. The main purpose of concluding the agreement, as stated in the preamble, is "establish[ing] the juridical framework of relations between the Catholic Church and Bosnia and Herzegovina". In addition, the preamble invokes the principles of separation of religion and the state and freedom of religion, and emphasizes the traditional character of the CC in BiH and its role in the social, cultural, and educational fields.[21]

Provisions contained in the BAHS can be classified into two basic categories. The first category consists of provisions that merely confirm or further elaborate the guarantees contained in the LFR. These include provisions on the CC public legal personality[22] and its freedom of (a) communication with the Holy See and other ecclesiastical organizations in the country and abroad,[23] (b) apostolic mission, including freedom of worship,[24] (c) broadcasting of its own media and access to public media,[25] (d) running its own schools and their equal treatment compared to public schools,[26] (e) teaching Catholic religious education in public schools and kindergartens,[27] (f) running charities and social care institutions,[28] (g) the protection of the CC property[29] and autonomy in appointing and dismissing its personnel,[30] and (h) freedom of Catholics to associate and its limitations.[31]

The second category consists of additional guarantees of religious rights that have not been treated by the LFR. Some of these guarantees are also relevant to other religious communities, such as those concerning the right to build new and renovate existing churches and other religious facilities.[32] Similarly, the guarantees of the right to pastoral care of Catholics in the army, police, prisons, hospitals, and orphanages[33] and the equal treatment of Catholic religious education with other school subjects[34] can be applied by analogy to other religious groups, following the principle of equality of religious communities. The remaining additional guarantees of religious rights in the BAHS are specific to Christian doctrine and canon law. Thus, for example, the inviolability of the seal of confession is

20 Parolin, "Temeljni ugovor."
21 See the preamble of the BAHS.
22 Art. 2, BAHS.
23 Art. 3, BAHS.
24 Arts. 4, 7, BAHS.
25 Art. 12, BAHS.
26 Art. 14, BAHS.
27 Art. 16, BAHS.
28 Art. 17, BAHS.
29 Art. 10, BAHS.
30 Art. 6, BAHS.
31 Art. 13, BAHS.
32 Art. 11, BAHS.
33 Art. 15, BAHS.
34 Art. 16, para. 1. BAHS.

protected[35] and it is envisaged that a special law will recognize Sundays and five Catholic festivals as non-working days for Catholics.[36]

The importance of concluding the BAHS goes beyond the normative regulation of the position of the CC. With this agreement, the Bosnian public authorities have opened a process of contractual regulation of relations with major religious groups in the country, which is still ongoing and which will determine the character of the relationship between the state and religion in BiH. This document served as a basis for drafting agreements of BiH with both the SOC and the IC and as an important reference in cases where certain dilemmas arose during the negotiations on the said drafts.

The Basic Agreement between BiH and the SOC (BASOC), signed in Sarajevo on 3 December 2007,[37] generally followed the structure and content of the previously signed agreement with the CC. Since both documents deal with the legal status of Christian denominations, the harmonization of their texts has been facilitated. Therefore, Arts. 1–12 and 14–29 of BASOC conceptually follow the structure and content of BAHS. The only exception is Art. 13, which guarantees the SOC the freedom to display its flag and other symbols, and prohibits unauthorized persons from showing them publicly. Besides, the preamble of the BASOC points out the role of the SOC in preserving the national unity of the Serb people, a claim that resonates closely with the cited Art. 28, para. 3, of the RS Constitution.[38]

4 The Draft Basic Agreement of BiH and the Islamic Community in BiH

At the time of concluding the agreements between the state and the two major churches, the leadership of the Islamic Community in BiH (IC) had shown no interest in concluding a similar agreement with the state. Mustafa Cerić, the former grand mufti (or *ra'is al-'ulama*) of the IC, argued that Bosnian Muslims, as the country's autochthonous majority, should not have negotiated their position with their home country.[39] Such an attitude will prove wrong for both pragmatical and essential reasons. Namely, reaching a political consensus on concluding the agreement between the state and the IC in a complex system of public decision-making in BiH would be far easier to achieve if it was on the agenda of

35 Art. 8, para. 2. BAHS.

36 Art. 9, BAHS.

37 With the authorization of the PBiH, the Agreement was signed by Safet Halilović, the then Minister for Human Rights and Refugees of BiH, and on behalf of the SOC, the Serb Patriarch Mr Pavle. At its 37th session held on 7 May 2008, the PBiH adopted a decision on ratification of this Agreement.

38 See preamble and Arts. 1–20 of the BASOC. The text of the BASOC received from the archives of Dr Ahmet Alibašić, a member of the Commission of the IC for negotiations with government representatives on the Basic Agreement between BiH and the IC.

39 V. Zija Dizdarević, "Zvona nad državom," [Bells Over the State] accessed 20 August 2019, www.pcnen.com/portal/2007/08/21/zvona-nad-drzavom/; Parolin, "Temeljni ugovor."

state authorities in a package with the remaining two agreements. In addition, concluding an agreement with the state proved more important for the IC than for the other two main religious communities, as it would create the basis for the accommodation of Islamic practices that are lacking in the laws currently in force.

The activities on concluding the agreement, which started in 2010, can be divided into three stages. In the first, the two negotiating parties formally expressed their readiness to start negotiations and carried out the necessary preparatory actions. It should be noted that the PBiH, even during the adoption of the BAHS, reached a conclusion on initiating the procedure of concluding similar agreements with other major religious communities.[40] However, it was only an attempt to weaken the status of the subject of religious education in public schools of Sarajevo Canton, initiated by Emir Suljagić, the then Cantonal Minister of Education, that led the leadership of the IC to amend its position on the need to conclude an agreement with the state. Thus, on 6 January 2010, Cerić submitted an initiative to Haris Silajdžić, a Bosniak member of the PBiH, to conclude an agreement, together with the first draft of this document, prepared by the Legal Service of the *Riyasat* (Presidency) of the IC.[41] The CMBiH adopted the Basis for Negotiations prepared by the MHRR[42] and appointed a Negotiating Team that included four representatives each from both the CMBiH and the IC.[43]

From the very beginning of this process, the relevant state bodies decided to conduct negotiations with the IC "on the same principles" that were applied in the contractual regulation of the state's relations with the Holy See and the SOC.[44] Namely, the agreements with the two churches were ratified by the PBiH, after previously obtaining the consent of the Parliamentary Assembly of BiH (PABiH).[45] When concluding the BAHS, there was no doubt that this was an international agreement, given the international legal subjectivity of the Holy See. Similarly, when it comes to the BASOC, the prevailing view was that it should also have the status of an international agreement, given that the seat

40 MHRR, Proposal of Basis for Negotiations with the Islamic Community in Bosnia and Herzegovina for Conclusion of the Basic Agreement between Bosnia and Herzegovina and the Islamic Community in Bosnia and Herzegovina: A Letter to the CMBiH, 22 August 2011.

41 The Draft was accepted at the session of the *Riyasat* of the IC on 20 October 2009 (see Cabinet of the *ra'is al-'ulama* of the IC, Conclusion of the Agreement between Bosnia and Herzegovina and the Islamic Community in Bosnia and Herzegovina: A Letter to the PBiH, no. 01/R-09/10, 6 January 2010).

42 The document was adopted at the 166th session of the CMBiH on 9 November 2011 (MHRR, Appointment of a Negotiating Team on behalf of the Islamic Community in Bosnia and Herzegovina: A Letter to the IC, no. 07–07–4546–1/11, 14 November 2011).

43 MHRR, Letter to the IC, no. 07–07–4546–1/11, 14 November 2011. The co-authors would like to thank Dr Ahmet Alibašić for providing insight into the materials created during the work of the negotiating team.

44 MHRR, Proposal for regulating the procedure of concluding the Basic Agreement between Bosnia and Herzegovina and the Islamic Community in Bosnia and Herzegovina: A Letter to the CMBiH, document not numbered or dated.

45 Such a procedure for ratification is provided for in Arts. 15–17 of the Law on the Procedure for Concluding and Executing International Agreements, *Official Gazette of BiH*, 29/00.

of this church is in another state (i.e. Serbia) and to ensure the equality of religious communities.[46] Although the IC was based in the country, it was proposed "equal treatment of the Islamic Community in Bosnia and Herzegovina in terms of content and procedure for concluding the Basic Agreement". The dilemma of whether the agreement of BiH and the IC should be recognized as a contract of international law arose only later, when its draft was submitted to the PBiH for consideration. After a remark was sent from the Cabinet of Dragan Čović, the Croat member of the PBiH that "the Islamic Community is not, nor can it be treated as an international entity with the necessary elements of foreignness",[47] the representatives of the IC in the Negotiation Team had to provide justification for such a treatment. The argument was found in the organizational structure of the IC, which, according to its Constitution, included the Islamic Community in Serbia, based in Novi Pazar, the Islamic Community in Croatia, the Islamic Community in Slovenia, and the Islamic Community of Bosniaks in the European Union, North America, and Australia.[48]

The first version of the DBAIC mostly follows the structure and content of previously concluded agreements with the two churches. However, additional accommodations of specific Islamic practices were provided, including, for example, the right of Muslims to a halal diet in the armed forces, police service, prisons, hospitals, schools, kindergartens, and other public institutions.[49] Further, the guarantees which strengthen the institutional authority of the IC and its role in terms of organizing religious life and representation of Bosnian Muslim community were envisaged, including the provisions of the IC exclusive responsibility for certification of halal products and services,[50] its autonomy in financial operations (except in relations to financial resources allocated to it by the state)[51] and regulating the labour of its employees,[52] and even the ban of registration of associations of Muslim believers without the prior written consent of the IC.[53]

In the second stage of activities the Negotiation Team, with the expert support of the MHRR, worked on harmonizing the text of the DBAIC. After reaching

46 Two members of the PBiH voted for the adoption of the BASOC, while the Bosniak member Haris Silajdžić abstained, disputing the international legal character of the agreement (see Dizdarević, "Zvona nad državom").

47 Čamdžić, Elvir, employee of the PBiH, e-mail correspondence with Mensur Karadža, Member of the Negotiation Team and Rifat Fetić, Chief of Staff of the *ra'is al-ʿulama* of the IC, 8 June 2017.

48 This argument was offered after consultations with some prominent lawyers (interview with Dr Ahmet Alibašić, Member of the Negotiating Team, 30 June 2019; notes by Ahmet Alibašić from the meeting of the *Riyasat's* Commission for Negotiations with the CMBiH held on 19 July 2016). Art. 1 of the 2014 Constitution defines the IC as "one and unique community of Muslims in Bosnia and Herzegovina and Sandžak, Croatia, Slovenia and Serbia, Bosniak Muslims outside their homeland and other Muslims who accept it as their own".

49 Art. 22, the initial Draft Basic Agreement between BiH and the IC.

50 Art. 15, the initial Draft Basic Agreement between BiH and the IC.

51 Art. 5, the initial Draft Basic Agreement between BiH and the IC.

52 Art. 7, para. 4., the initial Draft Basic Agreement between BiH and the IC.

53 Art. 16, para. 2., the initial Draft Basic Agreement between BiH and the IC.

consensus on work methodology, the Team discussed in detail each individual provision of the Draft.[54] During the negotiations, the original version of the Draft underwent numerous changes and reformulations, as a result of suggestions from both negotiating parties.

The Negotiating Team worked constructively and with full respect for the objections of both parties, so that the media were informed after the sixth meeting held on 22 October 2013 that the negotiations "are going smoothly and are in the final phase".[55] The beginning of political obstructions to the conclusion of the agreement can be traced from June 2014 when the BiH Ministry of Justice (MJ) and Ministry of Civil Affairs (MCA) submitted negative opinions on the text of the draft which was already agreed on 27 January 2014 with the participation of representatives of these ministries and was expected to be forwarded to the CMBiH for adoption.[56]

The MJ opinion argued that BiH was a "secular state, which is why it advocates the separation of religion and diminishing its importance of religion in public life".[57] This argument reflects the understanding of religion as a private matter that prevailed during the communist era and does not correspond to the real changes that have taken place in Bosnian society since the 1990s, in terms of reaffirming religious identities and the social importance of religious communities, nor existing constitutional and legal standards, relating to state-religion relations. It has already been mentioned that the Constitution of BiH did not explicitly regulate the relationship between religion and the state. Similarly, the LFR did not declare the secularity of the state, although it allowed for the separation of the state and religious communities. While the choice of words may seem random, it is actually closer to the concept of positive secularism that recognizes the possibility of cooperation between the state and religious communities. The MJ arguments would make at least some sense if the state had not previously entered into agreements with the remaining two major religious communities.

Furthermore, the opinions of the two ministries challenged the possibility of implementing the provisions of the draft agreement concerning the accommodation of Islam in the workplace (e.g. those pertaining to prayer, religious dress, etc.), given the alleged lack of mechanisms of state influence on the private employment sector, as well as the requirement of uniformity in the existing dress codes for public employees (e.g. in the armed forces, police service, judiciary, etc.).[58] The IC's representatives in the Negotiating Team put forward

54 A total of seven regular Team meetings were held. The first meeting was held on 19 April 2012 and the seventh on 27 January 2014.

55 Alibašić, Ahmet, Member of the Negotiating Team, e-mail Correspondence with Amila Kahrović-Posavljak, Journalist of Magazine *BH Dani*, 21 October 2013.

56 At that time, the function of the Minister of Justice of BiH was performed by Bariša Čolak, a member of the Croatian Democratic Union of BiH (HDZ), and the Minister of Civil Affairs Sredoje Nović, a Member of the Alliance of Independent Social Democrats (SNSD).

57 MJ, Opinion on the Basic Agreement between Bosnia and Herzegovina and the Islamic Community in Bosnia and Herzegovina: A Letter to the MHRR, no. 08–02–4–4320/14, 4 June 2014.

58 Opinion, no. 08–02–4–4320/14, 4 June 2014.

the counter-argument that the state in fact regularly impacts the private employment sector through labour laws and various bylaws. They also pointed out that "efficiency", in terms of the implementation of guarantees of religious rights, and "uniformity", in the context of dress codes in the public employment sector, are not legitimate reasons *per se* for restricting the expression of religion, that is, that those restrictions would be justified only if the conditions laid down in Art. 9, para. 2 of the ECHR were met. That the opinions of the two ministries were not guided exclusively by legal arguments was evident from the fact that they disputed even those provisions of the DBAIC that were identical to the formulations of the agreements previously concluded with the two churches or had an explicit ground in the 2004 LFR.[59]

Another key issue raised by the two ministries was whether the DBAIC should be harmonized with existing state and entity laws or, conversely, should be true. For example, the MCA challenged a clause in the agreement that obliges the state to regulate the provision of pension, disability, and health insurance to employees of the IC, arguing that the relevant entity authorities refused to establish a unified system of insurance for "religious officials" at the state level. An objection was also raised to the draft's provisions on the accommodation of Islam in the workplace, as they have no basis in the civil service law in force.[60] The IC's negotiating commission sharply criticized this approach, arguing that it neglects the state's positive obligation to ensure the effective enjoyment of the right to freedom of religion. In order to fulfil the obligation, the state should harmonize its legislation with the provisions of the agreement.[61] Otherwise, concluding an agreement that would not expand the scope of religious rights in relation to the existing legislation would be pointless.

After additional consultations,[62] requests,[63] and acceptance of compromise solutions,[64] the consensus was finally reached on the DBAIC, which the CMBiH adopted on 29 September 2015 and submitted to the PBiH for consideration. The third phase of negotiation activities followed, in which the politicization

59 Thus e.g. the provision obliging the state to finance the pension, disability, and health insurance of religious staff of the IC was derived from the Art. 13, para. 4 of the LFR, while the clauses dealing with the inviolability of Islamic religious facilities, restitution of the nationalized property of the IC, Islamic religious education in schools and the status of charitable organizations owned by the Community were analogous to those contained in agreements with the Holy See and the SOC.

60 MCA, Basic Agreement Between Bosnia and Herzegovina and the Islamic Community in Bosnia and Herzeogivna – Opinion: A Letter to the MHRR, no. br. 04–14–1–2394-EM/13, 11 June 2014.

61 Alibašić, Ahmet, e-mail Correspondence with Semiha Borovac, Minister of Human Rights and Refugees of BiH, 28 September 2014.

62 The Negotiating Team Held Additional Meeting on 27 November 2014 that discussed negative opinions of the MJ and MCA.

63 *Ra'is al-ʿulama* Husein-ef. Kavazović sent a letter to Vjekoslav Bevanda, the then chairman of the Council of Ministers, and Zlatko Lagumdžija, his deputy, urging the final adoption of the DBAIC by the CMBiH.

64 MJ in letter no. 09–02–4–5353/15 of 27 May 2015 gave a positive opinion on the DBAIC, stating that its previously given suggestions were included in it.

of the agreement with the Islamic Community in Bosnia and Herzegovina completely came to the surface. In order to understand the broader context of this politicization, it is useful to refer to the media reports on the adoption of the DBAIC. Radio-Television of the RS (RTRS) commented on the adoption of the DBAIC as "departure from a secular state" and the "path to a theocratic state dominated by religion".[65] Other media reported that Milorad Dodik, then RS president, opposed the adoption of the DBAIC, calling it a "dictation of Sharia" and accusing the rival political coalition "Alliance for Change" of its subservience to Bosniak political parties in Sarajevo by adopting the document.[66] At the same time the Sarajevo-based information portal "Klix" criticized state institutions and the IC for alleged hiding the DBAIC from the public.[67]

During 2016 and 2017, the text of the DBAIC was the subject of additional negotiations between the Office of the *ra'is al-'ulama* of the IC and the PBiH.[68] The Office sought to clarify any ambiguities that the members of the PBiH had regarding the Draft and expressed readiness to accept a number of suggestions made by them. For example, Art. 13, para. 2, provided that, when drawing up urban plans, the needs of the IC for the construction of new mosques and other religious facilities would be taken into account. Responding to the objection of Mladen Ivanić, then a member of the PBiH, that this provision was discriminatory for the CC and SOC because it was not included in their agreements with the state, the Office of *ra'is al-'ulama* proposed one of two alternatives, that is, to remove the provision from the text or to keep it, and to supplement the other two agreements with similar provisions. Nevertheless, the Office of the *ra'is al-'ulama* announced that a compromise regarding Art. 11 guaranteeing the accommodation of Islam in the workplace was not possible, as it was a "core

65 RTRS, "Ugovor sa IZ – BiH se udaljava od sekularne države," [Agreement with the IC – BiH Is Moving Away from a Secular State] accessed 21 August 2019, www.frontal.ba/novost/81161/ugovor-sa-iz-bih-se-udaljava-od-sekularne-drzave; RTRS "Uzbuna u Srpskoj: Sarajevo želi šerijatske propise na nivou BiH," [Alert in Srpska: Sarajevo Wants Sharia Regulations at the BiH Level] accessed 21 August 2019, www.kurir.rs/region/bosna-i-hercegovina/uzbuna-u-srpskoj-sarajevo-zeli-serijatske- propise-na-nivou-bih-clanak-1958623.

66 E. Mušinović, "O navodnom uvođenju šerijata u BiH: Kako su regulisana prava na hadž, džumu i odijevanje," [Alleged Introduction of Sharia in BiH: How the Rights to Observe Hajj, Jumu'a and Dress Were Regulated] accessed 21 August 2019, www.klix.ba/vijesti/bih/o-navodnom-uvodjenju-serijata-u-bih-kako-su-regulisana-prava-na-hadz-dzumu-i-odijevanje/151009046.

67 Er. M., "Poslije nekoliko mjeseci skrivanja dokumenta: Pogledajte Ugovor Islamske zajednice i BiH," [After a Few Months of Hiding the Document: See the Agreement of Islamic Community and BiH] accessed 21 August 2019, preuzeto sa: www.klix.ba/vijesti/bih/poslije-nekoliko-mjeseci-skrivanja-dokumenta-pogledajte-ugovor-islamske-zajednice-i-bih/151108064.

68 The Office conducted unofficial e-mail communication with Mladen Ivanić and Dragan Čović, the Serb and Croat members of the PBiH, conducted via the Cabinet of Bakir Izetbegović, a Bosniak member of the PBiH, occasionally consulting the *Riyasat*'s Commission for Negotiations with the state.

article in this agreement". When Bakir Izetbegović, a Bosniak member of the PBiH, proposed that the issue of the adoption of the DBAIC be included on the agenda of the session of the collective head of state, the other two members rejected it.[69]

The provisions contained in the DBAIC can be classified into three categories. The first includes provisions which have a clear basis in the LFR and are similarly worded in the agreements with the Holy See and the SOC. These include the continuity of the IC's legal personality, the right to communicate with other religious organizations at home and abroad, the freedom to carry out religious mission, autonomy in the internal organization and management of community affairs, the protection of religious sites, the right to own media and access to public media, the right to establish and manage of educational, charitable and social care institutions, as well as to provide for Islamic religious education in schools, and so on.

The second category includes provisions that are not explicitly based on the LFR, but have precedents in two previously concluded agreements. These include mandatory notification of the IC's authorities of court proceedings against its officials, the right of Muslim employees to take days off to celebrate their religious holidays, the right to build mosques and other religious facilities, the provision of Islamic pastoral care in the military, police, prisons, hospitals, orphanages, and social care institutions, equal status of Islamic religious education with other school subjects, and so on.

The third category includes provisions on the accommodation of religion in the workplace that do not have counterparts in earlier agreements. Art. 11 of the DBAIC provided:

1. In the public and private sectors, the right to free time (break) for performing Jumu'a prayer will be provided, as well as the right to free time for performing Iftar and Sahur during the month of Ramadan.
2. In the public and private sectors, the right to leave from work for the purpose of performing Hajj rites will be provided.
3. In the public and private sectors, the right of Muslim believers to manifest their religion, such as through performing prayers, choosing food, clothing and appearance in accordance with their religious beliefs, will be respected.
4. The rights referred to in paragraph (3) of this Article may be subject only to such limitations provided by law as are necessary in a democratic society in the interests of public security, protection of public order, health or morals, or protection of the rights and freedoms of others.

It was these provisions that were singled out by two non-Bosniak members of the PBiH as an obstacle to the adoption of an agreement with the IC. They

69 S. H., "Čović i Ivanić zvanično odbili podržati ugovor države s Islamskom zajednicom u BiH," [Čović and Ivanić Officially Refused to Support the State's Agreement with the Islamic Community in BiH] accessed 25 August 2019, www.klix.ba/vijesti/bih/covic-i-ivanic-zvanicno-odbili-podrzati-ugovor-drzave-s-islamskom-zajednicom-u-bih/180419073.

asserted that these provisions "(a) introduce Sharia into the legal order of BiH, (b) bring non-Muslims into a discriminatory position since Muslims are granted rights that are not provided for in the previously signed agreements with the Holy See and the SOC and (c) are difficult to implement, particularly in the private sector".[70]

Contrary to the first assertion, it may be argued that the specific accommodations of Islamic observances proposed in the text of the agreement are encompassed by the right to manifest religion in the light of Art. 9, para. 1, of the ECHR, as interpreted in the case law of the ECtHR. Otherwise, comparable accommodations in previously signed agreements "could be regarded as introducing canon law into the legal order of BiH".[71]

The allegation of the discriminatory nature of the contract is also untenable. Namely, the concept of discrimination refers to unjustifiably different treatment of individuals or groups of people who are in a comparable situation,[72] which is not the case here. For example, the need for a Muslim employee to abstain from work to offer Friday prayers is specific to Islam in a similar way to Sunday as a non-working day and the inviolability of the seal of confession – both recognized in agreements with the two churches – specific to Christianity. While this argument insists on the "formal equality of Muslims and other employees", the intention of the proposed agreement is to achieve a substantial equality that will provide equal opportunities to all employees, regardless of their religion or belief.[73]

Finally, the argument about the difficulties in applying these provisions, especially in the private sector, carries some weight. However, the problem could be solved by formulating Art. 11 in terms of the right to "reasonable accommodation" which is already a recognized concept in comparative law.[74] This would require that the scope of the restriction clause contained in Art. 11, para. 4 be extended to the entire text of the article. Such an approach would be in line with the recent jurisprudence of the ECtHR, which requires a careful balance between the freedom of religion of employees and the legitimate interests of employers to restrict the freedom if it interferes with the normal functioning of work or violates the rights of other employees.[75]

70 Nedim Begović, "Freedom of Religion in the Workplace: The European Court of Human Rights Decisions on Applications Made by Muslim Appellants," *Journal of Muslims in Europe* 10, no. 1 (2020): 183.

71 Begović, "Freedom of Religion in the Workplace," 184.

72 On treating like cases similarly and different cases differently see e.g. Christopher McCrudden and Sacha Prechal, *The Concepts of Equality and Non-Discrimination in Europe: A Practical Approach* (European Network of Legal Experts in the Field of Gender Equality, 2009), 11–13.

73 Begović, "Freedom of Religion in the Workplace," 184.

74 Begović, "Freedom of Religion in the Workplace," 18.

75 See European Court of Human Rights – Research Division, *Overview of the Court's Case-Law on Freedom of Religion*, 2013, para. 83, accessed 25 August 2019, www.echr.coe.int/Documents/Research_report_religion_ENG.pdf; *Eweida and Others v. the United Kingdom*, nos. 48420/10 and 3 others, ECHR 2013.

5 Implementation of the signed basic agreements

The implementation of the signed agreements between the state and the two churches involves three types of normative activity, namely (a) adopting implementing protocols on specific issues, (b) enacting new laws, and (c) adopting amendments to existing laws. In order to carry out these activities in relation to the signed agreement with the Holy See, a joint commission was formed in December 2008, which included representatives of the two parties.[76] The commission has so far prepared a series of documents aimed at elaborating the provisions of the BAHS, including the agreement on the pastoral care of Catholics in the military, concluded between the Holy See and BiH.[77] In contrast, no consensus has yet been reached on the proposed draft agreements on the pastoral care of Catholics in health and social care institutions, as well as in the police service and penitentiaries.[78] There has been even less success in passing new and amending existing laws. For example, the bill on non-working days during religious holidays, prepared with the aim of implementing the relevant provisions of the agreements guaranteeing the rights of Catholics and Orthodox, did not receive support in the PABiH. Also, the initiatives launched to adopt amendments to the criminal procedure codes have not yet yielded concrete effects.[79]

When it comes to the implementation of the BASOC, in April 2010 the CMBiH passed a decision on the establishment of the Mixed Commission, which, however, was never constituted, explained by the MHRR as a lack of interest and greater engagement of the contracting parties. In December 2016, the Ministry again prepared the Proposal of the Decision on the Establishment of the Mixed Commission, but it was never adopted by the CMBiH. Given that, in the meantime, there have been personnel changes in the SOC and the CMBiH, new activities are ahead in terms of forming the Commission.[80]

Thus, the conclusion can be made that no significant progress has been visible yet in the implementation of the concluded agreements, given that they have not resulted in expected adoption of new laws or amending existing laws and regulations.[81]

76 Its establishment was provided by Art. 18, para. 2, of the BAHS.

77 It was signed on 8 April 2010. See Agreement on the Pastoral Care of Catholic Believers, Members of the Armed Forces of BiH, Concluded Between the Holy See and BiH, accessed 25 August 2019, www.bkbih.ba/info.php?id=233.

78 Draft Agreement between the Holy See and BiH on the Pastoral Care of Catholic believers, members of the Armed Forces of BiH, letter from the MHRR sent to the CMBiH, No. 01–38–7238/09, 12 December 2009.

79 Adopting these amendments is necessary to bring the current laws on criminal procedure in accordance with the agreement's provisions concerning a judicial inquiry into offences committed on that part of a member of the clergy, and the protection of the inviolability of the seal of confession. In addition, amendments to the laws on spatial planning and the laws on public media need to be adopted to bring them into line with the provisions of the agreed agreements. See Information of MHRR, no. UP-I-05–07–7–25–3/19, 26 July 2019.

80 Information of MHRR, no. UP-I-05–07–7–25–3/19, 26 July 2019.

81 Information of MHRR, no. UP-I-05–07–7–25–3/19, 26 July 2019.

6 Conclusion

This chapter has analysed the constitutional/legal framework and the judicial doctrine in order to establish which system of state-religion relations BiH opted for in the post-war period. The analysis focused on the constitutional texts, the 2004 law on religions, relevant decisions of the Constitutional Court of BiH, and the agreements concluded between the state and the two major churches in BiH, but also the difficulties in both negotiating an agreement with the IC, as well as implementing already signed agreements.

This analysis suggests that in post-war BiH a cooperative model of state-religion relations has been emerging. This model is characterized by the structural and functional separation of the state and religious communities, but also enables their mutual cooperation in various societal fields, such as education, culture, charity, and so on. The 2004 law on religions provides for separation of the state and religion and upholds equal treatment of all religious communities. At the same time, it envisages the possibility of concluding agreements between the state and religious communities which will regulate issues of common interest. So far, these agreements have been concluded by two major churches, that is, the CC and the SOC. The process of establishing cooperative relations between the state and religion has been hampered on the level of practical politics which is best seen in the example of challenging the draft agreement between the state and the IC and the poor implementation of already signed agreements with the CC and the SOC.

II

Law, state, and religion in Bosnia and Herzegovina

Thematic studies

4 Religious rights in specialized regulatory contexts

1 Introduction

This chapter discusses the extent to which constitutional guarantees of the right to freedom of religion or belief have been implemented in specialized regulatory contexts in Bosnia and Herzegovina (BiH or Bosnia), such as military life, police service, prisons, the health sector, the employment, and the judiciary. Members of different religions, when found in institutionalized environments regulated by the state, face various challenges related to aspects of religious practice such as performing prayers during working hours, adhering to religious dietary requirements, wearing religious clothing and symbols, and so on.

The aforementioned discussion is relied on in-depth analysis of the normative framework applicable in various contexts such as military, police and civil service, prisons, healthcare, employment and the judiciary, as well as data collected under the laws on the right of access to information of public importance. Further, bilateral agreements of BiH with religious communities, human rights reports and the relevant case materials of the Constitutional Court of BiH and the Institution of Ombudsman for Human Rights of BiH (IOHR) have been consulted.

The chapter argues that in some regulatory contexts such as the armed forces, prisons, and, in part, hospitals, the accommodation of religious beliefs and practices is satisfactory. In contrast, it is necessary to ensure a greater scope of protection of religious rights for both private and public employees, including officers in the police force and the judiciary.

2 Armed forces

The exercise of religious rights of members of the Armed Forces of Bosnia and Herzegovina (AFBiH) is specifically regulated by the Law on Service in the Armed Forces of Bosnia and Herzegovina,[1] the Rulebook on the organization and functioning of the religious service in the Ministry of Defense of Bosnia and Herzegovina

1 Law on Service in the AFBiH, *Official Gazette of BiH*, 88/05, 53/07.

DOI: 10.4324/9780429266683-7

(MDBiH) and the Armed Forces of Bosnia and Herzegovina[2] and bilateral agreements of the state with three major religious communities.[3] It should be noted that the service in the AFBiH is of a professional nature, that is, that the obligation to serve military service was abolished in BiH as of 1 January 2006,[4] so that in practice there was no need to invoke conscientious objection to military service. Since the Law on Freedom of Religion (LFR) was passed before the abolition of military service, it had provided that religious officials and students of religious seminaries were exempt from military service, but could join the military at personal request.[5]

The Law on Service in the AFBiH stipulates that a military person "has the right to perform religious activities for the purpose of exercising religious freedoms in accordance with the specifics of each religion". The MDBiH, in cooperation with registered religious communities, prescribes the organization of religious activities and the manner of exercising the religious rights of members of the AFBiH.[6] The religious service forms an integral part of the structure of the MDBiH and the AFBiH and is composed of four organizational units, i.e. Military Muftiate, Orthodox Pastoral Care, Catholic Pastoral Care, and units of other religious communities. The latter are constituted at the request of any "other" religious community, provided that its members make up more than 2% of the total military personnel.

Two important factors could have contributed to the quality of protection of religious rights in the AFBiH. The first factor was the participation of the U.S. military legal experts in the preparation of the Bill on the Service in the AFBiH, which encouraged the adoption of standards on the accommodation of religion originating from the U.S. military's legal tradition. As another contributing factor, at the time of drafting the outlined bill, the Law on Freedom of Religion[7] was adopted at the state level, which had positive implications for the regulation of religious rights in the military environment.

2 Rulebook on the Organization and Manner of Operation of the Religious Service in the MDBiH and in the Armed Forces of Bosnia and Herzegovina, no. 06–38–5133/07, 12 November 2007.

3 On 11 September 2007, the Council of Ministers of BiH concluded the agreements with the authorities of the three major religious communities, i.e. the Islamic Community in BiH (IC), the Serb Orthodox Church (SOC) and the Catholic Church (CC) on the establishment, organization, and functioning of their organizational units of unified religious service in the MD and the AFBiH. Later, on 7 July 2010, the Presidency of BiH ratified the Agreement Between BiH and the Holy See on the Pastoral Care of Catholic Believers, Members of the AFBiH, which was concluded on 8 April 2010. The Agreement provided for the establishment of the Military Ordinariate for the Pastoral Care of Catholic believers in the AFBiH, instead of the former Office of Catholic Pastoral Care. See Decision on Ratification of the Agreement Between BiH and the Holy See on the Pastoral Care of Catholic Believers, Members of the AFBiH, *Official Gazette of BiH – International Agreements*, 8/10.

4 Art. 2, para. 1 and Art. 79, Law on Defense of Bosnia and Herzegovina, *Official Gazette of BiH*, 88/05.

5 Art. 6, para. 2 (d), Law on Freedom of Religion and the Legal Status of Churches and Religious Communities, *Official Gazette of BiH*, 5/04.

6 Art. 29, para. 1, 4, Law on Service in the AFBiH.

7 Law on Freedom of Religion and Legal Status of Churches and Religious Communities, *Official Gazette of BiH*, 5/04.

The appointment of military imams, priests and chaplains is a collaborative process between the state and religion in the sense that the Minister of Defense of BiH appoints members of the religious service on the basis of a decree of the head of a respective religious community.[8] Members of religious service have the status of civilians in the MDBiH, while in the AFBiH they form part of the military staff.[9] Salaries of members of the religious service in the AFBiH, as well as all other costs of its operation, are borne by the state.[10] In terms of overseeing the religious service, its members are subordinate to both the military and their religious authority.[11]

A range of religious activities of the military personnel is accommodated, including regular performance of religious rites of all three denominations, organization of pilgrimages to Mecca (*hajj*), as well as joint iftars and other activities during the holy month of Ramadan for Muslim members of the AFBiH, organization of pilgrimage to the monasteries and celebration of baptismal feasts for the Orthodox members of the AFBiH, that is, the pilgrimage to Lourdes, France, for the Catholic members of the AFBiH and so on.[12] In addition, military personnel have the right to use four days off during one calendar year to celebrate religious festivals, two of which are paid.[13]

Compliance with religious dietary requirements is regulated in detail by the relevant provisions of the Rulebook on Nutrition in the Armed Forces of Bosnia and Herzegovina in Peace. Accordingly, military personnel are entitled to a diet in accordance with norms or customs of their religion (halal products, halal slaughter, kosher meat, fasting food, vegetarian food, etc.). Special attention is paid to adjusting the diet of members of the AFBiH on fasting days, as well as on religious holidays.[14]

Two cases related to restrictions on the exercise of religious rights in the military environment can be singled out, one of which received an epilogue at the Bosnian Constitutional Court. In the first case, the Parliamentary Military Commissioner received a complaint from a member of the AFBiH who was banned from wearing a beard, although he did so for medical reasons. The prohibition was based on Art. 12 of the Rules of Service in the Armed Forces of Bosnia and

8 Art. 10, Rulebook on the Organization and Manner of Operation of the Religious Service.

9 Art. 4, para. 1, Art. 5, para. 1–2, Art. 7, para. 1–2, Rulebook on the Organization and Manner of Operation of the Religious Service.

10 See e.g. Art. 20, Agreement on the Establishment, Organization and Manner of Operation of the Military Muftiate as an Integral Part of the Unified Religious Service in MDBiH and AFBiH, 11 September 2007.

11 Art. 16, 17, Rulebook on the Organization and Manner of Operation of the Religious Service.

12 Nermin Lapandić, "Pravo vojnih lica na slobodu vjere u oružanim snagama Bosne i Hercegovine" [The Right of Military Personnel to Freedom of Religion in the Armed Forces of Bosnia and Herzegovina], *Context* 1, no. 2 (2014): 58–59.

13 Art. 57, Law on Service in the AFBiH.

14 See Art. 13 and annexes IX-XI, Rulebook on Nutrition in the AFBiH in Peace, no. 11-02-3-2923/15, 3 August 2015.

Herzegovina, which prohibit the wearing of beards by members of the military, except for religious officials. The Parliamentary Military Commissioner held that it was necessary for the MDBiH to consult all the necessary experts, including specialist doctors and members of religious service of the AFBiH, who could give a valid argument for or against introduction of the said restriction.[15]

The second case related to the removal of a female member of the AFBiH from her duty as a non-commissioned officer for intelligence affairs due to wearing a headscarf. After disciplinary proceedings were instituted against her for violating the relevant provisions of the Standard Operating Procedures governing the wearing of military uniforms,[16] she was transferred by order of the MDBiH to another barracks where she was allowed to wear a headscarf. By a decision of 22 March 2013, the Second Instance Chamber of the Court of BiH ruled that the MDBiH had not discriminated against the appellant by transferring her to another position in the AFBiH. As arguments, the Court stated that the contract of enlistment in the military service did not guarantee the appellant permanent engagement in a certain place, and that by signing that contract she voluntarily subjected herself to a situation in which "certain restrictions on the ability to manifest religious beliefs are justified".[17] These arguments determined the Constitutional Court of BiH to reject the appellant's allegations of violation of her rights to freedom of religion and non-discrimination on the grounds of religion.[18] Applying the so-called "special situation rule"[19] in a military context, the Court too easily came to the conclusion that there was no interference with the appellant's right to freedom of religion in this case. The court could instead have opted to follow the approach of recent ECtHR case law which requires a careful weighing between the employee's right to religious manifestation and the interests of the employer.[20] In the light of this principle, it was necessary to

15 Office of Parliamentary Military Commissioner of Bosnia and Herzegovina, Report on the Work of the Parliamentary Military Commissioner of Bosnia and Herzegovina for 2013, 2 February 2014, p. 13, accessed 17 May 2021, file:///C:/Users/Nedim/Downloads/Izvjestaj%20o%20radu%20Parl.vojnog%20pov.%20za%202013.-B.pdf.

16 These procedures provide that members of the AFBiH are not allowed to wear civilian items of clothing with uniforms, i.e. that they are allowed to carry religious symbols or not to carry the prescribed uniforms only while attending a religious rite or during prayer. See Constitutional Court of BiH, no. AP 2190/13, 9 July 2015, para. 32.

17 Constitutional Court of BiH, Case no. AP 2190/13, 9 July 2015, para. 22, 24.

18 Constitutional Court of BiH, Case no. AP 2190/13, 9 July 2015, para. 55, 56, 60.

19 This rule, which was developed in the early Strasbourg jurisprudence on religion, in reality operates as a limitation on the freedom to manifest religion that is distinct from the restrictions laid down in the second paragraph of Art. 9 of the ECHR. See Norman Doe, *Law and Religion in Europe: A Comparative Introduction* (New York: Oxford University Press, 2011), 52.

20 In his dissenting opinion, Judge Ćeman pointed out, *inter alia*, to the Court's reductionist approach in interpreting the ECtHR's recent case law on freedom of religion in the workplace, in particular the landmark case of *Eweida and Others v. the UK*. See Constitutional Court of BiH, Case no. AP 2190/13, 9 July 2015, Separate dissenting opinion of the Court's president Mirsad Ćeman.

assess whether the provisions of the MDBiH bylaw restricting the right to dress in accordance with the requirements of religion are in accordance with the constitutional guarantees of religious freedom.[21]

3 Police service

The current legislation on police officers in BiH contains a blanket ban on the manifestation of religious beliefs during the performance of their official duties.[22] Given its broad formulation, this prohibition can be interpreted "in such a way that police officers, upon taking office, completely give up the enjoyment of the constitutional right to freedom of religion while on duty".[23]

In February 2014, an employee of State Investigation and Protection Agency (SIPA) of BiH addressed the IOHR and the Ministry of Human Rights and Refugees of BiH with a question about "how employees of the police agency can exercise their constitutional right to manifest religion by performing daily and Friday prayers during working hours".[24] Both the Ministry and the Ombudsman responded that, under existing laws, institutions of BiH have no obligation to provide prayer facilities for their employees. Instead, they suggested either that employees perform religious rites during breaks during working hours or that the employer make a "reasonable accommodation" of their religious needs through a reorganization of the work schedule so that "it does not adversely affect the institution's work".[25]

21 This is in line with the Venice Commission's recommendation that restrictions on religious freedom in public institutions such as prisons, the military and state hospitals should be enacted only after careful "limitation analysis". See The Advisory Panel of Experts on Freedom of Religion or Belief of the Office for Democratic Institutions and Human Rights (ODIHR) of the Organization for Security and Co-operation in Europe (OSCE) in consultation with the European Commission for Democracy Through Law (the Venice Commission) of the Council of Europe, *Guidelines for Review of Legislation Pertaining to Religion or Belief*, June 18–19, 2004, 22.

22 Art. 36, para. 3 of the Law on Police Officers of the BiH, *Official Gazette of BiH*, 27/04, 63/04, 5/06, 58/06, 15/08, 50/08, 63/08, 35/09, 7/12 and 42/18; Art. 36, para. 3 of the Law on Police Officers of the FBiH, *Official Gazette of the FBiH*, 27/05 and 70/08; Art. 56, para. 3 of the Law on Police and Internal Affairs, *Official Gazette of the RS*, 57/16, 110/16, 58/19 and 82/19; Art. 48, para. 3 of the Law on Police Officers of the BD BiH, *Official Gazette of the BDBiH*, 41/07, 04/08, 36/09, 60/10, 37/14, 13/16, 14/19.

23 In his separate opinion in case U 8/17 (Constitutional Court of BiH, 30 November 2017), Judge Tudor Pantiru noted the possibility of such an interpretation and stressed the necessity to examine the compatibility of the ban on religious manifestation for the police officers with Art. 9, para. 2 of the ECHR. See Nedim Begović, "Freedom of Religion in the Workplace: The European Court of Human Rights Decisions on Applications Made by Muslim Apellants," *Journal of Muslims in Europe* 10, no. 1 (2021): 179–180.

24 Begović, "Freedom of Religion in the Workplace," 180.

25 Ministry for Human Rights and Refugees – Department for Human Rights, Response to the Request for Information on the Issue of the Free Manifestation of Religion, no. 07–38–701714, 11 March 2014; Institution of Ombudsman for Human Rights of BiH, Response, no. Ž-SA-05–229/14, 3 March 2014.

In January 2017, the new director of the BiH Border Police passed changes to the rules on wearing uniforms, which prohibit employees of this state agency from wearing beards at work.[26] Several police officers have filed complaints about the new rules, claiming they are violating their right to exercise their faith by wearing a beard. Safet Softić, Deputy Speaker of the House of Peoples of the Parliamentary Assembly of BiH, submitted a request to the Constitutional Court of BiH to review the constitutionality of the provision of the Rulebook on wearing a uniform, which reads: "Police officers in uniform must have their beards shaved."[27]

The focus of the decision of the Constitutional Court of BiH in this case was on the assessment of whether the ban on wearing a beard as a manifestation of religion (Art. 9) and as an aspect of private life (Art. 8) is justified by the protection of some legitimate aims. The Director of the Border Police stated that the reasons for introducing the ban were to achieve an orderly and uniform appearance of police officers and the fight against corruption that occurs in connection with the performance of police officers, due to difficulties in identifying people wearing beards. As to the first reason, the Court stated that it was reasonable that any police should look "neat and uniform" but that the Director of the Border Police did not explain why, in the case of permission to wear a well-groomed beard – as prescribed by the previous Rulebook on wearing a uniform – the mentioned general goal was violated. When it comes to the second reason, the Court was of the opinion that this is a flat claim that can be opposed by another, namely that, in fact, it is easier to identify a person wearing a beard because it "affects the physiognomy of the face of the person wearing it".[28] In view of this, the Court ruled that a total ban on the wearing of beards by officers of the Border Police could not be justified by any of the legitimate aims of restricting the right to privacy and the right to religion under Arts. 8 and 9 of the ECHR.[29]

Given that the Rulebook, which was the subject of the Constitutional Court's assessment, relied on the state Law on Police Officers, this decision served as a precedent for the accommodation of the right to wear a beard on employees of other state police agencies. In contrast, police officers whose work is regulated by entity and cantonal legislation are still not allowed to wear beards for religious or private reasons while in the workplace.[30]

26 Rulebook on Amendments to the Rulebook on Wearing Uniforms, no. 17–07–02–1161–7/06, 30 January 2017.
27 Art. 1, para. 1 (7), Rulebook on Amendments to the Rulebook on Wearing Uniforms.
28 Constitutional Court of BiH, Case no. U 8/17, 30 November 2017, para. 43.
29 Constitutional Court of BiH, Case no. U 8/17, 30 November 2017, para. 44.
30 In *Brulić v. the FBiH* (Case no. 65 0 P 733856 18 P, 9 January 2020) by the first instance decision of the Municipal Court in Sarajevo discrimination was found due to the ban on wearing beards by uniformed police officers in the Federal Police while at work. This decision is not final and the decision of the appellate court on appeal is pending.

4 Prisons

The right of prisoners to free excercise of their faith, without discrimination, is recognized by global and European international laws. This includes the accesss to religious care, services, and literature, as well as the diet in conformity with religious prescriptions.[31] The legislation governing the execution of criminal sanctions in BiH incorporates relevant international standards aimed at ensuring that prisoners meet their religious and spiritual needs. Accordingly, there must be no discrimination on the basis of religion or belief in the treatment of convicted persons.[32] Prisoners have the right to meet their religious needs,[33] and the conditions for this are provided by the prison authorities in collaboration with representatives of the registered religious communities in BiH.[34] This may include participation in collective prayer, attendance at religious ceremonies, and gatherings organized within the penitentiary institution, as well as access to religious literature.[35] Further, the nutrition of prisoners must be compatible with their religious and cultural requirements.[36] In addition, prison authorities may allow them to move freely outside the prison for up to two days during one year to celebrate their religious holidays.[37]

In order to ensure the religious rights of inmates, all penitentiary institutions in the RS provide the necessary conditions, including prayer rooms, religious inventory and literature. They also allow for unhindered visits by religious officials, not only for the purpose of performing collective prayer and celebrating religious holidays, but also at the individual request of prisoners. According to information received from the Ministry of Justice of the RS, in the period 2014–2018, there were no cases "where a prisoner was denied the right to exercise his religious needs or was discriminated against on religious grounds".[38] The largest and the oldest penitentiary institution in FBiH, located in Zenica, has been cooperating successfully for a long time with representatives of the IC, the SOC, and the CC in order to ensure the enjoyment of religious right of its prisoners. Within the penitentiary institution, prayer

31 European Prison Rules, para. 13, 22.1., 29.1., 29.2., 29.3., 35.1., accessed 18 May 2021, https://rm.coe.int/european-prison-rules-978-92-871–5982–3/16806ab9ae. See also Doe, *Law and Religion in Europe*, 203.

32 Art. 11, para. 3, Law on Execution of Criminal Sanctions in the FBiH, *Official Gazette of the FBiH*, 44/98, 42/99, 12/09; Art. 3, para. 5, Law on Execution of Criminal and Misdemeanor Sanctions of the RS, *Official Gazette of the RS*, 63/18.

33 The manner and conditions of satisfying religious needs are regulated in more detail by the prison house rules. Art. 100, Law on Execution of Criminal Sanctions in the FBiH.

34 Art. 12, Law on Execution of Criminal Sanctions in the FBiH; Art. 104, para. 2, Law on Execution of Criminal and Misdemeanor Sanctions of the RS.

35 Art. 86, para. 2, Art. 104, Law on Execution of Criminal and Misdemeanor Sanctions of the RS.

36 Art. 44, para. 1, Law on Execution of Criminal Sanctions in the FBiH; Art. 92, para. 1, Law on Execution of Criminal and Misdemeanor Sanctions of the RS.

37 Art. 89 e), Law on Execution of Criminal Sanctions in the FBiH; Art. 141, para. 1 (5), Law on Execution of Criminal and Misdemeanor Sanctions of the RS.

38 Ministry of Justice of the RS, Information no. 08.030/240–123/19, 3 October 2019.

rooms have been established, namely a masjid for Muslim and separate chapels for Orthodox and Catholic convicts. Imams, priests, and chaplains regularly visit this institution, lead religious ceremonies for prisoners, and provide them with religious instruction. Religious festivals are celebrated in a solemn manner, with an appropriate ceremony performed by the convicts, and attended by the prison educators and representatives of the prison authorities and religious communities. The ceremony is followed by a holiday greeting and a festive lunch. In order to meet the religious and cultural requirements regarding the nutrition of prisoners, the prison is equipped with two kitchens. One of them serves pork as part of the menu, while in the other food is prepared without pork products, so convicts have the right to choose which one to use.[39] When it comes to violations of the right to freedom of religion or beliefs of prisoners, only sporadic cases have been reported.[40]

5 Hospitals

Among the general principles on which the provision of healthcare is based is respect for the patient's "privacy, worldview, and moral and religious beliefs".[41] The accommodation of religious activities in hospitals may include the provision of spiritual care to patients,[42] the performance of religious rites in premises intended for that purpose, as well as the management of the dead bodies at the hospital's morgue in conformity with religious prescriptions.[43]

According to information obtained from the federal and cantonal ministries of health, these bodies have so far not received any complaints of violations of the right of patients or medical staff to freedom of religion or belief, nor did they enact any bylaws that would regulate the protection of the religious rights of

39 Zenica Penitentiary, Information no. 01–12–2154/19, 20 August 2019.

40 Thus, in 2015, a Turkish convict at the Zenica Penitentiary filed a complaint with the BiH Human Rights Ombudsman, alleging that his roommate in the prison, who was serving a sentence for war crimes against the Muslim population in the 1992–1995 war, obstructed him from performing prayers and humiliated his religion, nation and language. Their conflict was resolved by the prison administration placing them in different prison rooms. See Zenica Penitentiary, Information: A Letter to the Institution of the Human Rights Ombudsman of BiH, no. 01–12–2344/15, 13 March 2015.

41 Art. 30, Law on Rights, Obligations and Responsibilities of Patients of the Federation of Bosnia and Herzegovina, *Official Gazette of the FBiH*, 40/10. See also Art. 17, Law on Health Care of the RS, *Official Gazette of the RS*, 106/09, 44/15.

42 Art. 15 of the Basic Agreement Between the Holy See and BiH (BAHS) (*Official Gazette of BiH – International Agreements*, 10/07) stipulates that BiH recognizes to the CC the right to spiritual care of Catholic faithful who are members of the armed and police forces, and of those who are resident in penal institutions, hospitals, orphanages, and in any institution for the health and social care, whether public or private. However, the draft agreement on the implementation of this provision prepared by the Joint Commission for Monitoring the Implementation of the BAHS has not yet been adopted.

43 Art. 47, Law on Rights, Obligations and Responsibilities of Patients of the Federation of Bosnia and Herzegovina; Art. 27, para. 2, Law on Health Care of the FBiH, *Official Gazette of the FBiH*, 46/10.

patients and healthcare workers.[44] However, the situation is more complicated when it comes to data on the availability of prayer rooms in hospitals, the provision of spiritual care to patients, and the sources of its funding.

Although there is a legislative basis for the accommodation of patients' religious rites in hospitals, distinct prayer rooms are provided only in certain healthcare institutions, most often to meet the religious needs of patients belonging to the majority religious group at the local level. Thus, the University Clinical Hospital Mostar has a chapel for Catholic patients, but not for the employees of this institution. In the event that patients belonging to other religious communities request that they be provided with the conditions to perform the prayer, the hospital administration allows them to perform the prayer in an empty room, and if it is not available, the patient is fenced off so he can perform his religious duty in peace.[45] In the Central Bosnia and Tuzla Cantons, confessional prayer rooms have been established in two hospitals in each of them. These are the Travnik Hospital and the Croatian Hospital "Dr Fr. Mato Nikolić" in Nova Bila, Travnik, General Hospital "Dr Mustafa Beganović" in Gračanica, and the Center for Physical Medicine and Rehabilitation "Ilidža" in Gradačac.[46] Furthermore, the Cantonal Hospital "Dr Mihovil Sučić" in Livno, Hercegbosna Canton, has a chapel for Catholic patients, while the Clinical Center of the University of Sarajevo has a masjid for the needs of Muslim patients.[47] So far, the University Clinical Center of Republika Srpska in Banja Luka has received only a request from the SOC to provide a distinct prayer room for Orthodox patients. This request dates from 2014, but so far it could not be met due to the ongoing reconstruction of the clinical centre facilities.[48] Foča University Hospital also does not have confessional prayer rooms, however patients are allowed to perform prayer in the existing premises of the hospital at their personal request.[49]

Similarly, the issue of providing spiritual care to patients is not regulated in a systematic way. Some hospitals have full-time chaplains who usually belong to the local majority denomination and whose work is funded by their community.[50]

44 Federal Ministry of Health, Information no. 01–37–4342/19, 25 July 2019; Herzegovina-Neretva Canton – Ministry of Health, Labor and Social Welfare, Information no. 06–02–39–1532/19, 23 July 2019; Herceg-Bosna Canton – Ministry of Labor, Health, Social Welfare and Refugees, Information no. 09–01–49–46/18, 30 October 2018; Bosnian-Podrinje Canton of Goražde – Public Relations Service, Information no. 18–49–161–3/19, 15 August 2019; Central Bosnia Canton Travnik – Ministry of Health and Social Policy, Information no. 03–37–436/19–3, 3 October 2019.

45 University Clinical Hospital Mostar, Information no. 5393/19, 8 August 2019.

46 Central Bosnia Canton Travnik – Ministry of Health and Social Policy, Information no. 03–37–436/19–3, 3 October 2019.

47 Herceg-Bosna Canton – Ministry of Labor, Health, Social Welfare and Refugees, Information no. 09–01–49–46/18, 30 October 2018.

48 University Clinical Center of Republika Srpska, Information no. 01–10216–2/19, 8 August 2019.

49 Foča University Hospital, Information no. a-1185/2, 23 July 2019.

50 Central Bosnia Canton Travnik – Ministry of Health and Social Policy, Information no. 03–37–436/19–3, 3 October 2019; The University Clinical Hospital Mostar, Information no. 5393/19, 8 August 2019.

Others allow for visits and pastoral work by religious officials, in some cases even without the prior consent of the hospital management. In all cases, the work of these religious ministers is funded by their denominations.[51] In accordance with the relevant legislative provisions,[52] patients are provided with nutrition in health-care facilities in accordance with their religious beliefs.[53]

The ministries of health and university hospitals administration responded differently to the inquiry whether they recorded cases of medical workers who refused to provide certain services to the patients (e.g. performing an abortion, etc.) by invoking conscientious objection based on their religious beliefs. These responses ranged from not having information on such cases[54] to recognizing the right of health professionals to conscientious objection[55] or noting that the provisions of the relevant laws apply to the specific issue of abortion.[56] Further, ministries of health and hospitals most often do not have data on patients who complained of non-compliance with their religious beliefs when providing health services. However, there have been cases in which patients belonging to Jehovah's Witnesses have been denied the right to refuse a blood transfusion. The Cantonal Court in Tuzla upheld the lawsuit filed by a Jehovah's Witness and ordered the University Clinical Center Tuzla to provide her with surgery without a blood transfusion, thereby acknowledging her conscientious objection based on religious beliefs.[57] The verdict refers, *inter alia*, to the case of *Jehovah's Witnesses of Moscow and Others v. Russia*, in which the ECtHR took the position that the refusal of blood transfusions freely consented by Jehovah's Witnesses is, in principle, a matter for the individual's personal autonomy and as such is protected by Arts. 8 and 9 of the ECHR. The Strasbourg court further elaborated that refusing a transfusion could not be equated with suicide because the Jehovah's Witnesses did not refuse medical treatment in general; transfusion was the only medical procedure which they rejected on religious grounds.[58]

51 Herceg-Bosna Canton – Ministry of Labor, Health, Social Welfare and Refugees, Information no. 09–01–49–46/18, 30 October 2018; Foča University Hospital, Information no. a-1185/2, 23 July 2019.

52 Art. 45, Law on Rights, Obligations and Responsibilities of Patients of the Federation of Bosnia and Herzegovina.

53 Foča University Hospital, Information no. a-1185/2, 23 July 2019; University Clinical Hospital Mostar, Information no. 5393/19, 8 August 2019.

54 Herzegovina-Neretva Canton – Ministry of Health, Labor and Social Welfare, Information no. 06–02–39–1532/19, 23 July 2019; Bosnian-Podrinje Canton of Goražde – Ministry of Social Policy, Health, Displaced Persons and Refugees, Information no. 08–49–1195–3/19, 30 July 2019; Central Bosnia Canton Travnik – Ministry of Health and Social Policy, Information no. 03–37–436/19–3, 3 October 2019.

55 Herceg-Bosna Canton – Ministry of Labor, Health, Social Welfare and Refugees, Information no. 09–01–49–46/18, 30 October 2018.

56 Foča University Hospital, Information no. a-1185/2, 23 July 2019.

57 Cantonal Court in Tuzla, Case no. 03 0 U 016754 17 U, 10 October 2017.

58 *Jehovah's Witnesses of Moscow and Others v. Russia*, no. 302/02, § 131–133, 10 June 2010.

6 Employment

The development of new legislation pertaining to religion or belief has not been accompanied by due recognition of religious rights of the employees. The current labour and civil service laws still reflect the concept which dominated in the former communist regime that religion is solely a private matter of the individual rather than advanced standards for protecting freedom of religion, both in the private and public spheres. In the following, we will briefly look at three legislative areas that could potentially serve as a basis for claiming religious rights in the employment sector, that is, religious freedom law, non-discrimination law and employment, that is, labour and civil service law.[59]

The LFR protects a range of religious expressions, but does not address the protection of religion in the workplace. In practice, employees may not claim specific accommodations of their religious practices (e.g., performing daily and congregational Friday prayers, wearing religious clothing and symbols etc.) by invoking the said law. A rare example of the accommodation of religion in the workplace based on the LFR is provided by the conclusion of the Sarajevo Canton Government ordering public institutions and companies founded by this canton to adjust the menus in their canteens to "traditional and religious customs of the citizens", including, for example, halal, vegetarian, and kosher food, and so on.[60]

Regarding labour and civil service legislation, their provisions on the accommodations of religious beliefs and actions are rare and mainly limited to the allowance of days off for celebrating religious festivals,[61] that is, an hour off during the work week that can potentially be used by employees to meet their religious needs.[62] In addition, the Civil Service Law of the FBiH stipulates that a civil servant is impartial and, in this context, "does not abuse religious beliefs".[63] While the implications of this restriction on the freedom of religion of civil servants are not entirely clear, it's wording is reminiscent of former communist legislation on religion.[64]

59 This section is particularly based on: Begović, "Freedom of Religion in the Workplace," 177–184.

60 S. H., "Vlada u Sarajevu naredila: Jelovnike u javnim ustanovama prilagoditi vjerskim običajima," [The Government in Sarajevo Has Ordered: Menus in Public Institutions to be Adjusted to Religious Customs] accessed 24 May 2021, www.google.com/search?q=google+translate&oq=goo&aqs=chrome.1.69i60j69i59j0j69i59j69i57j69i60l3.1395j0j9&sourceid=chrome&ie=UTF-8.

61 See the book's chapter on religious symbols and festivals.

62 Art. 44, para. 2, Labour Law of the FBiH, *Official Gazette of the FBiH*, 26/16, 89/18.

63 Art. 17, para. 3 a), Law on Civil Service in the FBiH, *Official Gazette of the FBiH*, 29/03, 23/04, 39/04, 54/04, 67/05, 8/06, 77/06, 34/10, 45/10, 4/12, 99/15 i 9/17.

64 In contrast, related laws at the state and sub-state levels do not indicate religious beliefs, but are limited to the public expression of political opinions of civil servants. See Art. 14, para. 3 a), Law on Civil Service in the Institutions of Bosnia and Herzegovina, *Official Gazette of BiH*, 19/02, 35/03, 4/04, 17/04, 26/04, 37/04, 48/05, 2/06, 32/07, 43/09, 10/08 and 40/12; Art. 6, para. 3, Law on Civil Service in the RS, *Official Gazette of the RS*, 118/2008, 117/2011, 37/2012 i 57/2016; Art. 4, para. 9, Law on Civil Service in the Public Administration Bodies of the BDBiH, *Official Gazette of the BDBiH*, 9/14.

Eventually, the prohibition of indirect discrimination in the workplace which is contained in both employment and non-discrimination law could potentially serve as a legal tool for recognizing the right to reasonable accommodation of religion in the workplace.[65] However, according to the analyses so far, the courts' case law in this domain is still under-developed. A small number of cases concerning discrimination in employment are brought before the courts, among other things, due to the high costs and length of proceedings.[66] According to the findings of these analyses, discrimination (in the workplace) is widespread in Bosnian society and many cases go unreported.[67]

The Constitutional Court of BiH has so far indirectly dealt with the accommodation of religion in the workplace in three cases whose merits were decided on the ground of the provisions of the ECHR to a fair trial (Art. 6), freedom of religion (Art. 9), and non-discrimination based on religion or belief (Art. 14). The first case concerned a nun who applied for the position of the director of the public kindergarten in Glamoč. However, the city's Municipal Council refused to confirm her appointment, because she was a nun. After a six-year legal battle, she won her case before the Constitutional Court of BiH which found that her right to fair trial (Art. 6) was violated.[68] In the second case – discussed in more detail in the section on police service – the Constitutional Court took the position that it "sees no special reasons that could justify the 'necessity' of interfering" in the public employee's right to manifest his religion by wearing a beard.[69] This was, in fact, the first decision of the Constitutional Court finding a violation of Art. 9 of the ECHR and could potentially serve as an important precedent for the accommodation of religion in the workplace. The third case concerned the prohibition of members of the AFBiH to wear the headscarf and has already been discussed in the first section of this chapter.[70]

7 Judiciary

In September and October 2015, the High Judicial and Prosecutorial Council of BiH (HJPC) issued a circular stating that judges, prosecutors and other employees of judicial institutions are forbidden to wear religious symbols in the course

65 Arts. 2 and 3, Law on prohibition of discrimination in BiH, *Official Gazette of BiH*, 59/09, 66/16; Art. 8, Labour Law of the FBiH, *Official Gazette of the FBiH*, 26/16, 89/18; Arts. 19 and 20 of the Labour Law of the RS, *Official Gazette of the RS*, 1/16; Arts. 7 and 8, Labour Law of BD BiH, *Official Gazette of BD BiH*, 34/19).

66 Faris Vehabović, Midhat Izmirlija and Adnan Kadribašić, *Komentar Zakona o zabrani diskriminacije sa objašnjenjima i pregledom prakse u uporednom pravu* [Commentary on the Law on Prohibition of Discrimination with Explanations and Review of Practice in Comparative Law] (Sarajevo: Center for Human Rights of University of Sarajevo, 2010), 5.

67 Elma Demir, *Diskriminacija u oblasti rada u Bosni i Hercegovini* [Discrimination in the Field of Work in Bosnia and Herzegovina] (Sarajevo: Association for Democratic Initiatives, 2015), 4, 6, 15, 17–18.

68 *Janja Martina Katović v. Municipality of Glamoč*, Decision made by Supreme Court of the Federation of BiH no. 68 O P 017561 17 Rev 2 from 11 July 2017.

69 Constitutional Court of BiH, Case no. U 8/17, 30 November 2017, para. 43.

70 Constitutional Court of BiH, Case no. AP 2190/13, 9 July 2015.

of their duties (hereinafter the "circular"),[71] referring, *inter alia*, to the relevant provisions of the judiciary laws in the three administrative units of BiH. According to Art. 13 of the Law on Courts in the FBiH,

> Judges and court officials must not express any religious, political, national or other affiliation during the performance of official duties.
>
> Insignia of religious, political, national or other affiliation must not be displayed in court buildings or on court premises. The prohibition referred to in paragraph 1 of this Article shall not apply to the parties to the dispute and third parties.[72]

With regard to wearing religious symbols by other persons, such as parties, lawyers or witnesses, who are present in the courtroom, the circular gives judges discretionary power to decide the matter on a case-by-case basis, balancing the parties' rights to freedom of religion or belief and equal access to court, on the one hand, and preserving the reputation of the judiciary institutions, on the other hand.[73]

The circular was fiercely criticized by several important domestic actors, including the IC,[74] a number of NGOs[75] and some government bodies.[76] They assessed

71 HJPC's letter sent to the heads of courts and prosecutor's offices drew attention to "to the ban on the wearing of religious characteristics in judicial institutions for all employees and asked for appropriate measures to overcome the perceived problem with the aim of strengthening public confidence in the impartiality of the judiciary." See HJPC, Letter no. 08–02–1–3163–1/2015, 21 October 2015.

72 Art. 13, Law on Courts in the FBiH, *Official Gazette of the FBiH*, 38/05, 22/06, 63/10, 72/10, 13/07, 7/13, 52/14. Similar provisions are contained in the RS and BDBiH laws on courts. See Art. 14, Law on Courts in the RS, *Official Gazette of the RS*, 37/12, 14/14, 44/15, 39/16, 100/17; Art. 14, Law on Courts in the BDBiH – Consolidated Text, *Official Gazette of the BDBiH*, 18/20. In contrast, the laws governing the work of the Court of BiH and prosecutors' offices do not contain provisions of this type. See Law on the Court of BiH, *Official Gazette of BiH*, 49/09, 74/09, 97/09; Law on the Prosecutor's Office of BiH – Consolidated Text, *Official Gazette of BiH*, 49/09; Law on the Federal Prosecutor's Office of FBiH, *Official Gazette of the FBiH*, 19/03; Law on Public Prosecutor's Offices of RS, *Official Gazette of the RS*, 69/16.

73 HJPC, Memorandum, "Wearing Religious Marks in Judicial Institutions – Analysis," published on 19 February 2016, accessed 25 May 2021, https://translate.google.com/translate?hl=bs&prev=_t&sl=bs&tl=en&u=www.pravosudje.ba/vstv/faces/vijesti.jsp%3Fid%3D59614.

74 *Riyasat* of the IC, Letter to the HJPC, no. 05–03–1476/16, 3 March 2016.

75 These NGOs included, among others, Sarajevo Open Center, Women to Women Sarajevo, Budućnost Modriča, United Women Banja Luka, Woman-Victim of the War Sarajevo, Girls Foundation Sarajevo, etc. See Redaction, "Brojne reakcije javnosti zbog zabrane nošenja vjerskih obilježja," [Numerous Reactions from the Public Due to the Ban on Wearing Religious Symbols] accessed 25 May 2021, www.diskriminacija.ba/vijesti/brojne-reakcije-javnosti-zbog-zabrane-no%C5%A1enja-vjerskih-obilje%C5%BEja.

76 Agency for Gender Equality of BiH, "Reakcija na postupanje VSTV," [Reaction to the HJPC's Actions] accessed 25 May 2021, https://arsbih.gov.ba/reakcija-na-postupanje-vstv-bih/; The Assembly of Sarajevo Canton called for the withdrawal of the decision to ban the wearing of religious symbols in judicial institutions. See Sevima Sali Terzić, "Manifestacija vjerskih uvjerenja u pravosuđu: legitimno ograničavanje ili diskriminacija," [Manifestation of

it as discriminatory because it affected only one group of employees in the judiciary, that is, Muslim women wearing the headscarf (*hijab*), and violated their right to freedom of religion or belief. The circular also provoked a strong reaction from the general public manifested in the protests held in Sarajevo on 7 February 2016, in which, according to media reports, about 2,000 Muslim women wearing the headscarf took part.[77]

The HJPC offered an explanation that the circular only initiated the implementation of the judiciary laws and other regulations outlined earlier, which prohibit employees of the judicial institutions to display religious insignia or to abide by certain dress code. The essential reason was, as argued by the HJPC, the need to ensure the protection of the principle of impartiality of judicial institutions in secular BiH. Despite the reactions and calls for the withdrawal of the disputed Conclusion, the HJPC did not give up on its implementation. Opening the space for public debate on this issue,[78] the HJPC published on its website a memorandum, "Wearing religious symbols in judicial institutions", with an analysis that was the basis for issuing a circular.[79]

Participants in the academic debate, sparked by the adoption of the HJPC's circular, presented a number of arguments for or against the display of religious symbols in judicial institutions. Their views ranged from almost complete approval of the circular to criticism of its incompatibility with the constitutional right to freedom of religion or belief. Those who defended the circular argued that banning the display of religious symbols stimulates public perceptions of the impartiality and neutrality of judicial institutions, in line with the principle of secularism proclaimed by the LFR and the case law of the Constitutional Court of BiH. They further emphasized that this goal is particularly important in a multi-confessional society of BiH which is still burdened by a war past, including a large number of war crimes cases pending before the courts, as well as constant political, ethnic, and religious tensions.[80]

Critics of the circular, on the other hand, argued that the state enjoys a margin of appreciation in regulating the presence of religious symbols in the public institutions as evidenced by the ECtHR judgment in the landmark case of *Lautsi and Others v. Italy*.[81] Although this judgment does not concern the wearing of religious symbols and clothing in the workplace, its significance transcends the public school environment. Its particular importance lies in the affirmation of the

Religious Beliefs in the Judiciary: Legitimate Restriction or Discrimination] *Sveske za javno pravo* 7, no. 24 (2016): 8–9.

77 U.S. Department of State – Bureau of Democracy, Human Rights, and Labor, *2016 Report on International Religious Freedom: Bosnia and Herzegovina*, 5, accessed 25 May 2021, https://d2v9ipibika81v.cloudfront.net/uploads/sites/270/2017/08/2016-International-Religious-Freedom-Report-BiH.pdf; "Bosnia women protest at ban on headscarf," accessed 25 May 2021, www.bbc.com/news/world-europe-35518768.

78 Some members of the HJPC, including its vice-president Ružica Jukić, opposed any public discussion on the issue.

79 HJPC, Memorandum, "Wearing Religious Marks in Judicial Institutions – Analysis."

80 Terzić, "Manifestacija vjerskih uvjerenja u pravosuđu," 17.

81 *Lautsi and Others v. Italy* [GC], no. 30814/06, § 70, ECHR 2011.

concept of an inclusive public sphere in which different worldviews (secular, Jewish, Christian, Islamic, etc.) coexist and enter into mutual dialogue.[82] Further, it recognizes an important distinction between the secular model of state-religion relations and secularism as a philosophical worldview that strives for the absence of religion from the public sphere of democratic societies.[83] In the light of this judgment, the state's neutrality, as argued by the critics of the circular, should be the inclusive one which would enable various both religious and non-religious convictions to coexist in the public sphere, as long as they respect shared principles and values.[84] Regarding the impartiality argument, they claimed that the subjective perception about the bias of a judge wearing a religious symbol is not sufficient to justify a restriction of his or her right to freedom of religion or belief. Only in specific court cases (e.g., those involving incitement to religious hatred, etc.), as critics argued, could a judge be disqualified if there is a fear that his or her wearing religious clothing or symbols could affect the fairness of the trial.[85]

It should be noted that even supporters of the circular challenged its part by which the ban on wearing religious symbols potentially extends to litigants, including lawyers as their legal representatives.[86] For instance, it was argued by one author that

> after establishing the identity (*of parties*, author's remark) in an appropriate manner, out of respect for freedom of religion, I think that there is no basis in the laws on the courts in the entities, and in my opinion, in the European Convention for restriction in a way that would jeopardize the very approach to justice to everyone who manifest his or her religious belief by clothing, symbol, or otherwise.[87]

This part of the circular had a kind of epilogue in the reasoning of the Constitutional Court of BiH in the *Hamidović* case that "the restriction of the right to freedom of religion, manifested through the punishment of witnesses in criminal proceedings for refusing to remove a religious symbol – a Muslim skullcap, passed

82 *Lautsi and Others v. Italy* [GC], no. 30814/06, § 74, ECHR 2011.
83 *Lautsi and Others v. Italy* [GC], no. 30814/06, § 58, ECHR 2011.
84 Emir Kovačević, "Za ili protiv vjerskih obilježja u pravosudnim institucijama u BiH," [For or Against Religious Symbols in Judicial Institutions in BiH] *Sveske za javno pravo* 7, no. 24 (2016): 30, 31–32. This opinion is supported by the resolution of the Parliamentary Assembly of the Council of Europe and the comparative practice from the U.S., where e.g. a Muslim woman wearing a headscarf is allowed to work as a judge, despite the constitutional principle of separation of state and church. See Parliamentary Assembly of the Council of Europe, *Resolution 2076 (2015): Freedom of Religion and Living Together in a Democratic Society*, accessed 25 May 2021, https://assembly.coe.int/nw/xml/XRef/Xref-XML-2HTML-en.asp?fileid=22199&lang=en.
85 Kovačević, "Za ili protiv vjerskih obilježja," 29, 32.
86 See e.g. Jasmin Muratagić, "Implikacije zaključka Visokog sudskog i tužilačkog vijeća BiH o zabrani isticanja vjerskih obilježja u pravosudnim institucijama," [Implications of the Conclusion of the High Judicial and Prosecutorial Council of BiH on the Prohibition of Display of Religious Insignia in the Judicial Institutions] 15–19, accessed 25 May 2021, http://fcjp.ba/templates/ja_avian_ii_d/images/green/Jasmin_Muratagic3.pdf.
87 Terzić, "Manifestacija vjerskih uvjerenja u pravosuđu," 15.

the test of proportionality".[88] The case concerned the refusal of Mr Hamidović to take off his skullcap while testifying before the criminal court that investigated the case of the terrorist attack on the U.S. Embassy in Sarajevo in 2011. The presiding judge explained the witness that wearing the skullcap was contrary to the dress code for judicial institutions and that no religious symbol or clothing was allowed in court. However, the witness refused to obey the judge's order, claiming he wore the skullcap for religious reasons. The judge expelled him from the courtroom, convicted him of contempt of court and sentenced him to a fine.[89] Contrary to the findings of the Constitutional Court of BiH, the judgment of the ECtHR established that in the given case there was a violation of the applicant's right to freedom of religion.[90] The Court pointed out that a distinction must be made between this case and another concerning the wearing of religious symbols or clothing in the workplace, especially by public officials who may be bound by a duty of discretion, neutrality and impartiality, including the duty not to wear such symbols and clothing during the exercise of official authority. Unlike public servants, citizens in a private capacity, like the applicant, do not have such a duty. In its analysis of proportionality, the ECtHR took into account that the applicant, unlike some other members of the local Wahhabi community to which he belonged, responded to the court's summons and stood up when asked to do so, clearly submitting to the country's secular laws and courts.[91]

The case that took place at the Municipal Court in Sarajevo in February 2018 once again raised the question of whether the HJPC's circular was neutral in the sense that it is applicable to all religious insignia.[92] A judge of the Municipal Court in Sarajevo was reported to Janja Jovanović, the court's president and to the HJPC, because she kept Easter eggs on her desk. The report stated that the judge violated the prohibition to manifest religion in judicial institutions. In her statement for the media, Ružica Jukić, vice-president of the HJPC, stated that the circular did not specify what the religious insignia were, but that it was "certainly not food standing on the table". Instead, as Jukić claimed, they may include clothing and items of religious significance.[93] No disciplinary proceedings were instituted against the judge on this occasion.[94]

88 Amila Kurtović, "Zabrane nošenja vjerskih obilježja na radnom mjestu," [Prohibitions on Wearing Religious Symbols in the Workplace] (Sarajevo: Analitika – Center for Social Research, 2018), 10.

89 *Hamidović v. Bosnia and Herzegovina*, no. 57792/15, § 7–9, 5 December 2017.

90 The ECtHR decision in this case was commented as "a rare case of mandatory accommodation of Islamic religious practice". See Eva Brems, "Skullcap in the Courtroom: A Rare Case of Mandatory Accommodation of Islamic Religious Practice," accessed 26 May 2021, https://strasbourgobservers.com/author/ebrems/.

91 *Hamidović v. Bosnia and Herzegovina*, no. 57792/15, § 40–42, 5 December 2017.

92 According to the information received by the HJPC from the courts and prosecutor's offices, all cases of violation of the ban on wearing religious symbols concerned the wearing of headscarf (*hijab*). Furthermore, only one case involved a judge and the remaining ten cases related to court clerks. See *Hamidović v. Bosnia and Herzegovina*, no. 57792/15, § 14, 5 December 2017.

93 BLIC, "A Judge in Sarajevo Was Reported for an Easter Egg on the Table," 6 February 2018, accessed 11 February 2021, www.blic.rs/vesti/republika-srpska/sudiju-u-sarajevu-prijavili-zbog-vaskrsnjeg-jajeta-na-stolu/x19s6qb.

94 HJPC, Letter no. 03–09–6–2008–2/2019, 5 June 2019.

8 Conclusion

In some of the specific regulatory contexts covered in this chapter, the protection of religious rights is at a very satisfactory level. This statement applies in particular to the military and prisons. It is safe to say that the provisions on the religious rights of military personnel are designed in accordance with the highest standards in this area. In the MDBiH and AFBiH a regular religious service has been established, which includes representatives of the three major religious communities. Similarly, the regulatory framework for the accommodation of religion and belief in prisons is appropriate and the prison authorities collaborate with religious communities to provide religious assistance for their inmates. However, problems have been identified with regard to the accommodation of religious practices which are specific to a particular confession and do not have comparable counterparts in other religious groups, such as wearing a beard or headscarf.

When it comes to the accommodation of religion in the healthcare sector, it is necessary to work on improving the regulatory framework for providing religious spiritual care, but also on harmonizing the internal rules and practices of hospitals to ensure the religious rights of both patients and health workers. At the same time, it is necessary to ensure equal treatment of members of the majority and minority religions, which is often not the case now.

The most challenging issues of the accommodation of religion are related to employment, both in the private and public sectors. The courts' case law has so far provided no guidance on whether the prohibition of discrimination that forms part of domestic law implies a duty or a right to a reasonable accommodation of religion or belief in the workplace. However, the Constitutional Court of BiH has indirectly tackled this issue, providing effective protection against discrimination based on religion in employment (refusal to appoint a nun as director of a public kindergarten), as well as the accommodation of religious practice of a public employee (by declaring the unconstitutionality of the ban on wearing beards for the officers of the Border Police of BiH). The latter case was in fact the first one in which the Constitutional Court of BiH found the violation of Art. 9 of the ECHR. The Court's decision is a good example that the legal battle for the exercise of religious rights in the workplace can bear fruit, meaning that the legal system in BiH has the potential to provide their protection.

Following the ECtHR judgment in *Hamidović v. Bosnia and Herzegovina* which found violation of the right to freedom of religion or belief, it became clear that private citizens in democratic societies are permitted to wear religious clothing or symbols in the courtroom. However, the debate over whether judges, prosecutors, and court officers have the right to manifest religion in the course of their duties remains open.

5 Legal status of religious communities

1 Introduction

The achievement of freedom to manifest religion in community with others largely depends on the ability of believers to freely associate and establish religious organizations. Most religious groups today wish to be recognized and gain legal personality, so that they can reap the benefits that such status brings. Namely, a religious community that has the status of an independent legal entity has the opportunity to enter into various legal affairs and relationships that are a prerequisite for its successful operation, from concluding employment contracts with its staff, through buying or renting facilities for conducting worship and providing religious instruction to filing lawsuits in court to protect their rights.[1]

The benefits that religious communities acquire on the basis of having the status of a legal entity in various constitutional models of the relationship between the state and religion have already been noticed in the scholarly literature. These benefits include state administration and collection of "church tax" (e.g. in Germany), state funding of priests' salaries (in Slovakia), donations for the maintenance of religious buildings (France), cooperation in providing religious education (in Spain) and others.[2] Obtaining a legal personality in the state religion law of Bosnia and Herzegovina (BiH or Bosnia) allows religious communities to "enjoy such concessions and privileges as are characteristic of non-profit organizations".[3] The scope of rights acquired by registered churches and religious communities is very wide and they include, among other things, founding their own companies and associations, owning property, establishing educational, cultural, health and humanitarian institutions and carrying out "all such activities as are not prohibited by positive law".[4]

1 W. Cole Durham, Jr., "Facilitating Freedom of Religion or Belief Through Religious Association Laws," in *Facilitating Freedom of Religion or Belief: A Deskbook*, eds. Tore Lindholm, W. Cole Durham, Jr. and Bahia G. Tahzib-Lie (Leiden: Martinus Nijhoff Publishers, 2004), 321–322.

2 Durham, "Facilitating," 328.

3 Art. 9, Law on Freedom of Religion and Legal Status of Churches and Religious Communities in Bosnia and Herzegovina, *Official Gazette of Bosnia and Herzegovina*, 5/04.

4 Art. 10, Law on Freedom of Religion.

DOI: 10.4324/9780429266683-8

In many national legal systems, including Bosnian, the acquisition of legal personality by the religious community is a prerequisite for the issuance of approval by the competent authorities for the construction of religious facilities, the organization of pastoral care in hospitals, prisons and the army, obtaining exemptions from some taxes, performing religious education in public schools, and so on.[5]

This chapter explores the legal position of religious communities in the national legislation and case law. For these purposes, an analysis has been conducted of the relevant provisions of the 2004 Law on Freedom of Religion and the Legal Status of Churches and Religious Communities (LFR), bylaws, including the Instruction on the Application of the LFR and the Rulebook on Establishing and Maintaining a Unified Register of Churches and Religious Communities in BiH (hereinafter: Rulebook on the Register), and of bilateral state agreements with particular religious communities. In addition, an insight was gained into the practice of keeping the Register at the Bosnian Ministry of Justice (MJ). Finally, reports on BiH that include sections on religious freedom issues and the case law of national courts have been examined. The chapter shows that the criteria for acquiring legal personality, that is, registration of religious entities in BiH are largely compatible with international human rights standards and serve to facilitate communal aspects of freedom of religion. However, some domestic laws and bylaws are problematic in terms of these standards, in particular the European Court of Human Rights (ECtHR) jurisprudence.

2 The right of religious communities to legal personality in international law

The human rights instruments of the United Nations (UN) and the European Convention on Human Rights (ECHR) do not explicitly mention the freedom of religious association, the right of religious communities to exist, nor their right to legal subjectivity.[6] Focusing on the protection of individual rights, these instruments guarantee the right of the individual to freedom of thought, conscience, and religion. However, they also recognize the collective dimension of this right, as can be seen from Art. 18, para. 1 of the International Covenant on Civil and Political Rights (ICCPR) of 1966 and Art. 9, para. 1 of the ECHR, which proclaims freedom to manifest religion or belief "in community with others". According to R. Minnerath, although the ICCPR does not explicitly mention religious communities as right holders, "corresponding protections can be derived from the rights granted to individuals".[7] The same impression is gained after reading the UN Declaration on the Elimination of All Forms of Discrimination Based on Religion or Belief of 1981. This document addresses the problem of discrimination that can affect not only individuals but also the overall membership of a religious community. Furthermore,

5 Durham, "Facilitating," 323–324.

6 Rolland Minnerath, "The Right to Autonomy in Religious Affairs," in *Facilitating Freedom of Religion or Belief: A Deskbook*, eds. Tore Lindholm, W. Cole Durham, Jr. and Bahia G. Tahzib-Lie (Leiden: Martinus Nijhoff Publishers, 2004), 292–293.

7 Minnerath, "The Right to Autonomy," 310.

all the particular forms of expression of religion mentioned in Art. 6 of the Declaration presuppose action through religious communities and their right to autonomy in the conduct of their affairs.[8] Furthermore, freedom of association in religious communities has its basis in Art. 22 of the ICCPR and Art. 11 of the ECHR which provide a general guarantee of the right to association. Holders of this right are both an individual (in terms of the right to form an association with other people or to join an existing association) and an association (in terms of the rights to perform activities necessary to achieve the interests of its members). Thus, the right to associate in religious communities can be treated as a distinct form of the right to freedom of association, while members of a religious community are holders of that right.[9]

The ECtHR case law has significantly contributed to the consolidation of the right to religious association and the right of religious organizations to legal personality in international law.[10] Churches and other religious organizations may seek the assistance of the ECtHR as victims of violations of the right to freedom of religion or other rights guaranteed by the ECHR within the meaning of Art. 34.[11] They appear as holders of rights guaranteed by Art. 9 of the ECHR on behalf of their followers.[12] Based on the combined reading of Arts. 9 and 11 of the ECHR, the ECtHR has taken the unequivocal position that the protection of the collective freedom of religion includes the right of religious organizations to recognition of legal personality, as it is a precondition for their efficient operation and protection of their own legal interests before judicial authorities.[13]

3 Recognition of legal personality of religious communities

The instruments by which religious communities are recognized in BiH are the law (specifically the LFR), the Register (at the MJ), and the bilateral agreements of the state with religious communities. In terms of terminology, unlike the previous Bosnian Law on the Legal Status of Religious Communities of 1976, the current state religion law adopts a more inclusive term "churches and religious communities". According to the LFR, "churches and religious communities have the status of legal/juristic persons".[14]

8 Minnerath, "The Right to Autonomy," 310.

9 See Durham, "Facilitating," 368–369.

10 See W. Cole Durham Jr. and Brett G. Scharffs, *Law and Religion: National, International, and Comparative Perspectives* (New York: Aspen Publishers, 2010), 428.

11 Jim Murdoch, *Protecting the Right to Freedom of Thought, Conscience and Religion Under the European Convention on Human Rights: Council of Europe Human Rights Handbooks* (Strasbourg: Council of Europe, 2012), 24.

12 *Metropolitan Church of Bessarabia and Others v. Moldova*, no. 45701/99, § 101, ECHR 2001-XII.

13 *Metropolitan Church of Bessarabia and Others v. Moldova*, no. 45701/99, § 118, ECHR 2001-XII. See also Lance S. Lenhof, "Freedom of Religious Association: The Right of Religious Organizations to Obtain Legal Entity Status Under the European Convention," *BYU Law Review*, no. 2 (2005): 600–606, accessed 23 March 2020, https://digitalcommons.law.byu.edu/lawreview/vol2002/iss2/16.

14 Art. 8, para. 1, Law on Freedom of religion.

Regarding the criteria for recognition of legal personality as well as the manner of registration, the Law provided for three categories of religious communities. The first category consists of traditional religious communities of long historical duration in BiH, namely the Islamic Community in BiH (IC), the Serb Orthodox Church (SOC), the Catholic Church (CC), and the Jewish Community in BiH (JC). The second category consists of other religious communities that acquired legal personality before the law's entry into force. Regarding the first two categories, the law confirmed the continuity of their previously acquired status of a legal entity with the obligation to register in the national Register of Churches and Religious Communities.[15] The third category consists of new religious communities that acquire legal personality by registering with the fulfilment of special conditions prescribed by the law's Art. 18.

According to Vukšić, the previous Law on Religious Communities of the Socialist Republic of Bosnia and Herzegovina (SRBiH) required all religious communities to submit a mandatory application for registration. Given that traditional religious communities have been operating in BiH for centuries, some of them have never filed this application, nor have they formally had the status of a legal entity, which has certainly produced a number of problems in the daily activities of these communities. This is probably one of the main reasons why the LFR recognized the continuity of religious communities with a long history in the country. In all other provisions, the Law does not differentiate between traditional and new religious communities, but all registered religious communities are treated in the same way and with the same rights and obligations.[16]

4 Registration of religious communities

As in most European countries, the registration authority is a national administrative body, that is, the MJ.[17] Religious communities whose legal personality was recognized by the LFR are registered on the basis of an application containing basic information about the community (name, seat, contact telephone, stamp and sign) and the person authorized to represent it (name and surname, signature, and ID number).[18] New religious communities, in order to register and thus acquire legal personality, must prove the fulfilment of additional conditions by attaching the appropriate documentation when submitting the application for entry in the Register. The first condition concerns the possession of an internal regulatory instrument in the form of a statute or other general act. This general act is certified by the MJ and should make visible "content and method of

15 Art. 8, para. 2, 8, Law on Freedom of Religion.

16 Tomo Vukšić, ed., *Crkva i država u Bosni i Hercegovini: Zakoni, podzakonski akti, ugovori i komentari* [Church and State in Bosnia and Herzegovina: Laws, By-Laws, Agreements and Comments] (Sarajevo: Bishops Conference of Bosnia and Herzegovina, 2007), 48.

17 Rulebook on the Establishment and Management of Single Register of Churches and Religious Communities, their associations and organizational forms in Bosnia and Herzegovina, *Official Gazette of Bosnia and Herzegovina*, no. 46/04.

18 Art. 5 para. 1, 2, 3, Rulebook on the Register.

practice of religion and confession, scope and manner of activities" of a religious community.[19] It is common for the internal regulatory instruments of religious communities in European national legislations to state the name, objectives, seat, and organizational structure of the religious community, including its governing bodies.[20] The second condition is the submission of "a statement of its official religious doctrines". The third and fourth conditions concern the numerical size of the group that is to be registered in the form of a religious community. Thus, a new religious community is required to submit a list of at least 300 adherents accompanied by their signatures, as well as a decision on establishment of a community with signatures of at least 30 founders. The law explicitly stipulates that these 300 followers must be Bosnian citizens, which is problematic from the perspective of the ECtHR case law given that the right to freedom of religion or belief is a fundamental human right whose enjoyment is not limited to citizens.[21] The fifth condition is the submission of data on persons authorized to represent the religious community in the state legal sphere.[22] The length of existence of a religious community in a country is not prescribed as a condition for its registration, as is the case in a small number of national legislations in Europe (e.g. in Slovenia).[23] Setting this condition is contrary to the ECtHR practice, according to which there are no " 'relevant' and 'sufficient' reasons which could justify the lengthy waiting period that a religious organization had to endure prior to obtaining legal personality."[24]

Among the mentioned conditions for recognition, two have been the subject of criticism by some international and domestic commentators. The first is to prescribe the numerical size of a religious group, which can be an objective obstacle to small religious communities in acquiring legal personality and depriving them of the benefits that more numerous religious groups enjoy. The second concerns the competence of public authorities to examine the doctrine of religious groups when considering their applications for registration,[25] which is deemed as contrary to the principle of "autonomous existence of religious communities". According to the ECtHR case law, the principle is "at the very heart of the protection which Art. 9 affords" and it excludes "assessment by the state of the

19 Art. 18, para. 2, Law on Freedom of Religion; Art. 7, The Rulebook on the Register.

20 Norman Doe, *Law and Religion in Europe: A Comparative Introduction* (Oxford: Oxford University Press, 2011), 106.

21 See OSCE Office for Democratic Institutions and Human Rights (ODIHR) and Venice Commission, *Guidelines on the Legal Personality of Religious or Belief Communities* (Warsaw: OSCE Office for Democratic Institutions and Human Rights (ODIHR), 2014), para. 29, accessed 23 March 2020, www.osce.org/odihr/139046?download=true.

22 Art. 18, para. 1–2, Law on freedom of religion; Art. 6, para. 2, Rulebook on the Register.

23 Doe, *Law and Religion in Europe*, 105.

24 *Kimlya and Others v. Russia*, nos. 76836/01 and 32782/03, § 100, ECHR 2009.

25 Commission on Security and Cooperation in Europe, *Bosnia and Herzegovina's Draft Religion Law: Draft Text Fails to Meet OSCE Commitments on Religious Freedom* (Washington: Commission on Security and Cooperation in Europe, 2003), 2; Ivan Cvitković, "Sloboda podrazumijeva ne samo slobodu religije već i slobodu od religije," [Freedom Entails Not Only Freedom of Religion but also Freedom from Religion] *Diskursi* 3, no. 4 (2013): 15.

legitimacy of religious beliefs or the ways in which those beliefs are expressed".[26] However, it should be noted that the LFR does not differ significantly from most other national religious laws in Europe in relation to the criteria for registration of religious organizations, which include, for example, a minimum number of followers[27] and the provision of information on the doctrine, rites, and mission of the religious organization.[28] Nevertheless, it belongs to the group of European countries that set a fairly high numerical criterion for the registration of a religious organization in the status of a legal entity.

The LFR protects religious communities from unnecessary bureaucratic procedures and uncertainties regarding registration, in line with the recommendations of the UN Special Rapporteur on Freedom of Religion or Belief, as well as the Guidelines on the Legal Subjectivity of Religious or Community Organizations of the Organization for Security and Cooperation in Europe (OSCE) – the Office for Democratic Institutions and Human Rights (ODIHR) and the Venice Commission.[29] It is explicitly prescribed that the MJ makes a decision on the entry of a religious community in the register within 30 days from the submission of the application for registration.[30] Additional protection is provided by the provision according to which the religious community will be considered automatically registered, if the Ministry does not make any decision within 60 days from the submission of the application for registration.[31]

In fulfilling its obligation under international law to allow religious communities access to legal personality, BiH has a duty to respect the autonomy of these communities in terms of their internal organization.[32] According to the LFR, religious communities "may establish, alter and dissolve existing internal bodies that have the status of legal/juristic person". Respecting the principle of religious autonomy, the state recognizes the application of canonical or religious community regulations on the legal subjectivity of its internal organizational forms within the secular

26 *Metropolitan Church of Bessarabia and Others v. Moldova*, no. 45701/99, § 117–118, ECHR 2001-XII.

27 European countries significantly differs with regard to numerical criterium for registration of religious organizations. For instance, a religious group in Germany must have eight members in order to register as a legal person of private law, i.e. must have at least one adherent per 1,000 inhabitants of a certain lander in order to qualify for registration in the status of public law corporation; in Hungary it must have ten members (to register as an association), i.e. 100 (to register as a "church"); in Finland 20; in Austria 300; in Slovakia 20,000 etc. See Doe, *Law and Religion in Europe*, 103–104.

28 See Nedim Begović, "Ustavni okvir i Zakon o slobodi vjere i pravnom položaju crkava i vjerskih zajednica u BiH," [Constitutional Framework and Law on Freedom of Religion and Legal Status of Churches and Religious Communities: Normative Projection of Bosnian-Herzegovinian Secularism] in *Sekularnost i religija: BiH i* regija, eds. Edin Šarčević and Drago Bojić (Sarajevo: Fondacija Centar za javno pravo, 2015), 88–89.

29 United Nations General Assembly: Human Rights Council, *Report of the Special Rapporteur on Freedom of Religion or Belief, Heiner Bielefeldt*, 22 December 2011, para. 55, accessed 23 March 2020, file:///C:/Users/User/Downloads/A-HRC-19-60_en.pdf.; ODIHR and Venice Commission, *Guidelines*, para. 25.

30 Art. 18, para. 3, Law on Freedom of Religion.

31 Art. 18, para. 6, Law on Freedom of Religion.

32 Art. 18, para. 4, Law on Freedom of Religion.

legal order.[33] To illustrate, faced with inquires of some lower courts who, while dealing with property disputes, sought to determine who were the legal predecessors of the currently registered organizational forms of religious communities in the land registry, the MJ sent to all courts the letter which clarified that only religious communities can provide such an information.[34] The dispute over the juristic personality of the Old Catholic Church in Donje Dubrave, the Municipality of Živinice, shows which implications can arise when state authorities interfere, even accidentally, in intra-religious issues through the registration process.[35] This religious organization has been operating under the "umbrella" of the Old Catholic Church in Zagreb since 1924. In 2006, the church was re-registered with the MJ as the Bosnian Old Catholic Church, which provoked strong opposition from the authorities of the umbrella church in Zagreb.[36]

The Register is kept separately for each religious community and their organizational forms that have the status of legal entities.[37] It is not allowed to register a new religious community under a name that is identical or similar to the name of an already registered religious organization,[38] nor to use the official signs of those organizations.[39] Decision-making on the establishment of legal entities within religious communities can be more or less centralized.[40] As of 21 August 2019, a total of 1,100 legal entities of religious communities have

33 Art. 8, para. 5, 6, Law on Freedom of Religion. As an example of acting of the MJ on grounds of autonomous decision of a registered religious community, take the case of removing the Islamic cultural centre in Mostar from the Register (previously recorded under no. 111/07, the Book no. 1, 6 June 2007) by the Ministry's decision no. 08–38–3–23/07 of 6 February 2014, issued on the basis of the petition of *Riyasat* of the IC of 9 January 2014, supplemented on 4 February 2014. The aforementioned decision was made on the basis of Art. 8, para. 5 of the LFR and Art. 13, para. 4 of the Rulebook on the Register.

34 Interview with Slavka Alagić, chief of Department for Registers of the MC, Sarajevo, 21 August 2019.

35 Interview with Slavka Alagić.

36 H. Ibišević, "Previranja u Starokatoličkoj crkvi kod Živinica prijete da prerastu u međunarodni skandal," [The Turmoil in the Old Catholic Church Near Živinice Threatens to Grow into an International Scandal] published on 17 June 2014, accessed 21 March 2020, http://tip.ba/2014/06/17/previranja-u-starokatolickoj-crkvi-kod-zivinica-prijete-da-prerastu-u-medunarodni-skandal/.

37 The Register's books are numbered as follows: The Book no. 1 – the IC, the Book no. 2 – the CC, the Book no. 3 – the SOC, the Book no. 4 – the JC and the Book no. 5 – Other churches and religious communities.

38 So far there have been no applications for the registration of parallel Islamic or Muslim communities, while the majority of so-called "other religious communities" (the Register's Book no. 5) represent different Christian denominations (Slavka Alagić, chief of Department for Registers of the Ministry for Justice of BiH, interview by coauthors, Sarajevo, 21 August 2019).

39 Art.18, para. 1, Law on Freedom of Religion.

40 According to Art. 19 of Constitution of the IC, "The Assembly of the Islamic Community Shall Determine Which Organizational Units, Bodies and Institutions of the Islamic Community Have the Status of a Legal Person," (Ustav Islamske zajednice u Bosni i Hercegovini – prečišćeni tekst [Constitution of the Islamic Community in Bosnia and Herzegovina – Consolidated Text] accessed 23 March 2020, https://islamskazajednica.ba/images/stories/

been entered in the Register. Of that number, 120 are legal entities within the IC, 526 legal entities within the SOC, 399 legal entities within the CC and eight within the JC. As for other religious communities, a total of 47 subjects are entered in the Register.[41] Although the LFR allows for the establishment of alliances of religious communities, so far no such alliance has been entered in the Register.[42]

The reasons for refusing registration can be procedural or essential in nature. The application for registration will be rejected for procedural reasons if it is not submitted in accordance with the terms of the Rulebook on the Register or if the necessary documents have not been submitted according to the instructions of the MJ.[43] The substantive grounds for rejecting the application are not regulated in detail and include general grounds for restricting freedom of religion or belief under Art. 9, para. 2 of the ECHR. Consequently, the MJ is authorized to reject the application for registration if "the content and manner of worship and other manifestation of religion is contrary to the legal order, public morals or is damageable to the life and health or other rights and freedoms of believers and citizens".[44]

In case of refusal of registration, the religious community has the possibility to file an appeal to the Council of Ministers of BiH within 60 days from the date of refusal of registration. The Council of Ministers may decide to register or reject the appeal, and its decision is final. In addition, the religious community may initiate a dispute against the decision of the Council of Ministers within three months from the date of its adoption before the administrative department of the Court of BiH.[45]

According to the information obtained from the MJ, laws and bylaws on the registration of religious communities are applied in a way that seeks to facilitate the acquisition of legal personality by these communities, thus effectively contributing to the institutional aspects of religious freedom. This refers to the fulfilment of both procedural and essential conditions for registration. The Department for Registers at the MJ perceives its role in terms of a service that helps representatives of religious communities to properly submit applications for registration and submit the necessary documentation.[46] The applications, as claimed by the

Ustavi/Ustav_IZ-e_preciscenі_tekst_2014.pdf). In the SOC and the CC in BiH the decision to assign legal personality to church entities is more decentralized.

41 Among these are the Evangelical Church Sarajevo, Christian Baptist Church, Victory Celebration Center, Christian Adventist Church, Old Catholic Church in BiH, Christ's Pentecostal Church, Krishna Awareness Society, Church of God in BiH, Protestant Community "The Word of Life", Mormon Church etc. (Interview with Slavka Alagić).

42 Interview with Slavka Alagić.

43 Art. 9, para. 1–3, Rulebook on the Register.

44 Art. 18, para. 5, Law on Freedom of Religion.

45 Art. 18, para. 7–8, Law on Freedom of Religion; Art. 11, para. 4–6, Rulebook on Register.

46 It should be noted that a low amount of fees is prescribed for registering religious communities as well as gaining insight into this Register. Hence, they do not constitute an objective obstacle to the registration process (see Arts. 15 and 20, Rulebook on Register).

Department, are being considered logically and legally, not in terms of review of religious doctrine, which is in line with the recommendations of the OSCE and the Venice Commission.[47] In other words, the teachings and doctrines of religious communities wishing to register are not subject to the state "inquisition". In support of the claims from the Department is the fact that so far there has been no case of rejection of the application for entry in the Register. Consequently, there was no need to appeal to the BiH Council of Ministers, nor to initiate administrative disputes before the courts for refusing registration, which are legal options available to religious groups. However, it is an interesting fact that about 95 percent of religious entities were entered in the Register according to the principle of continuity of previously acquired legal subjectivity, meaning that there were only a few cases of registration of new religious communities.[48] It is difficult to draw any definitive conclusion as to whether the numerical criterion for the registration of new religious groups could constitute an objective obstacle to freedom of religious association.

5 Non-recognized religious groups and their freedom of religious manifestation

One of the questions that arises in the context of considering the legal status of religious communities is whether the state religion law in BiH respects the right to freedom of religion, including its manifestation in community with others, of those religious groups that do not desire to register or do not meet the conditions prescribed for registration. The LFR generally guarantees the freedom to manifest religion in its collective dimension without making its enjoyment conditional, at least not explicitly, on the mandatory registration of a religious group, that is, by acquiring legal personality.

The original draft Law on Freedom of Religion contained a provision allowing the establishment of associations for the collective expression of religion, regardless of whether they are registered as legal entities. However, such associations would not have the status of religious communities or the rights and privileges granted to them by law.[49] However, the drafters of the Law decided to exclude this provision from the final text, possibly because of criticism of the CSCE Report and some other legal commentators about unequal treatment of religious associations and registered religious communities.[50] Therefore, there is a loophole in the adopted text of the LFR regarding the regulation of the issue of organized religious activity by religious associations.

The Instruction on the Implementation of the LFR contains a provision that "religious activity may be performed by churches and religious communities on the territory of Bosnia and Herzegovina that have the status of a legal entity

47 ODIHR and Venice Commission, *Guidelines*, para. 31.

48 Interview with Slavka Alagić.

49 The provision was contained in Art. 5, para. 3 of the Draft Law.

50 See e.g. CSCE, *Bosnia and Herzegovina's Draft Religion Law*, 2, 4.

and are registered in the Register of Churches and Religious Communities in Bosnia and Herzegovina". This provision is not compatible with international human rights law. Namely, freedom of religion or belief is a right that belongs to individuals and communities on the basis of human dignity and its enjoyment does not depend on the approval of the state. Therefore, legally prohibiting or sanctioning the religious activities of an unregistered group or community of believers is not compatible with international standards, unless the criteria of the restrictive clause of Art. 9, para. 2 of the ECHR are met. The ECtHR noted in *Masaev v. Moldova* that it

> does not contest the State's power to put in place a requirement for the registration of religious denominations in a manner compatible with Articles 9 and 11 of the Convention. However, it does not follow, as the Government appear to argue, that it is compatible with the Convention to sanction the individual members of an unregistered religious denomination for praying or otherwise manifesting their religious beliefs. To admit the contrary would amount to the exclusion of minority religious beliefs which are not formally registered with the State and, consequently, would amount to admitting that a State can dictate what a person must believe.[51]

At the end of 2015 and the beginning of 2016, the question was raised in BiH whether the religious activities of unregistered local Muslim congregations (jamaats) operating outside the structure of the state-recognized IC are legal within the meaning of the LFR and whether the state can prevent these activities, especially if extreme or radical interpretations of religion are preached in some of these congregations.[52] While most of the unregistered congregations belong to various branches of the Salafi movement, there are also some Sufi zawiyas that are not included in the Tariqah Center controlled by the IC, as well as several Shi'i educational and cultural institutions. It should be noted that the overwhelming majority of Bosnian Muslims are Sunnis following the Maturidi school of thought in theology and Hanafi madhhab in Islamic law.[53]

In the period between 14 December 2015 and 25 March 2016, IC conducted an extensive dialogue with representatives of unregistered congregations with the intention of integrating them into its structure.[54] In the event of a refusal to integrate, the intention was for the IC to distance itself from the activities of religious groups that promote radical interpretations of Islam and incite their

51 *Masaev v. Moldova*, no. 6303/05, § 26, 12 May 2009.

52 In the Report of the Directorate for Religious Affairs of the IC these congregations are termed as "para-jamaats", i.e. parallel or so-called congregations.

53 Muhamed Jusić, "Bosnia and Herzegovina," in *Yearbook of Muslims in Europe*, ed. Oliver Scharbrodt (Leiden: Brill, 2018), vol. 9, 129–130.

54 See Muhamed Jusić, Aid Smajić and Muhamed Fazlović, "Bosnia and Herzegovina," in *Yearbook of Muslims in Europe*, ed. Oliver Scharbrodt (Leiden: Brill, 2017), vol. 8, 132–133; Jusić, "Bosnia and Herzegovina," 129, 131.

members to violent extremism.[55] In addition, the intention was to leave it to the state authorities to examine whether the activities of unregistered communities are legal in terms of the LFR.[56] On 25 April 2016, the report of the Directorate for Religious Affairs of the *Riyasat* of the IC was presented indicating that interviews were conducted with representatives of 38 unregistered congregations, of which 29 used facilities that were not registered with the IC. The Jumuah prayer was performed in 19 facilities, and the five daily prayers in 20 facilities. Of the total number of unregistered congregations, 14 decided to join the IC, while the remaining unregistered groups continued to operate independently.[57] So far, however, the state authorities have not imposed a requirement on these groups to register as religious communities, but have qualified their activities as illegal and supported the internal efforts of the officially recognized IC to integrate them into its own structures.[58]

The issue of the legality of the activities of unregistered religious groups was also raised in the case ruled by the Basic Court in Kotor Varoš, that is, in the second instance procedure, the District Court in Banja Luka. The Basic Court fined Ivica Ackovic for running the unregistered monastery of St. George in Jošavka, Municipality of Čelinac, as well as for falsely presenting himself as a monk of the SOC, thus acting contrary to the decision of the church's Grand Ecclesiastical Court depriving him of that rank.[59] The court applied Art. 23 of the Law on public order of the Republic of Srpska (RS) he who impersonates as "a representative of an international or other organization" shall be punished "by a fine ranging from 500 BAM to 1,500 BAM or imprisonment for up to 40 days".[60] The District Court upheld the first instance court's decision, arguing that the municipality of

55 Some right-wing politicians in Europe, such as Kolinda Grabar-Kitarović, former president of the Republic of Croatia, expressed in their public statements opinions about the alleged radicalization of Bosniaks and the "change of Islam" in BiH. Dr. Husein Kavazović, the Grand Mufti of the IC, responded to these statements by criticizing the politicization of the radicalization of small groups of extremists with the aim of weakening the position of Bosniaks. See Nedim Begović, "Bosnia and Herzegovina," in *Yearbook of Muslims in Europe*, ed. Oliver Scharbrodt (Leiden and Boston: Brill, 2019), vol. 10, 132–133.

56 According to a statement given by Ahmed Adilović, Mufti of Travnik (a town in central Bosnia), to Radio Free Europe, the goal of the campaign is to "try to talk to them, to invite them to join the legal system of the IC, and in case there are those who refuse it, they will be no our responsibility and we will be no responsible for their actions. In that case, the state authorities have the power to review their work, their registration, whether they are working legally or not, and what to do in that case." Marija Augustinović, "Travnički muftija: Nelegalni vjerski objekti biće birga države," [Mufti of Travnik: Illegal Places of Worship Shall Be the State's Concern] February 2, 2016, accessed 21 March 2020, www.slobodnaevropa.org/a/travnicki-muftija-nelegalni-vjerski-objekti-bice-briga-drzave/27527745.html.

57 Jusić, "Bosnia and Herzegovina," 130–131.

58 Ministry for Human Rights and Refugees of BiH (MHRR), Information no. UP-I-05–07–7–25–3/19, 26 July 2019.

59 Basic Court in Kotor Varoš, Case no. 73 0 Pr 025108 17 Pr 2, 23 November 2017, pp. 1, 14.

60 Art. 23, Law on Public Order of the RS, *Official Gazzette of the Republic of Srpska*, no. 11/15.

the SOC in Jošavka represents an "organization" in the sense of the stated legal provision, because is registered with the MJ.[61]

These court decisions raise two important issues of the right to freedom of religion. The first concerns respect for the autonomy of the religious community to decide on the appointment and removal of its own staff.[62] The second concerns freedom of religion of an unregistered, schismatic religious group and its leader. The Banja Luka District Court did not accept the convict's appeal that the Basic Court's decision violated his right to freedom of religion.[63] However, in the proceedings before the court, this issue was actualized both in the allegations of the parties in the misdemeanour dispute and testimonies of witnesses. The Basic Court's decision states that a representative of the RS Ministry of Internal Affairs – Čelinac Police Station, in his closing argument at the oral hearing, asked the Court not only to hold the defendant responsible for impersonation, but also to prohibit the operation of monastery on private property until its registration at the MJ.[64] Dragan Davidović, Director of the Secretariat for Religions of the Government of the Republika Srpska, in his capacity as a witness, agreed that the activities of the monastery were illegal, given that it did not have a recognized legal personality. However, he also pointed out the inviolability of the right to freedom of religion, even for unrecognized religious groups. For the sake of comparison, he pointed to the activities of the Salafi-Wahhabi movement as an unrecognized religious group in private premises in certain settlements in BiH, including the RS entity.[65] Eventually, both the Basic and District Courts refrained from taking a position on this sensitive issue, limiting themselves to sanctioning false representation as a violation within the meaning of the RS Law on Public Order.

6 Conclusion

In accordance with international human rights standards, and in particular the case law of the ECtHR, the state religion law of BiH guarantees legal personality to all registered religious organizations, assigning them special names, namely "churches and religious communities". Unlike the constitutions of BiH, FBiH,

61 District Court in Banja Luka, Case no. 73 0 Pr 025108 17 Pžp 2, 28 February 2018.

62 Art. 11, para. 3, Law on Freedom of Religion; Art. 6, Basic Agreement of BiH and the SOC.

63 In *Şerif v. Greece*, no. 38178/97, ECHR 1999-IX, the ECtHR considered whether criminal conviction of a mufti in Rodopi, supported by at least part of local Muslim community, for usurping the functions of "a minister of the Greek Orthodox Church or another known religion" (Art. 175, para. 2 of the Criminal Code) and "public wearing the dress or the insignia of a minister of religion" referred to in Art. 175 § 2 without having the right to do so (Art. 176 of the Criminal Code) was compatible with the protections afforded by Art. 9 of the ECHR. The ECtHR expressed the opinion that "punishing a person for merely acting as the religious leader of a group that willingly followed him can hardly be considered compatible with the demands of religious pluralism in a democratic society" and found violation of Art. 9 (see in particular § 29, 31, 51). The same reasoning of the ECtHR was applied in *Agga v. Greece* (no. 2), no. 50776/99 and 52912/99, 17 October 2002.

64 Basic Court in Kotor Varoš, Case no. 73 0 Pr 025108 17 Pr 2, 23 November 2017, p. 3.

65 Basic Court in Kotor Varoš, Case no. 73 0 Pr 025108 17 Pr 2, 23 November 2017, pp. 7, 11.

and Brčko District of Bosnia and Herzegovina (BDBiH) which contain general guarantees of the right to freedom of religion or belief, the RS Constitution contains an additional provision on the rights and privileges that religious communities enjoy in exercising their legal personality. The instruments by which the legal personality of religious communities is confirmed or recognized are the LFR, the Register, and the bilateral agreements between the state and religious communities. The registration authority is the state administrative body, that is, the MJ. The LFR provides for two basic criteria for recognizing legal personality and regulating the legal status of religious organizations: (a) long historical duration in the country or continuity of acquired legal personality before the law's entry into force; and (b) meeting distinct criteria for new religious organizations (e.g. the number of adherents, submission of internal regulatory act, and the statement on religious doctrine, etc.). In most matters concerning the recognition, registration and regulation of the legal status of religious communities, Bosnian religion legislation is compatible with international standards of religious freedom and comparable to other national religion laws of European countries. The practice of registering religious communities with the MJ has been facilitated, thus respecting the autonomous decisions of these communities regarding their internal organization, and serving to facilitate religious freedom rather than control the work of religious associations. However, there are some aspects of national legislation that raise dilemmas about their compliance with international standards. This primarily refers to prescribing a relatively high criterion regarding the numerical size of the registration group as well as the related issue of the legality of the activities of small religious groups that operate informally or are registered under the laws on associations and foundations. The biggest challenge seems to be to strike a balance between preserving religious pluralism as an essential feature of a democratic society, according to ECtHR case law, and the need to ensure the accountability of religious communities for their activities that must not violate public order, security, and rights of others.

6 Autonomy of religious communities

1 Introduction

Religious autonomy, as R. Minnerath has rightly pointed out, represents "one of the crucial features of any meaningful system of freedom of religion or belief".[1] All the more, in the broadest sense, it can be used as a synonym for the general right to freedom of religion or belief.[2] However, in this chapter it will be used in a more specific meaning of the right of religious communities to autonomy in their own affairs. As a corporate right, it is not explicitly recognized in any of the major international instruments which are permeated by an individualistic vision of fundamental human rights. Having said that, it has been widely acknowledged as crucial for the protection of both religious beliefs of individual believers and the corporate dimension of religious liberty. The way religious communities are organized and function can often be a matter of religious doctrine. Also, defining the scope of autonomy of religious communities is important for the proper structuring of relations between the state and those communities.[3]

There are two dimensions of religious autonomy that are closely intertwined: (a) autonomy of belief in a sense of "the right of a religious organization to define, elaborate, and control its own doctrine" and (b) institutional autonomy as the right of a religious organization to manage its own affairs in accordance with religious prescriptions.[4] While defining "internal affairs" of a religious community is not an easy task, they can be categorized into three broad areas of legislation, administration, and adjudication.[5]

Religious autonomy issues may arise in a variety of contexts, including freedom to teach the faith, internal organization of a religious community, free appointment

1 Roland Minnerath, "The Right to Autonomy in Religious Affairs," in *Facilitating Freedom od Religion or Belief: A Descbook*, eds. Tore Lindholm, W. Cole Durham Jr. and Bahia G. Tahzib-Lie (Leiden: Martinus Nijhoff Publishers, 2004), 291.

2 W. Cole Durham, Jr. and Brett G. Scharffs, *Law and Religion: National, International and Comparative Perspectives* (New York: Aspen Publishers, 2010), 371.

3 Minnerath, "The Right to Autonomy," 291–292.

4 Minnerath, "The Right to Autonomy," 292.

5 Norman Doe, *Law and Religion in Europe: A Comparative Introduction* (Oxford: Oxford University Press, 2011), 123.

DOI: 10.4324/9780429266683-9

and dismissal of the clergy, managing educational, charitable, and other institutions established by religious organizations, and so on.[6] This chapter aims to investigate to what extent the right of religious autonomy has been protected in the areas discussed in the national legislation and the courts case law in Bosnia and Herzegovina (BiH). For these purposes, an analysis has been conducted of the primary sources, that is, the relevant provisions of the 2004 Law on Freedom of Religion (LFR),[7] bylaws, including the Instructions on the Application of the LFR,[8] and of bilateral state agreements with particular religious communities. In addition, an insight was gained into the courts' decisions in disputes concerning the applicability of civil labour law on religious ministers. The chapter traces the growing recognition of the principle of religious autonomy in the new regime of state-religion relations in BiH.

2 The right to religious autonomy in international law

The right to religious autonomy in international law is largely inferred from the guarantees of collective religious freedom and freedom of association. The International Covenant on Civil and Political Rights (ICCPR) and the European Convention on Human Rights (ECHR), for example, envisage the freedom to manifest religion "in community with others",[9] while the UN Declaration on the Elimination of All Forms of Intolerance and Discrimination Based on Religion or Belief enlists the examples of religious practice which are inconceivable without religious autonomy.[10] In a series of decisions concerning registration of religious communities and state involvement into their internal disputes, the ECtHR affirmed the notion of religious autonomy, based on combined reading of Arts. 9 (freedom of religion) and 11 (freedom of association) of the ECHR. In *Metropolitan Church of Bessarabia v. Moldova* the ECtHR pointed out:

> since religious communities traditionally exist in the form of organised structures, Article 9 must be interpreted in the light of Article 11 of the Convention, which safeguards associative life against unjustified State interference.

6 See Minnerath, "The Right to Autonomy," 291–292; Brigite Schinkele, "Church Autonomy in Austria," in *Church Autonomy: A Comparative Survey*, ed. Gerhard Robbers (Frankfurt am Main: Peter Lang, 2001), accessed 9 March 2021, www.iclrs.org/church-autonomy-a-comparative-survey/.

7 Law on Freedom of Religion and Legal Status of Churches and Religious Communities in Bosnia and Herzegovina, *Official Gazette of Bosnia and Herzegovina*, 5/04.

8 Instructions on the Implementation of the Law on Freedom of Religion and Legal Status of Churches and Religious Communities in Bosnia and Herzegovina, *Official Gazette of BiH*, 28/19.

9 Art. 18, para. 1, International Covenant on Civil and Political Rights, accessed 9 March 2021, www.ohchr.org/en/professionalinterest/pages/ccpr.aspx; Art. 9, para. 1, European Convention on Human Rights, accessed 9 March 2021, www.echr.coe.int/Pages/home.aspx?p=basictexts&c.

10 Art. 6, Declaration on the Elimination of All Forms of Intolerance and of Discrimination Based on Religion or Belief, accessed 9 March 2021, www.ohchr.org/en/professionalinterest/pages/religionorbelief.aspx.

> Seen in that perspective, the right of believers to freedom of religion, which includes the right to manifest one's religion in community with others, encompasses the expectation that believers will be allowed to associate freely, without arbitrary State intervention. ***Indeed, the autonomous existence of religious communities is indispensable for pluralism in a democratic society and is thus an issue at the very heart of the protection which Article 9 affords.***[11]

The principle of religious autonomy dictates that "in exercising its regulatory power in this sphere and in its relations with the various religions, denominations and beliefs, the State has a duty to remain neutral and impartial".[12] This duty includes, *inter alia*, refraining the state from assessing the legitimacy of religious beliefs, not interfering in the election and appointment of heads of religious communities, and supporting one of the opposing factions within a divided religious community.[13] When faced with tensions caused by religious pluralism, the role of the state is not to eliminate pluralism, "but to ensure that the competing groups tolerate each other".[14]

In *Sindicatul "Păstorul cel Bun" v. Romania* the ECtHR recognized the choice not to apply the civil labour law regime to the regulation of the work of employees in a religious community as arising from the principle of religious autonomy. Accordingly, the principle implies that the state should accept the decision of a religious community not to allow the formation of a union of its staff without the prior approval of the authorities of that community.[15] The similar arguments were employed in *Fernàndez Martínez v. Spain* for the conclusion that autonomy of religious community implies the heightened expectation of loyalty from its employees. The case concerned the decision of a church not to renew a former priest's contract to teach religion and ethics in a public school after a local newspaper identified him as a married priest and a member of the celibacy movement. The ECtHR ruled that there was no breach of Art. 8 (the right to private and family life) of the applicant who knowingly placed himself in a situation that was incompatible with the church's precepts.[16]

3 Freedom to teach religious doctrine

The LFR provides broad guarantees of freedom of religious communities to teach the faith. These communities are, *inter alia*, free to advocate on a daily basis the principles of their religion and to act in accordance with them so as not to endanger the freedoms of others, perform religious rites in their own or

11 *Metropolitan Church of Bessarabia v. Moldova*, no. 45701/99, § 118, ECHR 2001-XII. Italics added.

12 *Metropolitan Church of Bessarabia v. Moldova*, no. 45701/99, § 116, ECHR 2001-XII.

13 *Hasan and Chaush v. Bulgaria* [GC], no. 30985/96, § 78, ECHR 2000-XI; *Supreme Holy Council of the Muslim Community v. Bulgaria*, no. 39023/97, § 93–96, 16 December 2004.

14 *Serif v. Greece*, no. 38178/97, § 53, ECHR 1999-IX.

15 *Sindicatul "Păstorul cel Bun" v. Romania* [GC], no. 2330/09, §163–165, ECHR 2013.

16 *Fernàndez Martínez v. Spain* [GC], no. 56030/07, ECHR 2014.

rented premises, as well as in homes and estates of their adherents, organize public religious celebrations, run the media and disseminate their announcements in all types of communications, write, translate, and publish books and freely organize religious ceremonies and visits of believers to holy places in the country and abroad.[17] However, the autonomy of religious communities in teaching the faith is not absolute. Thus, the state authorities may legitimately restrict the activities of religious communities if this limitation is prescribed by law and proved to be necessary for the protection of public safety, health, public morals or the rights and freedoms of others.[18] Specifically, religious communities are not allowed, when teaching religion or in other activities, "to disseminate hatred and prejudices against any other churches and religious communities or its members, or against the citizens of no religious affiliation".[19]

These legal guarantees are supplemented by the provisions of bilateral agreements between the state and the Holy See and SOC which provide for freedom of worship and inviolability of places of worship, including churches, chapels and other church premises.[20] The competent authorities of BiH are not even allowed to take security measures in the aforementioned religious facilities "without previous authorization from the competent ecclesiastical authority, unless such action is urgently needed for the defence of life or health or to preserve goods of particular artistic or historical value".[21] In addition, in the case of a judicial investigation against a cleric or a monk on charges of having committed a criminal offense, the judicial authorities will inform the competent church authorities in advance of their actions and only then take the measures provided by law.[22]

4 The right to self-governance in accordance with religious norms

As noted by some authors, the very word "autonomy" means "having one's own law" and its etymology is from Greek words *autos* (self) and *nomos* (law).[23] Thus, religious autonomy includes the right of religious organizations to legislate their own regulatory instruments or to abide by the known systems of religious law (e.g. Christian law, Islamic law, Jewish law, etc.). On one hand, religious communities

17 Art. 9, Law on Freedom of Religion.

18 Art. 14, para. 7, Law on Freedom of Religion.

19 Art. 4, para. 2, Law on Freedom of Religion.

20 Art. 7, Basic Agreement between the Holy See and Bosnia and Herzegovina (BAHS), *Official Gazette of BiH – International Agreements*, 10/07; Art. 7, Basic Agreement between Bosnia and Herzegovina and the Serb Orthodox Church (BASOC), *Official Gazette of BiH – International Agreements*, 6/08.

21 Tomo Vukšić, ed., *Crkva i država u Bosni i Hercegovini: Zakoni, podzakonski akti, ugovori i komentari* [Church and State in Bosnia and Herzegovina: Laws, By-Laws, Agreements and Comments] (Sarajevo: Bishops Conference of Bosnia and Herzegovina, 2007), 22.

22 Art. 8, BAHS.

23 Durham and Scharffs, *Law and Religion*, 371; N. Doe, *Law and Religion in Europe* (Oxford: Oxford University Press, 2011), 115.

function in compliance with the law of the state but, on the other hand, they also govern themselves based on regulations adopted without recourse to the state approval. The LFR explicitly recognizes the right of religious communities to self-governance on the basis of their internal regulations:

> Churches and religious communities shall be self-administering in accordance with their own laws and doctrines, which shall have no civil-legal effect and shall not be forcibly imposed by the public authorities nor applicable to non-members. Churches and religious communities shall autonomously regulate their internal organization in accordance with their internal regulations, laws and doctrines.[24]

The Constitutional Court of BiH in *the Parish of St. Anthony Padovanski of Bugojno, Fransiscan Province of Bosna Srebrenica v. Vladimir Batinić* dealt with the issue whether the civil-legal effects of religious norms can be recognized. According to the provisions of canon law, the inheritance of a monk belongs to his priestly order in accordance with his vow of poverty. While the lower courts fully accepted the church parish's claim and applied *the Codex Iuris Canonici*, the Supreme Court of the FBiH reversed their judgments and awarded the deceased priest's inheritance to his brother in accordance with the related provisions of civil law. The Constitutional Court upheld the decision of the FBiH Supreme Court, referring to the outlined provisions of the LFR. However, the Court's decision left the possibility of applying the internal norms of a religious community in the legal system of BiH if they are recognized through bilateral agreements of the state with those community.[25] Since the BAHS envisaged the church juridical persons may acquire, possess, use, and alienate property "according to the norms of canon law and the legislation of Bosnia and Herzegovina",[26] it is still unclear what practical implications this clause of the agreement will have.

There are two clear exemptions to the general rule that religious doctrines and laws have no civil-legal effects. First, the state authorities recognize the status of a legal entity to the bodies of religious communities which they declare as such by their autonomous decisions on the basis of canonical or other religious regulations.[27] Second, religious communities have the right to determine the need to build a place of worship in accordance with their internal regulations, while the state is obliged to enable the implementation of given decisions if they are not opposed by objective reasons.[28]

24 Art. 11, Law on Freedom of Religion.

25 Constitutional Court of BiH, Case no. AP 286/06, 29 September 2007.

26 Art. 10, para. 1, BAHS.

27 Art. 8, para. 5, 6, LFR. N. Miličević argues that this legal provision grants the religious communities a right that is "eminently the domain of exercising state power". See Neđo Miličević, "Sloboda vjere i vjeroispovijedanja," *Godišnjak Pravnog fakulteta u Sarajevu* (Sarajevo: Pravni fakultet, 2004), 265.

28 Art. 11, para. 2, BAHS.

5 Administrative autonomy

Administrative (or executive) activities are an important aspect of enjoying the autonomy of a religious community. They encompass a range of issues, including proclamation of the faith, worship and rituals, hiring and dismissal of staff, ordination of priests, educational and charitable work, administration of the property and finance, and so on.[29] As a general rule, the LFR prohibits the state from interfering in the affairs and internal organization of religious communities.[30] In particular, religious communities enjoy "autonomy in the selection, appointment and dismissal of their personnel in accordance with their respective requirements and regulations".[31] The separation of the sphere of the state and religious communities is manifested, among other things, through the inadmissibility of interference by public authorities in the selection and appointment of religious dignitaries.[32] The same applies to the conferral of religious or ecclesiastical services (such as through ordination) that should be decided upon on that basis of religious norms.[33]

Religious communities have an established code of religious rights and duties of their members that are in line with the nature of their mission, which indirectly gives religious communities the right to be guided by this internal code when hiring or firing their staff. The autonomy of religious communities in this regard is further confirmed by their exemption from the applicability of provisions of the Law on prohibition of discrimination.[34]

Respecting the autonomy of religious communities, the Bosnian courts regularly declare themselves as incompetent to resolve disputes regarding the appointment and dismissal of religious officials. For illustration, the Cantonal Court in Bihać in *V. A. v. the Islamic Community*[35] upheld the decision of lower court which proclaimed that the dispute between an imam and the Islamic Community in Bosnia and Herzegovina (IC) lies outside its jurisdiction. In its reasoning, the Court referred to the LFR[36] and the IC's Constitution, which states, *inter alia*, that the IC's *ra'is al-ʿulama* is responsible for the appointment and dismissal of imams and chief imams.[37]

Still, there is a dilemma regarding the issue whether the autonomy of religious communities extends to hiring and dismissal of the members of their staff which are not in the status of religious officials. Considering that the LFR enables religious communities to engage in all legal activities – economic, educational,

29 Doe, *Law and Religion in Europe*, 126.
30 Art. 14, para. 2, LFR.
31 Art. 11, para. 3, LFR.
32 Art. 14, para. 6, LFR.
33 Art. 6, Instructions on the implementation of the LFR; Art. 6, BAHS.
34 Art. 5, Law on Prohibition of Discrimination, *Official Gazette of BiH*, 66/16.
35 Cantonal Court in Bihać, Case no. 17 0 Rs 030553 12 RSŽ, 6 February 2012.
36 Art. 11, para. 1–3, Law on Freedom of Religion.
37 Art. 61, Constitution of the IC, accessed 7 February 2021, www.islamskazajednica.ba/images/stories/Ustavi/Ustav_IZ-e_precisceni_tekst_2014.pdf.

cultural, and so on– in practice the question arises as to who is considered a religious official whose election, appointment, or removal is subject to the principle of religious autonomy. According to the Instruction on the Implementation of the LFR, "religious officials are natural persons considered as such by their church or religious community. They perform activities that meet the religious, spiritual and special cultural needs of citizens." In certain cases, the courts have accepted the consideration of employees' lawsuits against their religious employers, thus distinguishing between religious and lay staff of religious communities, although this difference is not explicitly stated in the LFR or in the Instruction.[38]

6 Educational, health, and charitable institutions established by religious communities

The LFR recognizes the right of religious communities to undertake a range of activities which makes them easier to carry out their core faith mission. Thus, they may found business enterprises as well as acquire, administer, and dispose of property. In addition, they have the right to establish cultural, charitable, health and social care institutions, family counselling centres, as well as educational institutions that are equal in rights with institutions founded by the state.[39] The decision to establish these institutions is made autonomously by the relevant bodies and the membership of religious communities.[40] These possibilities represent a complete novelty in relation to the previous communist period when religious communities could only perform religious rites and other core religious affairs.

The status and autonomy of faith-based educational and charitable institutions is further regulated by the bilateral agreements signed between the state and religious communities. These documents specify that religious communities have the right to establish educational institutions at all levels and to administer them according to its own norms, while also respecting the relevant legal provisions of the state. The agreements further envisage that the said institutions will enjoy equal status with those established by the state in terms of state funding, recognition of academic degrees and university qualifications obtained, as well as the status of their both teaching and non-teaching staff.[41] Similar provisions on autonomy and equal status apply to charitable institutions established by religious communities.[42]

7 Conclusion

This analysis reveals the growing recognition of religious autonomy as an important feature of the post-communist restructuring of the state-religion relations

38 Art. 11, Law on Freedom of Religion; Art. 6, Instructions on the Implementation of the LFR.
39 Art. 10, Law on Freedom of Religion.
40 Art. 10, 14, Law on Freedom of Religion.
41 Art. 14, BAHS; Art. 15, BASOC.
42 Art. 17, BAHS; Art. 14, BASOC.

in BiH. Religious communities enjoy independence from the state in a variety of areas, such as adopting internal regulatory instruments, organization and structure, self-administration, management of religious affairs, and so on. Moreover, civil-legal effects of certain aspects of religious laws and regulations have been recognized, such as decisions on the juristic personality of the bodies of the religious community or the construction of church buildings or other religious facilities.

Significant advance, especially compared to the tight control of religious structures by the state during the communist period, relates to the current independence of religious communities in terms of the election, appointment and removal of their dignitaries and other religious officials. While the case law is still evolving in the area of religious autonomy, the courts have thus far made a clear line of judgment that labour disputes of religious staff of faith communities fall out of their jurisdiction. On the contrary, the courts have been willing to decide on appeals of those employees of religious communities who are not regarded as members of their religious personnel.

Ultimately, the new religion law of BiH provide a broad scope for religious communities for the social action necessary to accomplish their mission. Thus, the concept of religious autonomy takes on a broader meaning and implies the entry of religious communities into the fields that were previously under the exclusive jurisdiction of the state, such as, for example, education, health and social care, media, and so on.

7 Property and finances of religious communities

1 Introduction

Important puzzles in the mosaic of relations between the state and religious communities are issues concerning the property and finance of these communities.[1] As N. Doe noted, the dominant model of state-religion relations in Europe regarding the property and finances of religion is cooperation.[2] The European experience in this area differs significantly from that in the U.S., whose constitutional non-establishment clause imposes much stricter restrictions on public funding of religion.[3] There are various ways in which countries across Europe financially support their respective religious communities, and they can generally be classified as direct and indirect aid. While the former refers to the direct financial contributions of states to religion, the latter covers various types of tax exemptions and concessions for religious communities.

With regard to property, this chapter studies the right of religious communities in Bosnia and Herzegovina (BiH or Bosnia) to acquire, manage, and dispose of property. The study includes also civil and criminal law protection of places of worship, as well as the restitution of property of religious communities confiscated during the former communist regime. With regard to finance, the chapter explores the ways through which the state provides financial support to religious communities in BiH. One of the important issues is the criteria according to which different levels of government provide direct financial support to religious communities and their relation to the principle of equality of religious communities.

1 According to a group of coauthors, the activity of religious communities can be financed through different systems: (a) own revenues, (b) donations, scholarships, and collected funds, (c) financing from the state budget, (d) church foundations, and (e) church tax. However, one system does not exclude others and their combinations are possible in one country (see Silvija Marasović, Mirko Klarić i Ante Balić, "Crkveni porez kao oblik financiranja djelatnosti vjerskih zajednica" [Church Tax as a Form of Financing the Activities of Religious Communities], *Zbornik radova Pravnog fakulteta u Splitu* 44, no. 3–4 (2007): 573–596).

2 Norman Doe, *Law and Religion in Europe: A Comparative Introduction* (New York: Oxford University Press, 2011), 164.

3 W. Cole Durham, Jr. and Brett G. Scharffs, *Law and Religion: National, International, and Comparative Perspectives* (New York: Aspen Publishers, 2010), 452.

DOI: 10.4324/9780429266683-10

These analyses will be conducted based on insights into religion, property and tax law, the Constitutional Court's case law, reports of the Ombudsman for Human Rights of BiH, and data obtained from state authorities in accordance with the Law on Freedom of Access to Information in BiH. These data were collected from the state and entity ministries responsible for cooperation with religious communities and at the local government level from the municipality of Centar Sarajevo (in the Federation of Bosnia and Herzegovina) and the municipality of Srebrenica (in the Republic of Srpska).

The chapter argues that the property rights of religious communities are protected by general property rights, but also by the relevant provisions of the 2004 Law on Freedom of Religion (LFR) and bilateral protocols agreed between the state and religious communities. However, unsatisfactory results were observed when it comes to criminal prosecution and punishment of perpetrators of attacks on religious facilities and the absence of any significant progress in terms of restitution of nationalized property of religious communities. Further, it is noted that the state provides financial aid to religious communities through direct subsidies to religious objects and tax exemptions, but that the criteria for allocating funds at some levels of government raise the issue of equality of majority and minority religious groups.

2 State-religion financial relations in international law

Both the universal[4] and European systems for protecting human rights[5] respects the sovereign powers of states to regulate relations between the state and religious communities through their constitutions and sub-constitutional laws, provided that the protection of the right to freedom of religion or belief and the principle of non-discrimination on the basis of religion or belief is ensured. Among the main principles of the EU religion law is subsidiarity. It is best expressed in the Declaration on the status of churches and non-confessional organizations appended to the Treaty of Amsterdam 1997 and reads: "The European Union respects and does not prejudice the status under national law of churches and religious associations or communities in the Member States."[6] However, the principle of subsidiarity does not preclude the EU interference in the financial relations

4 According to para. 9 of the General Comment no. 22 of Art. 18 of the 1966 International Covenant on Civil and Political Rights (ICCPR): "the fact that a religion is recognized as a state religion or that it is established as official or traditional or that its followers comprise the majority of the population, shall not result in any impairment of the enjoyment of any of the rights under the Covenant, including articles 18 and 27, nor in any discrimination against adherents to other religions or non-believers". See UN Human Rights Committee (HRC), *CCPR General Comment No. 22: Article 18 (Freedom of Thought, Conscience or Religion)*, 30 July 1993, CCPR/C/21/Rev.1/Add.4, accessed 8 April 2021, www.refworld.org/docid/453883fb22.html.

5 See *Darby v. Sweden*, 23 October 1990, Series A no. 187.

6 European Union – Treaty of Amsterdam, accessed 28 September 2021, https://europa.eu/european-union/sites/default/files/docs/body/treaty_of_amsterdam_en.pdf.

between the state and religions in an effort to bring national tax legislation in line with relevant EU directives.[7]

The principle of subsidiarity has a prominent role in the European Court of Human Rights (ECtHR) jurisprudence on the financing and taxation of religious communities. The Member States of the European Convention on Human Rights (ECHR) enjoy a wide margin of appreciation with regard to state funding and the tax system applicable to religious communities.[8] Indeed, there are no common standards at European level on these issues which are closely linked to the history and tradition of each country.[9] Some countries with a state or national church (e.g. Finland, Denmark) or cooperation system (e.g. Germany, Austria) employ the so-called church tax system. In Germany, for instance, the state collects a church tax (*kirchensteuer*) as a proportion of the income tax of members of religious organizations possessing a public corporation status. In other groups of countries, such as in Italy, Spain, Hungary, Latvia, and so on, a taxpayer may voluntarily allocate a portion of his or her income tax, collected by the state, to a specific religious community.[10] The ECtHR has taken a clear position that the existence of a church tax regime is not contrary to the exercise of the right to freedom of religion as long as individuals are able to leave the church in question.[11] Moreover, the right of religious communities to levy such a tax may serve as a legitimate aim for restricting negative religious freedom in the light of Art. 9, para. 2 of the ECHR.[12] Freedom to manifest religion or belief does not empower religious communities to secure funds from the state budget. However, the financial benefits provided to religious societies facilitate the realization of their religious mission and the state is obliged to remain neutral when granting them. Accordingly, there must be clearly defined criteria on the basis of which cooperation between the state and religious communities is achieved in terms of funding in order to avoid situations in which members of some religious groups feel like second-class citizens.[13]

7 Françoise Curtit and Anne Fornerod, "State Support for Religions: European Regulation," in *Public Funding of Religions in Europe*, ed. Francis Messner (London and New York: Routledge, 2015), 3–22.

8 See *Alujer Fernández and Caballero García v. Spain* (dec.), no. 53072/99, ECHR 2001-VI.

9 On different aspects of state-religion financial relations see Francis Messner, ed., *Public Funding of Religions in Europe* (London and New York: Routledge, 2015); Michaela Moravčíková and Eleónora Valová, eds., *Financing Churches and Religious Communities in the 21st Century* (Bratislava: Institute for State-Church Relations, 2010); Jelena Ulić i Sandra Brajušković, *Pregled nacionalnih sistema ustavnopravnih odnosa između države i crkve i uređenje imovinskih pitanja u nekoliko zemalja EU* [An Overview of National Systems of Constitutional Relations Between the State and the Church and the Regulation of Property Issues in Several EU Countries] (Podgorica: Istraživački centar Skupštine Crne Gore, 2019).

10 Doe, *Law and Religion in Europe*, 177–179.

11 Durham, Jr. and Scharffs, *Law and Religion*, 455.

12 *Wasmuth v. Germany*, no. 12884/03, ECHR 17 February 2011.

13 *Magyar Keresztény Mennonita Egyház and Others v. Hungary*, nos. 70945/11 and 8 others, ECHR 2014.

3 Property and finances of religious communities

Although the right of religious communities to acquire, manage, and dispose of property is implicitly covered by general property law,[14] there are specific statements of this right in the Republic of Srpska (RS) Constitution, the LFR, and bilateral state agreements with religious communities. According to Art. 28, para. 2 of the RS Constitution, "religious communities ... may ... engage in economic and other activities, receive gifts, create endowments and manage them, in accordance with the law".[15] A more comprehensive statement is contained in Art. 12 of the LFR, which reads:

> Churches and religious communities may acquire property in accordance with the law. Churches and religious communities may own property and property rights, which they shall be free to use and administer.[16]

These provisions are further elaborated in the singed agreements between the state and religious communities.[17] Religious communities may have different sources of funding their activities, including donations and membership fees,[18] revenues they generate from their busines enterprises[19] or educational, cultural, and other activities, the sale of religious literature and souvenirs, the provision of religious services to its members,[20] as well as state financial subsidies,[21] and so on. The right of religious communities to property and peaceful enjoyment of possessions may be restricted for the protection of public interest. The Constitutional Court of BiH has taken the position that the disputed Arts. 13 and 16 of

14 "All persons within the territory of Bosnia and Herzegovina shall enjoy the human rights and fundamental freedoms ...; these include: ... k) The right to property" (Art. II, para. 3, Constitution of BiH, accessed 16 January 2021, www.ccbh.ba/public/down/USTAV_BOSNE_I_HERCEGOVINE_engl.pdf).

15 Constitution of RS, *Official Gazette of RS*, 21/92. Amendments of Constitution of RS, *Official Gazette of RS*, 28/94, 8/96, 13/96, 15/96, 16/96, 21/96, 21/02, 26/02, 30/02, 31/02, 69/02, 31/03, 98/03, 115/05 and 117/05.

16 Law on Freedom of Religion and Legal Status of Churches and Religious Communities, *Official Gazette of BiH*, 5/04.

17 "Ecclesiastical juridical persons may acquire, possess, use and usufruct or alienate moveable and immoveable goods, and may also acquire and alienate patrimonial rights, according to the norms of canon law and the legislation of Bosnia and Herzegovina. The juridical persons indicated in section 1 may institute foundations. Their activity, as far as its civil effects are concerned, is regulated according to the legal norms of Bosnia and Herzegovina." Art. 10, para. 1–2, Basic Agreement Between the Holy See and Bosnia and Herzegovina (BAHS), *Official Gazette of BiH – International Agreements*, 10/07. See also Art. 10, Basic Agreement Between Bosnia and Herzegovina and the Serb Orthodox Church (BASOC), *Official Gazette of BiH – International Agreements*, 6/08.

18 Art. 11, para. 4 and Art. 13, para. 2–3, Law on Freedom of Religion.

19 Art. 10, para. 1, Law on Freedom of Religion.

20 Art. 9, para. 1, Instructions on the Implementation of the Law on Freedom of Religion and Legal Status of Churches and Religious Communities in Bosnia and Herzegovina, *Official Gazette of BiH*, 28/19.

21 Art. 12, para. 4 and Art. 14, para. 4, Law on Freedom of Religion.

the Law on Cemeteries and Funeral Services of the RS are compatible with Art. 1 of Protocol no. 1 of the ECHR.[22] These articles stipulate that cemeteries, including those owned by religious communities, which have been put out of use, may be used for other purposes if it is determined by the documents on spatial and urban planning for which the general interest has been established.[23] The jurisdiction of religious communities does not extend to the personal property of their personnel. Therefore, the case law of the Bosnian Constitutional Court suggests that the church parish's claim for religious freedom does not include its right to inherit the personal property of its monk, despite his voluntary acceptance that his property belongs to the parish in accordance with canon law.[24]

The right to construct places of worship and other religious facilities as well as enlarging the existing ones is exercised through cooperation between the competent religious and public planning authorities.[25] The state guarantees the inviolability of places of worship which may be destined to other purposes only with explicit approval of authorities of a religious community. Security measures may not be carried out in these places without the prior approval of the competent ecclesiastical authorities, unless urgent action is required to protect life and health and to preserve property of historical or artistic importance.[26]

Attacks on holy sites and damage to religious buildings and other property of religious communities are explicitly prohibited by the LFR.[27] The initial draft of the law (June 2003) contained a special section on crimes against freedom of religion which prescribed stricter sanctions than those regulated by general criminal law. Thus, attacks on religious facilities, as well as other crimes against freedom of religion, were punishable by imprisonment for a term of three months to three years, and in the case of serious consequences resulting from the attack, for a period of six months to five years.[28] For comparison, the FBiH Criminal Code provides for a fine or imprisonment of up to one year for the criminal offense of damaging someone else's property used for religious purposes, which is most often a qualification for attacks on religious facilities.[29]

Religious freedom reports as well as information from the Bosnian MHRR indicate the continuity of attacks on places of worship, cemeteries, and property of religious communities in the post-war period, although their numbers have declined recently. The most common targets of attacks are the facilities of minority religious groups in a particular entity and "the results so far in identifying

22 Constitutional Court of BiH, Case no. U 19/14, 24 September 2014, para. 73–77.

23 Law on Cemeteries and Funeral Services of the RS, *Official Gazette of the RS*, 31/13, 6/14.

24 Constitutional Court of BiH, Case no. AP 286/06, 29 September 2007.

25 Art. 6, para. 6–8, Instructions on the Implementation of the Law on Freedom of Religion; Art. 11, BAHS; Art. 11, BASOC.

26 Art. 7, para. 2–4, BAHS.

27 Art. 5, para. 2.b., Law on Freedom of Religion.

28 The Commission on Security and Cooperation in Europe, *Bosnia and Herzegovina's Draft Religion Law: Draft Text Fails to Meet OSCE Commitments on Religious Freedom*, CSCE Report, Congress No. 108, Session No. 1 (30 September 2003), 12–13.

29 Art. 293, para 2, Criminal Code of the FBiH, *Official Gazette of the FBiH*, 36/03, 21/04, 69/04, 18/05, 42/10, 42/11, 59/14, 76/14, 46/16, 75/17.

the perpetrators are not effective enough to ensure the peaceful enjoyment of the religious freedoms guaranteed by the Constitution and laws of Bosnia and Herzegovina in force".[30] Out of a total of 219 cases of attacks on religious sites or personnel of religious communities registered by the Interreligious Council in Bosnia and Herzegovina (IRC) from 2010 to 2018, the police identified suspects in 75 cases and prosecuted only 23 perpetrators.[31] The IRC has repeatedly suggested that attacks on religious sites should be treated as hate crimes instead of the commonly used qualification of vandalism and damage to property.[32]

Another problem related to the property of religious communities that affects members of minority religions in certain localities is the denial of permits for the construction of new places of worship, as well as the illegal construction of religious buildings on private property. In such a way, Drvar municipal authorities continue to refuse to issue a permit to build a new Catholic church despite orders from the Ministry of Construction, Reconstruction, Space Planning and Environmental Protection of Hercegbosna Canton to issue the said permit.[33] On 1 October 2019, the ECtHR ruled that the state was obliged to remove an illegally built Orthodox church on Fata Orlović's property in Bratunac within three months, but the relevant authorities of the RS entity have only recently enforced the ruling. The SOC built a church in 1998 on the applicant's land in the immediate vicinity of the house where she and her family lived before they were expelled by the RS Army. The ECtHR found that "authorities had failed to comply with previous decisions by the Commission for Real Property Claims of Displaced Persons and Refugees in 1999 and the Ministry for Refugees and Displaced Persons of the RS in 2001 ordering that Orlović be granted full restitution of her land, the seizure of which resulted in a violation of the right to property".[34]

One of the key unresolved issues in the relations between the state and religious communities in BiH is the restitution of the property of those communities nationalized by the communist regime in the period after the end of the World War II.[35] As early as the 1990s, several political parties included the issue

30 Ministry for Human Rights and Refugees of BiH (MHRR), Information no. UP-I-05–07–7–25–3/19, 26 July 2019.

31 U.S. Department of State – Office of International Religious Freedom, *2019 Report on International Religious Freedom: Bosnia and Herzegovina*, accessed 25 April 2021, www.state.gov/reports/2019-report-on-international-religious-freedom/bosnia-and-herzegovina/.

32 E.g. when a group of five attackers threw stones at the Riječanska mosque in Zvornik on 24 July 2019, a police report recorded minor damage and did not treat the case as a hate crime. See IRC, "Osuda napada na Riječansku džamiju u Zvorniku," [Condemnation of the Attack on the Riječanska mosque in Zvornik] accessed 25 April 2021, https://avaz.ba/vijesti/bih/505172/osuda-napada-na-rijecansku-dzamiju-u-zvorniku.

33 U.S. Department of State – Office of International Religious Freedom, *2019 Report on International Religious Freedom: Bosnia and Herzegovina*.

34 *Orlović and Others v. Bosnia and Herzegovina*, no. 16332/18, 1 October 2019, accessed 25 April 2021, http://hudoc.echr.coe.int/eng?i=001-196155.

35 See Fikret Karčić, "Vakufi i reprivatizacija," [Waqfs and reprivatization] *Gazette of the Riyasat of the Islamic Community in the SFRY*, no. 3 (1991): 267–272. According to the data of the Commission for Religious Affairs of BiH, from 1946 to 1961, 53.7% of the buildings of the Islamic Community, 41% of the buildings of the Serb Orthodox Church (SOC), 36

of restitution in their programmes.[36] Later, the 2004 law on religions provided for the right of religious communities to "restitution of confiscated property throughout Bosnia and Herzegovina, without discrimination".[37] The state's obligation to pass a law on restitution was also confirmed by the agreements signed with religious communities.[38] Still, unlike other republics of the former Yugoslavia, BiH has not yet enacted a restitution law to alleviate decades of injustice inflicted on religious communities. So far, several drafts of this law have been made, but they have not been adopted, obviously due to the lack of political will of key state actors.[39] Due to this situation, the partial return of nationalized property to religious communities or its allocation for use until the final resolution of this issue often took place at the discretion of municipal authorities while favouring the dominant religion at the local level.[40] Thus, the Human Rights Chamber for BiH (HRCBiH) ruled that the Travnik Municipality discriminated against the Catholic Church (CC) in the enjoyment of the right to freedom of religion by allowing it to use only one part of the Catholic gymnasium building – nationalized during the communist period, while the entire *madrasa* building was returned to the IC and enabled the construction of an additional facility in its vicinity.[41] However, due to the failure of the authorities of the Central Bosnia Canton and the FBiH to implement the decision of the Human Rights Committee (HRC), the Roman Catholic Archdiocese of Vrhbosna filed an appeal against BiH before the ECtHR. The Court ruled that there was a violation of the right of the CC to the peaceful enjoyment of possession under Art. 1 of the Protocol no. 1 to the ECHR and obligated the respondent state to "secure the immediate and full enforcement of the Chamber's decision".[42]

---

buildings of the Catholic Church in BiH (CC) and four buildings of other religious communities were nationalized. The biggest victim of the nationalization process was the Islamic Community (IC). Of a total of 992 nationalized buildings owned by religious communities, 80.9% belonged to the IC. See Denis Bećirović, *Islamska zajednica u Bosni i Hercegovini za vrijeme avnojevske Jugoslavije (1945–1953)* [Islamic Community in Bosnia and Herzegovina During Avnojevska Yugoslavia (1945–1953)] (Zagreb and Sarajevo: Bosniak National Community for the City of Zagreb and Zagreb County, the Islamic Community in Croatia and the Institute of History Sarajevo, 2012), 231.

36 Drino Galičić, "Finansijski odnosi i imovina crkava i vjerskih zajednica," [Financial Relations and Property of Churches and Religious Communities] in *Doktrinarni i praktični aspekti odnosa između države, crkava/vjerskih zajednica i pojedinca*, ed. Nedim Ademović (Sarajevo: European Academy for Applied Research and Education in BiH, 2012), 51.

37 Art. 12, para. 3, Law on Freedom of Religion.

38 Art. 10, para. 3, BAHS; Art. 1–2, Additional Protocol to the BAHS, accessed 25 April 2021, www.kuvn.org/upload/file/Temeljni%20ugovor.pdf, Art. 10, para. 3, BASOC.

39 U.S. Department of State – Office of International Religious Freedom, *2019 Report on International Religious Freedom: Bosnia and Herzegovina.*

40 Nedim Begović, "Ustavni okvir i Zakon o slobodi vjere i pravnom položaju crkava i vjerskih zajednica u BiH," [Constitutional Framework and the Law on Freedom of Religion and the Legal Status of Churches and Religious Communities in BiH] in *Sekularnost i religija: BiH i* regija, eds. Edin Šarčević and Drago Bojić (Sarajevo: Fondacija Centar za javno pravo, 2015), 92.

41 Human Rights Chamber for BiH, Case no. CH/02/9628, 9 May 2003.

42 *Roman Catholic Archdiocese of Vrhbosna v. Bosnia and Herzegovina*, no. 40694/13, 5 June 2018.

4 Direct state aid to religious communities

The principle of state-religion separation does not prevent the state from financially supporting religious communities. Of the existing models of state aid to religious communities in various European countries,[43] church taxes and voluntary tax allocations for religious organizations have not been considered as options in BiH. The 2004 Law on Freedom of Religion allows the state to provide direct financial support to religious communities for the preservation of cultural and historical heritage sites, healthcare activities, educational, charitable, and social services. The provision of this support must be based on the principle of equal treatment of religious communities and is conditioned by the fact that they provide the said services without discrimination on any grounds, in particular on the grounds of religion or belief.[44] Such a provision is in line with the concept of the welfare state that provides various types of social services to its citizens through its own or civil society organizations. In this context, religious organizations that provide the said services (e.g. educational) have the same right to apply for support from the state budget as secular organizations.[45] The state provides salaries for teachers of religious education in public schools as well as funding of religious secondary and high schools.[46] Three Islamic faculties (in Sarajevo, Zenica and Bihać), as well as the faculties of Orthodox (Foča) and Catholic theology (Sarajevo), are members of respective public universities and their status, including state funding, is regulated by special protocols signed between the relevant education authorities and religious communities.[47]

Another area of direct state aid to religious communities concerns the financing of health, pension and disability insurance for religious officials. The LFR requires the state to enact special regulations on the pension, disability, and health insurance of "religious officials",[48] but this legal provision has not yet been implemented. There were no concrete responses from the state to several initiatives launched by religious communities through the IRC to ensure the implementation of the outlined provision.[49] However, the state does provide direct funding for chaplains in the Armed Forces of BiH, that is, staff of the Military Mufti Office, the Office of the Catholic Pastorship, and the Office of the Orthodox Pastor.[50] The basic agreements of the state with the Holy See and the SOC

43 See Doe, *Law and Religion in Europe*, 177–186.
44 Art. 14, para. 4, Law on Freedom of Religion.
45 Durham and Scharffs, *Law and Religion*, 453.
46 Art. 14 and 16, BAHS.
47 See e.g. Art. 144, para. (2), adents f) and o) and Art. 178, Law on Higher Education of Sarajevo Canton, 33/17.
48 Art. 13, para. 4, Law on Freedom of Religion.
49 Galičić, "Finansijski odnosi," 54–55.
50 See Art. 21, Rulebook on the Organization and Manner of Functioning of the Religious Service in the Ministry of Defense of BiH and the Armed Forces of BiH, no. 06–38–5113/07, 12 November 2007; Art. 10, 11, 15, 16, 20, Agreement on the Establishment, Organization and Manner of Functioning of the Military Mufti's Office in the Ministry of Defense and the Armed Forces of BiH, 11 September 2007; Art. 10, 11, 15, 16, 20, Agreement on the

envisage the establishment of pastoral service in police services, prisons, hospitals, orphanages, as well as all public and private health and social care institutions,[51] but this clause has not yet been implemented.

Providing financial support to religious facilities or projects of religious communities from the state budget seems quite appropriate in the context of BiH, especially given that the state has not restituted nationalized property that would be a significant source of funding for religion. However, this type of financial relations between the state and religion raises questions about the criteria on the basis of which the distribution of financial resources is made, that is, whether these criteria ensure equal treatment of various religious groups.

According to the Instruction on the Implementation of the LFR, all levels of government in BiH can allocate from the budget, on an annual basis, the amount for financing projects of religious communities in the field of education, culture, healthcare, social and humanitarian activities, cemetery maintenance, and so on. In addition to the principles of equality and transparency, there are three general criteria that must be met when allocating funds, that is, the type and significance of the project and its importance to citizens. Religious communities may also be awarded grants to maintain and renovate existing places of worship and build new ones. When deciding on the distribution of financial support, the authorities are required to consult with the competent ministry for cooperation with religious communities and the ministry of finance. These authorities have the right to receive information from religious communities on the manner and dynamics of spending funds allocated from the budget.[52]

The data obtained from different levels of government, based on the regulations on freedom of access to information, aim to illustrate what state funding of religious communities looks like in practice. The report submitted by the MHRR, the relevant state ministry for cooperation with religious communities, states that it allocated 70.000 BAM[53] from the 2016 budget and awarded it to religious communities through a public announcement. In accordance with the principle of equality, all religious communities registered with the MJ of BiH had the right to apply for the said grant funds. Pursuant to the Decision on Criteria for Awarding Grants to Religious Communities for 2016, the approved funds could be used to (a) strengthen religious freedoms and interreligious tolerance, (b) preserve cultural and historical heritage, and (c) support charitable and social services of religious communities. The decision also specified the scoring criteria

Establishment, Organization and Manner of Functioning of the Orthodox Pastoral Care in the Ministry of Defense and the Armed Forces of BiH, 11 September 2007; Art. 10, 11, 15, 16, 20, Agreement on the Establishment, Organization and Manner of Functioning of the Catholic Pastoral Care in the Ministry of Defense and the Armed Forces of BiH, 11 September 2007; Art. 10, Agreement on the Pastoral Care of Catholic Believers, Members of the Armed Forces of Bosnia and Herzegovina, accessed 26 April 2021, www.bkbih.ba/info.php?id=233.

51 Art. 15, BAHS.

52 Art. 9, para. 2–6. Instructions on the Implementation of the Law on Freedom of Religion.

53 1 BAM = 0,51 EUR.

for the evaluation of project proposals. Based on the report of the commission of the MHRR for project selection, the Council of Ministers of BiH (CMBiH) awarded grants to *Majlis* of the IC Srebrenik, Church Municipality Čajniče, Metropolitanate of Dabro-Bosnia Sokolac, Jewish Municipality Sarajevo, Church of St. Peter East New Sarajevo, Media Center of the Vrhbosna Archdiocese Sarajevo and *Majlis* of the IC Kiseljak.[54] Regarding the distribution of funds, it is noticeable that the MHRR has balanced between the principle of equal treatment (approximately equal amounts were given to four traditional communities) and the quality of the proposed projects.

Furthermore, according to the MHRR report all important issues of enjoyment of the right to freedom of religion are resolved through consultations with the IRC with which the said Ministry signed a Cooperation Agreement in 2008. The aim of the agreement is to support the IRC work in the field of interreligious dialogue, strengthening tolerance and coexistence in BiH.[55]

Unlike at the state level, the principle of equality, and sometimes transparency, does not play such a pronounced role in the distribution of funds to religious communities at some lower levels of government, especially in the RS entity. It is obvious that the criterion of statistics is of paramount importance here. Accordingly, a larger religious group more easily qualifies for state aid, even where its current numerical superiority is the result of ethnic cleansing and forced displacement in the past war.[56]

The distribution of funds from the grant that is allocated to religious communities within the annual budget of the RS is done by the Government of the RS, that is, since 2011. Republic Secretariat for Religions, taking into account the number, importance, and needs of religious organizations. By decisions of the entity government, funds are remitted to the SOC, the CC, the IC, Jewish municipalities and other religious organizations.[57] According to the information received from the Republic Secretariat for Religions, the amount of financial assistance of the RS entity to religion, the distribution of which is performed by this body in the period 2014–2018, was 300,000 BAM per year. The distribution is not done automatically, but on the basis of project funding applications that can be submitted by all registered religious communities. A special commission of the Secretariat decides on the approval of financing, based on the rulebook on the distribution of funds.[58] The key criterion for the distribution is the numerical size of the religious

54 All the mentioned subjects of religious communities were awarded grants in the amount of 10,000 BAM each, except for the Jewish Community in BiH (JC), which was approved 9,990 BAM. See MHRR, Information no. UP-I-05–07–7–25–3/19, 26 July 2019.

55 The agreement stipulates the obligation of the state to allocate 100,000 BAM every calendar year for the operation of the IRC. See MHRR, Information no. UP-I-05–07–7–25–3/19, 26 July 2019.

56 According to the 2013 census, 11 Bosniak majority municipalities and one Croat majority municipality from the 1991 census became Serb majority municipalities. See "Entity: RS," accessed 2 May 2021, www.statistika.ba/?lang=en#link3.

57 Constitutional Court of BiH, Case no. AP 2575/13, 26 October 2016, para. 67.

58 Unfortunately, the rulebook and data on the distribution of funds are not available on the website of the Government of the RS, which would require the principle of transparency.

group according to the first post-war census from 2013. The only exceptions are JC, whose municipalities in Banja Luka and Doboj receive an annual amount of 30,000 KM, as well as the CC, due to their small size, but long historical duration.[59]

However, the RS government provides additional aid to religious communities from its budget reserves. According to information made available to the public by the Center for Investigative Reporting, out of the total amount of 6,380,000 BAM allocated for the financing of religious communities in the period 2010–2012, as much as 6,000,000 BAM were awarded to the SOC, that is, 94.04%.[60] Even if the statistical criterion is applied as decisive, this percentage exceeds 81.39% of the RS inhabitants who declared themselves as Orthodox at the 2013 census.[61] In 2020, the RS government allocated about 10 million BAM to religious communities from a donation it received from the Republic of Serbia (7.8 million BAM), donation from the public company "Elektroprivreda of the Republic of Srpska" (1 million BAM) and the RS budget (1.1 million BAM). Of the total amount of financial assistance, 300,000 BAM related to the regular annual grant that the Republic Secretariat for Religions distributes to the four traditional and other religious groups. The entire remaining amount of about 9.6 million BAM was allocated to the SOC, of which only 5 million BAM for the construction of the Serbian-Russian temple in Banja Luka.[62]

The Government of the FBiH, through the Federal Ministry of Culture and Sports (FMCS), supports religious communities in accordance with the propositions and criteria of public announcements. All allocated funds are earmarked and the amounts of grants are determined in accordance with the available funds and with the prescribed general and special criteria for each transfer from the budget separately, taking

59 Republic Secretariat for Religions, Response to a request for access to information, e-mail sent to E. Kovačević on 8 October 2019.

60 Thus, in 2010 the RS government has allocated 1,200,000 BAM for funding religious communities, mainly for the renovation or construction of churches and temples. Of this amount, 200,000 BAM went to the CC, and the remaining 1,000,000 BAM to the dominant SOC. In 2011, the RS Government allocated a total of BAM 3,340,000 to finance religion. The entire amount was allocated to the SOC, except for 50,000 BAM, which was given in support of the work of the IRC. It is noteworthy that most of this support from the entity government (2,765,000 BAM) was spent on settling the previously incurred debts of the Metropolitanate of Dabro-Bosnia and the four dioceses of the SOC. In 2012 the RS government set aside 1,840,000 BAM for funding religious communities. Of the total amount, 80,000 KM went to the JC, 100,000 BAM for the CC, while the largest amount (i.e. 1,660.000 BAM) again awarded to the SOC. It is striking that in this period, the Government of RS did not provide any financial support to the IC, despite the fact that its members make up the second largest religious group in this entity. Namely, according to the 2013 census, Bosniak Muslims comprised 14% of the RS population, while according to the 1991 census, they made up 28% of the population in the territory where this entity was established. See "Entity: RS," accessed 27 April 2021, www.statistika.ba/?lang=en#link3.

61 *Census of Population, Households and Dwellings in Bosnia and Herzegovina: Final Results* (Sarajevo: Agency for Statistics of BiH, 2016), 68.

62 Svjetlana Šurlan, "Milionsku pomoć Srbije Vlada Republike Srpske podijelila crkvama," [The Government of the Republika Srpska Distributed Serbia's Million-Dollar Aid to Churches] accessed 2 May 2021, www.capital.ba/milionsku-pomoc-donacija-srbije-vlada-republike-srpske-podijelila-crkvama-video/.

into account the quality of the project, purpose, and urgency. Recipients of grants can be registered religious communities, and are realized through budget transfers for significant cultural projects, NGOs, youth support, sports, and restoration of cultural heritage. It is important to note that all budget transfers to religious communities are available to the public through the Ministry's website.[63]

In 2013 the FMCS allocated 326,000 BAM for religious communities, of which 199,000 BAM (61.04%) for the IC, 82,000 BAM (25.15%) for the CC and 45,000 BAM (13.80%) for the SOC. The following year, 2014, 358,100 BAM was distributed to the IC (190,800 BAM or 53.28%), the CC (87,300 BAM or 24.38%), and the SOC (80,000 BAM or 22.34%.[64] A comparison of these data with the number of FBiH residents who declared themselves as Muslims (71.28%), Catholics (22.10%), and Orthodox (2.57%)[65] in the 2013 census indicates that statistics were only one of several criteria on the basis of which decisions were made on the distribution of financial assistance.[66] This argument especially gains on importance after considering the 2015 data. That year, the FBiH allocated a total of 575,000 BAM to religious communities, of which 409,000 BAM to the CC (71.13%), 91,000 BAM (15.83%) to the IC, and 75,000 BAM (13.04%) to the SOC.[67]

To illustrate the mode of distribution of state financial aid to religious communities at the local level, the Municipality of Center Sarajevo (the FBiH) and the Municipality of Srebrenica (the RS) were selected. The former regularly plans two grants for religious communities in its annual budget, namely the current grant intended for co-financing the organization of religious events and celebrations of important religious holidays and the capital grant for co-financing the renovation, reconstruction, and equipping of religious facilities. Only traditional religious communities, that is, the IC, the SOC, the CC, and the JC are listed as beneficiaries of grants. Funds are allocated on the basis of individual requests from religious communities and their spending must be justified by narrative and financial reports. The allocation of funds is decided by the Municipal Commission for Relations with Religious Communities in accordance with the adopted neutral criteria such as, for example, detailed explanation of the religious community project, condition of the religious facility that is subject to renovation with an assessment of the planned works, number of facilities of religious communities in need of renovation, protection of the facility by the state, reports on previously approved funding, and so on.[68]

63 Federal Ministry of Culture and Sport, Decision on access to information, no. 01/02-1-4677/19, 19 July 2019.

64 Federal Ministry of Culture and Sports, "Pregled korisnika sredstava po transferima – 2014. god," [Review of Beneficiaries by Transfers – 2014] accessed 27 April 2021, www.fmks.gov.ba/download/2014/pregledkorisnikasredstava/ministarstvo/004.pdf.

65 *Census of Population*, 68.

66 "Entity: FBiH," accessed 27 April 2021, www.statistika.ba/?lang=en#link2.

67 Federal Ministry of Culture and Sports, "Pregled utroška sredstava transfera – 2015," [Overview of the Use of Transfer Funds] accessed 2 May 2021, https://fmks.gov.ba/download/2015/pregledkorisnikasredstava/ministarstvo/002.pdf. The last year for which the data was updated on the website is 2015.

68 Municipality of Center Sarajevo, Decision on access to information, no. 10-49-1355/19, 30 July 2019.

During the period 2015–2018, the Municipality of Srebrenica provided assistance to religious communities from the local community in the following proportions: the SOC 65,795.50 BAM (53.09%), the IC 52,135.00 BAM (42.07%), and the CC 6,000.00 BAM (4.84%).[69] The funds were allocated to religious entities at their request and were largely intended to rebuild the religious infrastructure devastated in the last war. All religious communities in Srebrenica can in principle be beneficiaries of budget assistance, while the approval of funds takes into account the criteria of real needs and the number of believers who will use the renovated religious facilities.[70]

The Greek Catholic Vicariate of the Diocese of Križevci in BiH – representing the religious communities of the Ukrainian national minority in BiH – raised the issue of the distribution of state financial assistance to religious communities in its appeal to the Constitutional Court of BiH on 12 June 2013 against the actions of the competent authorities of the RS entities. Earlier, the RS Secretariat for Religions rejected the appellant's request to be granted the status of a permanent grant beneficiary, which is awarded from the RS budget to religious communities. The Greek Catholic Vicariate was suggested to exercise its financial rights within the CC, given that it was registered within the Register of the said church at the MJBiH.[71]

The apellant alleged before the state Constitutional Court that it was discriminated in the exercise of the right to freedom of religion, given that it was denied regular financial support from the RS entity, unlike the four traditional religious communities, that is, the SOC, the IC, the CC, and the JC.[72] However, the court rejected the appeal as unfounded, arguing that any interference by the state authorities in the distribution of funds within the CC – in whose register the appellant was registered with the MJBiH – would constitute a "violation of the principle of neutrality of public authority, i.e. interference in the internal affairs of a given church".[73] It appears that the Court's decision in this case focused too much on the protection of ecclesiastical autonomy and that the Court, unfortunately, missed the opportunity to consider in great detail whether the existing way of allocating state aid to religious communities in RS was based on valid criteria and in accordance with the principles of equality and transparency.[74]

69 According to the 2013 census, Srebrenica is inhabited by 54.1% Muslims, 44.6% Orthodox, 0.1% Catholics, and 1.1% others. "Religion 2013," accessed 27 April 2021, www.statistika.ba/?show=8#link3.

70 Municipality of Srebrenica – Department for Social Affairs and Public Services, Response to a request for access to information, no. 06–1525/19, 22 July 2019.

71 On the facts of the case see Constitutional Court of BiH, Case no. AP 2575/13, 26 October 2016, para. 5–22.

72 On the allegations of the appellant see Constitutional Court of BiH, Case no. AP 2575/13, 26 October 2016, para. 23–31.

73 Constitutional Court of BiH, Case no. AP 2575/13, 26 October 2016, para. 60.

74 Admittedly, the Court agreed with the Ombudsman's Opinion no. P-185/14 of 10 September 2014 calling on the RS authorities to adopt clear criteria for the distribution of financial support to religious entities and the Recommendation of the Advisory Committee on the Framework Convention for the Protection of National Minorities that "the authorities of the Republika Srpska reexamine the provisions currently in force regarding the allocation

5 Indirect state aid to religious communities

Indirect state financial assistance to religious communities consists of various tax exemptions and concessions to religious communities. Generally, they "enjoy benefits based on their status and privileges that are characteristic of non-profit organizations", provided they do not distribute income or profits "for the benefit of private individuals, unless the distributions themselves have a legitimate charitable purpose".[75] Accordingly, "donations and revenues of churches and religious communities will be treated in accordance with laws and regulations relating to non-profit, educational and charitable organizations".[76]

Generally, registered religious communities and their institutions and enterprises are required to pay taxes and contributions to the income of their employees, that is, the health, pension, and disability insurance. However, they are exempt from the obligation to pay Value Added Tax (VAT) for "trade in goods and services directly related to the religious rites ... in accordance with the regulations governing the performance of that activity".[77] For instance, the IC does not pay VAT on its revenues earned through the performance of religious activities such as mebership fees, ***zakah*** (annual charity), ***sadaqah al-fitr*** (Ramadan charity), ***qurban*** (animal sacrifice), and so on. In contrast, it pays income tax on profitable activities such as, for example, renting business premises in their ownership.[78]

According to Dragan Davidović, director of the RS Secretariat for Religions, religious communities, that is, their lower organizational units in the RS, are registered with the entity's Tax Administration and receive their tax number. They

> do not pay taxes and similar duties to the state for activities in the spiritual domain (baptisms, weddings, funerals, holy water, prayers, confession, etc.). In all other matters, given the obligation to register trade, construction, establishment of companies, etc. they are obliged to pay taxes as well as all secular institutions, establishments, companies.[79]

---

of financial assistance under the Entity budget to churches and religious communities, in order to ensure that the rules in force do not discriminate, whether directly or indirectly, against persons belonging to national minorities". See Constitutional Court of BiH, Case no. AP 2575/13, 26 October 2016, para. 71; Advisory Committee on the Framework Convention for the Protection of National Minorities, *Third Opinion on Bosnia and Herzegovina Adopted on 7 March 2013*, accessed 2 May 2021, www.coe.int/en/web/minorities/bosnia-and-herzegovina.

75 Art. 9, Law on Freedom of Religion.

76 Art. 13, para. 3, Law on Freedom of Religion.

77 Art. 24, para. 7, Law on Value Added Tax of BiH, *Official Gazette of BiH*, 9/2005, 35/2005, 100/2008 and 33/2017.

78 Interview with Muhedin Garanović, head of the Accounting and Finance Department of the Directorate for Economic and Financial Affairs of the *Riyasat* of the IC, Sarajevo, 29 October 2019.

79 Mladen Obrenović, "Finansiranje vjerskih zajednica: od državne kase do prodaje vina, sira ...," [Funding of Religious Communities: From the State Treasury to the Sale of Wine, Cheese ...]

Having said that, religious communities do qualify for the exemptions from property tax[80] and real estate transfer tax[81]– often provided that they use the property for their own needs, that is, to perform worship, as well as from inheritance and gift taxes.[82]

Following a complaint from the religious community of Jehovah's Witnesses in BiH, the BiH Ombudsman Institution issued a recommendation to the state Ministry of Finance and Treasury to prepare information for the CMBiH on the compliance of BiH customs policy regulations with the LFR. The recommendation particularly emphasized the importance of exempting minority religious communities, including Jehovah's Witnesses and the Christian Adventist Church, from the obligation to pay customs duties on imports of religious literature, given the financial difficulties they face in carrying out their religious mission.[83]

6 Conclusion

The right of religious communities to acquire, manage, and dispose of property is guaranteed by the general property law, the LFR, and the state's bilateral agreements with the two traditional churches. It includes their right to build new and maintain existing places of worship and other religious facilities. Reports indicate a continuity of attacks on the property of religious communities, especially minorities in the given territory, in the post-war period and the absence of satisfactory results in detecting and sanctioning their perpetrators. There are also problems with the illegal construction of religious buildings and delays in issuing permits for the construction of religious buildings for minority groups. Due to the failure to pass a state law on the restitution of nationalized property of religious communities, in some places local authorities favoured the majority

accessed 27 April 2021, https://balkans.aljazeera.net/teme/2017/12/17/finansiranje-vjerskih-zajednica-od-drzavne-kase-do-prodaje-vina-sira.

80 See e.g. Art. 9, para. (1), adent 5), Real Estate Tax Act, *Official Gazette of the RS*, 91/15; Art. 6, Law on Property, Inheritance and Gift Tax, *Official Gazette of Zenica-Doboj Canton*, 9/09, 13/11; Art. 6, Law on Property, Inheritance and Gift Tax, *Official Gazette of Tuzla Canton*, 14/09, 3/10, 4/10, 8/14, 13/19, 8/20.

81 See e.g. Art. 14, para. (1) indent c), Real Estate Sales Tax and Inheritance and Gift Tax Act, *Official Gazette of the Canton Sarajevo*, 28/18; Art. 6, para. 1, indent h), Real Estate Sales Tax, *Official Gazette of Zenica – Doboj Canton*, 6/09, 6/13, 6/18, 12/20. Art. 6, para. 1, indent 14., Real Estate Sales Tax, *Official Gazette of the Tuzla Canton*, 5/21 – consolidated text; Art. 6 d), Tax Act, *Official Gazette of the Herzegovina-Neretva Canton*, 2/09, 3/09.

82 See e.g. Art. 22, para. (2), adent b), Real Estate Sales Tax and Inheritance and Gift Tax Act, *Official Gazette of the Canton Sarajevo*, 28/18; Art. 18, Tax Act, *Official Gazette of the Herzegovina-Neretva Canton*, 2/09, 3/09; Art. 18 e) and 19, para. (1), adent c), Law on Property, Inheritance and Gift Tax, *Official Gazette of Zenica-Doboj Canton*, 9/09, 13/11; Art. 18, Law on Property, Inheritance and Gift Tax, *Official Gazette of Tuzla Canton*, 14/09, 3/10, 4/10, 8/14, 13/19, 8/20.

83 Institution of Human Rights Ombudsman of BiH, Recommendation no. 238/18, 23 October 2018. See *2019 Annual Report on Results of the Activities of the Institution of Human Rights Ombudsman of Bosnia and Herzegovina* (Banja Luka, 2020), 131–132, www.ombudsmen.gov.ba/documents/obmudsmen_doc2020051813152592eng.pdf.

religion in making restitutions. Therefore, it is necessary to pass a law on restitution as soon as possible in order to alleviate the injustice done to religious communities in the previous regime, but also to ensure their equal treatment.

Religious communities receive both direct and indirect financial aid from the state. Direct financial assistance consists of budget allocations from different levels of government, that is, state, entity, canton (in FBiH), and municipalities that are allocated without the existence of uniform criteria. The criteria are often decided by the public authority allocating the funds, and in some cases they have not been made available to the general public as required by the principle of transparency. It has been noted that funding for religious entities in the RS entity is provided from various budget categories, some of which are used exclusively to fund the majority church, which puts other religious entities in a particularly unequal position. This is certainly not the best way of financially assisting religious communities as it opens up the possibility of political use of religious communities. Unlike the four traditional religious communities, small religious communities are almost completely absent among state grant beneficiaries. In view of all this, it is necessary to work on harmonization of criteria for financing religious communities in accordance with the principles of equality and non-discrimination as required by the LFR. When it comes to indirect financial aid from the state, religious communities enjoy various tax exemptions and privileges and no unequal treatment of religious communities was observed in this regard. On the other hand, the issue of harmonization of customs regulations with the LFR was raised, given their adverse effects on small religious communities.

8 Religious symbols and festivals in the public space

1 Introduction

Religious symbols occupy a significant place in debates across Europe on the scope of religious freedom in the public space, but also related topics on religious accommodation, identity, and multiculturalism, caused by the growing visibility of minority religions, especially Islam, in many European countries.[1] The approach of these countries in regulating this issue depends, *inter alia*, on the regime of state-religion relations and the public policy adopted by these countries toward the issues of immigration and growing religious, ideological, and cultural pluralism.[2] Ferrari identified three strategies of European countries in managing the problem of display of religious symbols in the public space, that is, emphasizing the secularity of the public sphere (France), favouring the dominant religion (Italy) or prohibiting "public institutions from displaying religious symbols", but allowing "public employees to wear them" (Great Britain).[3] Although the recognition and accommodation of religious festivals of minority cultures has not been given the same prominence in academia and the public discourse, it is closely linked to the discussions on the presence of religion in the public sphere and the challenge of achieving social cohesion in the context of the growing religious and ideological pluralism of European societies.[4]

1 For the scholarly accounts of these debates see e.g. Sylvie Bacquet, *Religious Symbols and the Intervention of the Law: Symbolic Functionality in Pluralist States* (London and New York: Taylor & Francis Limited, 2021); Erica Howard, *Law and the Wearing of Religious Symbols in Europe* (London: Routledge, 2019); Jeroen Temperman, ed., *The Lautsi Papers: Multidisciplinary Reflections on Religious Symbols in the Public School Classroom* (Leiden and Boston: Martinus Nijhoff Publishers, 2012); Piotr Stanisz, Michal Zawiślak and Marta Ordon, eds., *Presence of the Cross in Public Spaces: Experiences of Selected European Countries* (Newcastle upon Tyne: Cambridge Scholars Publishing, 2016); Erica Howard, *Law and the Wearing of Religious Symbols: European Bans on the Wearing of Religious Symbols in Education* (Abingdon: Routledge, 2012).

2 See Nedim Begović, "Vjerski simboli u javnoj sferi: uporednopravna perspektiva," [Religious Symbols in Public Sphere: A Comparative Legal Perspective] *Novi Muallim* 12, no. 45 (2011): 43–50.

3 Silvio Ferrari, "State-Supported Display of Religious Symbols in the Public Space," *Journal of Catholic Legal Studies* 52, no. 7 (2013): 11–12.

4 See Ruth Gavison and Nahshon Perez, "Days of Rest in Multicultural Societies: Private, Public, Separate?" In *Law and Religion in Theoretical and Historical Context*, eds. Peter Cane,

DOI: 10.4324/9780429266683-11

Debates on the display of religious symbols in the public space and the public recognition of religious festivals in the post-war Bosnia and Herzegovina (BiH or Bosnia) have emerged in a somewhat different context, in which religion is often used as a means of realizing political projects based on a nationalist agenda. This chapter's intent is to capture these domestic debates and discuss the arguments employed in them *vis-à-vis* the constitutional and legislative standards on freedom of religion and state-religion relationship. It draws on the analysis of the state regulations, the Bosnian Constitutional Court's case law, recommendations of the Institution of Ombudsman of BiH, international expert opinions, and relevant media articles.

The chapter reveals that much of the issues discussed had a political connotation and were related to the constant tensions, disputes, and disagreements between political forces seeking to preserve the multicultural character and integrity of the state and those seeking to divide it according to ethnic criteria. It also shows that events in Europe regarding the religious freedom and public visibility of Islam are reflected domestically where they are placed in a specific political context that is heavily burdened by interethnic relations. Finally, the chapter notes an asymmetry in the state-supported display of religious symbols and the public recognition of religious festivals in the two Bosnian entities. In contrast to the FBiH, the actions of the Republic of Srpska (RS) authorities were assessed as incompatible with the principles of state neutrality and equality of religious communities.

2 Religious symbols and festivals in international law

The core international human rights instruments recognize the freedom to manifest religion or belief both in private and public space, enumerating the four general forms of religious expression, that is, worship, observance, practice, and teaching.[5] The most explicit recognition of the right to wear or display of religious symbols and to celebrate religious festivals may be found in the General Comment no. 22 of Art. 18 of the UN International Covenant on Civil and Political Rights[6] and the 1981 UN Declaration on the Elimination of All Forms of Intolerance and of Discrimination Based on Religion or Belief.[7] However, these rights are not absolute and may be subject to restrictions in a national

---

Carolyn Evans and Zoë Robinson (Cambridge: Cambridge University Press, 2008), 186–213; Katayoun Alidadi, *Religion, Equality and Employment in Europe: The Case for Reasonable Accommodation* (Oxford and Portland: Hart, 2017).

5 Art. 18, para. 1, International Covenant on Civil and Political Rights (ICCPR), accessed 8 April 2021, www.ohchr.org/en/professionalinterest/pages/ccpr.aspx; Art. 9, para. 1, European Convention on Human Rights, accessed 8 April 2021, www.echr.coe.int/documents/convention_eng.pdf.

6 UN Human Rights Committee (HRC), *CCPR General Comment No. 22: Article 18 (Freedom of Thought, Conscience or Religion)*, 30 July 1993, CCPR/C/21/Rev.1/Add.4, accessed 8 April 2021, www.refworld.org/docid/453883fb22.html.

7 Art. 6(h), Declaration on the Elimination of All Forms of Intolerance and of Discrimination Based on Religion or Belief, accessed 8 April 2021, www.un.org/ruleoflaw/blog/document/

context if they are prescribed by law and necessary to protect public security and order, health, public morals, and the rights and freedoms of others.[8] In practice, the approaches of national policies, public opinion and the courts case law in various countries greatly affects the extent to which these rights are respected. Also, the case law of international human rights bodies reveals significant divergencies in the interpretation of the same human right.[9] Therefore, while the UN HRC is more willing to scrutinize the necessity of banning the wearing of religious symbols, the ECtHR is applying a deferential standard of judicial review which recognizes a wide margin of appreciation for States parties in regulating this issue.

3 Religious symbols in the public domain in BiH

Unlike the previous communist system which relegated religion to the private sphere, the current Bosnian religion law accentuates the public dimension of the right to freedom of religion or belief.[10] Echoing the formulations of major international human rights instruments, the 2004 LFR guarantees the right to religious expression both in private and *public*.[11] The guarantee is further concretized by the provision which stipulates the right of both individuals and religious groups to plead for their doctrines and beliefs in public, organize religious ceremonies and gatherings in public places, establish and run faith-based media, and disseminate informations and opinions through the public media.[12]

Although the right to wear religious symbols or religious attire is not explicitly mentioned in the LFR, based on the relevant interpretations of international human rights bodies, one may conclude that it is encompassed by the concepts of observance and practice, enlisted in the law's Art. 4. While the recognition of an individual right to display religious symbols has been a matter of inference and interpretation, the right of religious communities to publicly display their symbols and emblems has been explicitly mentioned in the LFR and bilateral agreements with religious communities. Namely, the prohibition of "the public use of religious symbols, signs, attributes or the name of a church or religious community without the consent of the said church or religious community" inevitably implies the right of religious communities to display their symbols in the public.[13]

declaration-on-the-elimination-of-all-forms-of-intolerance-and-of-discrimination-based-on-religion-or-belief/.

8 Art. 18, para. 2, ICCPR; Art. 9, para. 9, ECHR.

9 Stephanie E. Berry, "Freedom of Religion and Religious Symbols: Same Right – Different Interpretation?" accessed 8 April 2021, www.ejiltalk.org/freedom-of-religion-and-religious-symbols-same-right-different-interpretation/.

10 Begović, "Vjerski simboli u javnoj sferi: uporednopravna perspektiva," 48–49.

11 Art. 4, para 1, Law on Freedom of Religion and Legal Status of Churches and Religious Communities, *Official Gazette of BiH*, 5/04. English text of the law accessed 21 January 2021, https://mrv.ba/lat/clanci/vijesti/dokumenta/law-on-freedom-of-religion-and-legal-position-of-churches-and-religious-communities-in-bosnia-and-herzegovina/. Emphasis added.

12 Art. 7, Law on Freedom of Religion.

13 Art. 5, para. 2.e., Law on Freedom of Religion.

Three issues related to the display of religious symbols in public space attracted significant media attention and were the subject of discussion, namely: (a) the construction of large crosses at several locations in BiH, (b) a proposal to ban the wearing of the niqab in public places, and (c) a ban on the wearing of religious symbols in judicial institutions.[14] These debates, and especially the first two, had a pronounced political connotation. Besides, while the issues (b) and (c) can be easily placed within the human rights discourse, the issue (a) can hardly be formulated from the angle of the right to freedom of religion. On another side, the issues (a) and (b) raise the question on the compatibility of these actions with the principle of separation of state and religion, which has the less pronounced role in the issue (b).

The post-war erection of extremely large-scale crosses on the government-owned land around the cities of Mostar, Žepče, Stolac, and other locations is a glaring example of the political use of religious symbols with the support of local religious representatives of a dominant ethnic group. On one hand, the initiators and supporters of the erection of crosses present them either as purely religious symbols[15] or as monuments to the Croat population who perished in the last war.[16] On the other hand, this practice was criticized by political and religious representatives of Bosniaks,[17] NGOs,[18] academic commentators,[19] and religious freedom reports[20] as marking the territory by the dominant ethnic group, sending the message of intolerance to believers of minority communities or as a missionary message of the Catholic Church (CC). One of the most politicized cases concerns the illegal construction of crosses on the historic site of the Old Town of Stolac, which

14 The wearing or display of religious symbols in courts and prosecutors' offices is specifically addressed in the book's Chapter 4 dealing with religious rights in specialized regulatory contexts.

15 See e.g. "Stolac: Ne rušiti na Križevcu križa," [Stolac: Do Not Demolish the Cross on Križevac!] the Letter of Bishop Ratko Perić to Ramiz Mehmedagić, Minister of Spatial Planning of the FBiH of 17 July 2004, accessed 17 April 2021, www.md-tm.ba/clanci/stolac-ne-rusiti-na-krizevcu-kriza.

16 Begović, "Vjerski simboli u javnoj sferi: uporednopravna perspektiva," 49.

17 S. A., "Haos u Stocu: Nećete graditi nelegalne križeve po Starom gradu!" [Chaos in Stolac: You Will Not Build Illegal Crosses in the Old Town] accessed 17 April 2021, https://novi.ba/clanak/17334/12; "Izgradnja križeva u Stocu je kamen smutnje," [The Construction of Crosses in Stolac Is a Stone of Trouble] accessed 17 April 2021, https://tuzlalive.ba/izgradnja-krizeva-u-stocu-je-kamen-smutnje/.

18 "Stočani na nogama zbog izgradnje križeva oko grada: Falsificiranje historije i kulturocid," [The Citizens of Stolac Are Protesting Against the Construction of Crosses Around the City: Falsification of History and Culturicide] accessed 17 April 2021, www.klix.ba/vijesti/bih/stocani-na-nogama-zbog-izgradnje-krizeva-oko-grada-falsificiranje-historije-i-kulturocid/200128185.

19 See e.g. "Bosna se nastoji prikazati kao katolička zemlja u kojoj su Bošnjaci strani elemenat," [Bosnia Is Sought to Be Portrayed as a Catholic Country in Which Bosniaks Are a Foreign Element] accessed 15 March 2021, https://hamdocamo.wordpress.com/2017/04/05/bosna-se-nastoji-prikazati-kao-katolicka-zemlja-2/.

20 U.S. Department of State, Bureau of Democracy, Human Rights and Labor, *International Religious Freedom Report 2005, Bosnia and Herzegovina*, accessed 17 April 2021, https://2009-2017.state.gov/j/drl/rls/irf/2005/51544.htm.

was declared a National Monument of BiH in early 2003. Construction of these Catholic symbols began in 2001 with the significant return of Bosniak refugees to Stolac. The 2004 decision of the Federal Minister of Spatial Planning ordering the removal of the crosses could not be implemented due to opposition from local municipal and church authorities,[21] and the issue was brought up again in early 2020 after Stolac Municipality sold part of the National Monument to the Catholic Church to allow it to continue with the construction of crosses.[22] Apart from the fact that such actions of local governments encourage interethnic tensions and send messages about the domination of one nation, it also cannot be brought into line with the principle of secularism proclaimed in Art. 14 of the LFR.

In July 2010 the Alliance of Independent Social Democrats (*Savez nezavisnih socijaldemokrata*, SNSD), the dominant political party in the RS, proposed the adoption of a law banning the wearing of clothing which prevents a person from being identified in the public places, sparking debates about the practice of wearing the niqab. In fact, the proposal came in response to a previous initiative by the Social Democratic Party (*Socijalnodemokratska partija*, SDP) to ban fascist and neo-fascist organizations in BiH, including the Ravna Gora Chetnik Movement.[23] The SNSD's initiative was argued by the need to protect public safety through easier identification of people moving in public.[24] However, the initiative did not receive support in the Parliamentary Assembly of BiH, after the Constitutional-Legal Commission of the House of Representatives took the position that the proposed law would be in conflict with the constitutional guarantees of fundamental human rights.[25] In legal scholarship, three arguments have been proposed against the adoption of this proposal, namely the absence of a real threat to public

21 "HDZ u mukama: Federalna inspekcija naredila uklanjanje križeva u Stocu," [HDZ in Agony: Federal Inspection Orders Removal of Crosses in Stolac] accessed 13 April 2021, www.zasrcebrenicu.ba/hdz-u-mukama-federalna-inspekcija-naredila-uklanjanje-krizeva-u-stocu.za.

22 "Izgradnja križeva u Stocu upitna: Reagovalo Muftijstvo mostarsko, građani potpisuju peticiju," [The Construction of Crosses in Stolac Is Questionable: The Office of Mufti of Mostar Reacted, Citizens Sign a Petition] accessed 17 April 2021, https://okanal.oslobodjenje.ba/okanal/vijesti/izgradnja-krizeva-u-stocu-upitna-regovalo-muftijstvo-mostarsko-gradjani-potpisuju-peticiju-7843.

23 Dženana Halimović, "Prijedlog o zabrani nikaba podijelio političare u BiH," [The proposal to ban the niqab divided politicians in BiH] accessed 15 April 2021, www.slobodnaevropa.org/a/prijedlog_o_zabrani_nikaba_podijelio_politicare_u_bih/2112389.html.

24 Club of MPs of the SNSD, Proposal of the law on the prohibition of wearing clothes that prevent identification of 9 April 2010, accessed 15 April 2021, file:///C:/Users/Nedim/Downloads/Prijedlog%20zakona%20o%20zabrani%20no%C5%A1enja%20odje%C4%87e%20koja%20onemogu%C4%87ava%20identifikaciju.pdf. At the protests held in Sarajevo in front of the Parliamentary Assembly of BiH on the occasion of considering the outlined bill, women wearing niqab expressed the view that the ban, contrary to the claims of the proponents of the bill, would put them in a position not to go to school, work and sit at home. See Marija Arnautović, "Pokrivene žene: Zabrana nikaba je kršenje ljudskih prava," [Veiled Women: Banning the Niqab Is a Violation of Human Rights] accessed 16 April 2021, www.slobodnaevropa.org/a/nikab_sarajevo_zene_protest/2109951.html.

25 "Ustavnopravna komisija: Bez podrške zabrani nošenja odjeće koja onemogućava identifikaciju," [Constitutional and Legal Commission: No Support for a Ban on Wearing Clothing

safety because Bosnian security agencies have not confirmed the existence of genuine difficulties in identifying persons wearing the niqab; the political and ideological motivation of this proposal; and finally, although formulated in neutral terms, it targeted Muslim women wearing the niqab and there were fears that it would be applied in a discriminatory manner.[26]

We agree with the opinion that passing a law banning the wearing of clothing covering the face would be contrary to the right to freedom of religion or belief. Security protection is a legitimate reason to limit this right, especially in situations where it is necessary to establish the identity of the person covering the face, such as the airport, school, government institutions, and so on. However, in such situations, well-established security procedures are applied to establish the identity of women wearing the niqab. There are no concrete and convincing arguments that people wearing the niqab are more frequent perpetrators of crimes, nor that their clothing practices pose a particular problem in security checks.[27] In addition, the proposal, although formulated as neutral, targeted exclusively Muslim women, as evidenced by public debates focused on wearing the niqab, as well as media appearances by SNSD MPs who brought the proposal into the context of similar laws passed in some European countries.[28]

4 Religious festivals in the public domain in BiH

Due to the lack of political consensus, there is no single law on public holidays, including religious ones, at the state level. The LFR did not treat religious festivals either. By concluding bilateral agreements with the two churches, the state authorities undertook to enact distinct laws recognizing important Catholic and Orthodox holidays as non-working days for members of these religions,[29] but efforts to fulfil that obligation did not bear fruit.[30] The 2015 Bill on non-working days during religious festivals which provided for the right of both private and public employees from all religious denominations to an equal number of paid days off to celebrate their religious festivals received support from the Interreligious Council in BiH (IRC) and the Constitutional-Legal Commission of the

That Prevents Identification] accessed 15 April 2021, https://vijesti.ba/clanak/12007/ustavnopravna-komisija-bez-podrske-zabrani-nosenja-odjece-koja-onemogucava-identifikaciju.

26 Fikret Karčić, "Zašto ne treba zakonom zabraniti nikab," [Why Shouldn't the Niqab Be Banned by Law] accessed 24 January 2021, www.islamskazajednica.ba/aktuelno-arhiva/9294-zato-ne-treba-zakonom-zabraniti-nikab.

27 Nedim Begović, *Vjerska sloboda i muslimanske manjine u Evropi* [Religious Freedom and Muslim Minorities in Europe] (Sarajevo: El-Kalem, 2015), 162.

28 See Halimović, "Prijedlog o zabrani nikaba podijelio političare u BiH."

29 Art. 9 of Basic Agreement Between the Holy See and Bosnia and Herzegovina, *Official Gazette of Bosnia and Herzegovina–International Agreements*, 10/07; Art. 9 of Basic Agreement Between Bosnia and Herzegovina and the Serb Orthodox Church, *Official Gazette of Bosnia and Herzegovina–International Agreements*, 6/08.

30 Nedim Begović, "Freedom of Religion in the Workplace: The European Court of Human Rights Decisions on Applications Made by Muslim Apellants," *Journal of Muslims in Europe* 10, no. 1 (2021): 15.

Parliamentary Assembly of BiH, however it was not adopted in the further parliamentary procedure.[31]

Due to the absence of state regulation, public holidays are currently regulated at the entity level. The 1992 Law on Holidays of the Republic of Bosnia and Herzegovina continues to apply in the FBiH,[32] however it does not contain provisions on religious festivals. On the contrary, the RS has adopted in 2007 a new Law on Holidays which recognizes religious festivals of major religious denominations (i.e. the Orthodox and Catholic Christmas, Easter and Good Friday, Eid al-Fitr and Eid al-Adha). The employees belonging to respective denominations have the right to two days off with pay to celebrate their recognized festivals. Furthermore, they have the right to paid leave from work, of their choice, for up to two days during the calendar year, on the days of their other religious holidays.[33]

The labour and civil service laws of the entities and Brčko District of Bosnia and Herzegovina (BDBiH) represent another regulatory area dealing with this issue. The accommodations of religious festivals in the workplace provided in these laws are not harmonized and put employees in an unequal position. Thus, while the Labour law of the RS recognizes the employee's right to three non-paid days off to meet their religious needs,[34] the Labour law of the FBiH contains more favourable provisions on the employee's right to four days off in one calendar year to meet their religious or traditional needs, with up to two days' paid leave.[35] Even less harmonized are laws on the status of civil servants whose allocations of non-working days for celebrating religious festivals range from one day in a calendar year in the Law on civil service in the public administration bodies of the BD BiH[36] to six days off in the Law on labour in the institutions of BiH.[37] Unlike the RS and the FBiH where employees use leave during festivals of their respective denomination on an individual basis, in the BD BiH six religious festivals of major religious groups, that is, Eid al-Fitr, Eid al-Adha, the Orthodox

31 The Bill on non-working days during religious holidays, proposed by the Council of Ministers of BiH, was not passed by the BiH Parliamentary Assembly. This bill provided for the right of both private and public employees to five days off with pay to celebrate festivals of their religious traditions (see Council of Ministers of Bosnia and Herzegovina (CMBiH), The Bill on non-working days during religious holidays in BiH, no. 05–02–2513/13, 30 September 2013).

32 Law on Holidays of the Republic of Bosnia and Herzegovina, *Official Gazette of the Republic of Bosnia and Herzegovina* 2/92; 13/94.

33 Arts. 7 and 8, Law on Holidays of the RS, *Official Gazette of the RS*, 43/07.

34 Art. 92 of the Labour law of the RS, *Official Gazette of the RS*, 1/16 and 66/18.

35 Art. 54(3), Labour law of the FBiH, *Official Gazette of the FBiH*, 26/16, 89/18. Similarly, Art. 68(4) of the Labour law of the BD BiH provides up to two paid days off for religious reasons (*Official Gazette of Brčko District of Bosnia and Herzegovina*, 34/19).

36 Art. 78, para. 1, Law on Civil Service in the Public Administration Bodies of the BD BiH, *Official Gazette of BDBiH*, 09/14, 37/15, 48/16, 9/17 and 50/18.

37 Art. 30, para. 3, Law on Labour in the Institutions of BiH, *Official Gazette of BiH*, 26/04, 7/05, 48/05, 50/08, 60/10, 32/13 and 93/17.

and Catholic Christmas and Easter, were declared as non-working days by the decision of the District's Assembly.[38]

The Institution of Ombudsman for Human Rights of BiH had the opportunity to consider the issue of discriminatory application of the provisions of the FBiH Labour law regarding the exercise of the right to leave from work to celebrate a religious festival. The appellant, a professor of University of Tuzla, alleged that, as a non-Muslim employee, he had been discriminated against for refusing his oral request to be granted one paid day of leave to meet religious needs. Namely, unlike their non-Muslim counterparts, Muslim employees are not required to submit a written request to the rector of the university for approval of paid leave during the holidays in their denomination.[39] The Institution of Ombudsman issued a recommendation requiring university authorities to ensure equal treatment of their employees by issuing written consents on leave to celebrate religious festivals, regardless of their religious affiliation.[40]

5 Public recognition of religious festivals and discrimination against minorities

Another important issue that needs to be discussed within this chapter is the inclusion of the ceremonies of the SOC in the celebration of the Day of the RS as a public holiday, as well as the celebration of the festivals of the SOC as the baptismal feasts of the government and public institutions in the RS entity. As these practices clearly favour one religious community, they inevitably raise the question of the compliance of such practices with the principles of separation of state and religion, and the state neutrality towards various religious collectivities.

On 26 November 2015 the Constitutional Court of BiH issued a decision approving the request of Bakir Izetbegović, a member of the Presidency of Bosnia and Herzegovina, to review the constitutionality of Art. 3. b) of the Law on Holidays of the RS.[41] The applicant claimed that the RS "opted for 9 January as the Republic Day, a date which already chosen by the 'Assembly of the Serb People in BiH' in 1992, without the participation of Bosniaks and Croats". He

38 See e.g. Decision on Determining Non-Working Days in the Brčko District of BiH for the Period April 2019–January 2020, no. 01–02–573/19 of 10 April 2019, accessed 17 April 2021, https://skupstinabd.ba/2-registar/hr/Odluke/2019/573.%2045.%20Odluka%20o%20neradnim%20danima%202019-2020%20H.pdf.

39 Complaint to the Institution of the Ombudsman for Human Rights of BiH, no. Ž-BR-04–26/17, 30 January 2017.

40 Recommendation of the Institution of Ombudsman for Human Rights of BiH concerning case no. Ž-BR-04–26/17, 31 May 2017. On 6 September 2017, the Rector of the University of Tuzla informed the Institution of Ombudsman that the University of Tuzla harmonized its practice with the recommendation of 31 May 2017 by issuing decisions on paid days of leave for Muslim employees to celebrate Eid al-Adha. See University of Tuzla, Notice: A Letter to the Institution of Ombudsman for Human Rights of BiH, no. 01–4813/17–1, 6 September 2017.

41 Law on Holidays of the RS, *Official Gazette of the RS*, 43/07, 77/16.

also pointed out that on 9 January 1992 the Assembly of the Serb People in BiH adopted a "Declaration to proclaim the Republic of the Serb people of BiH" which provided for territorial demarcation with other two constituent peoples in Bosnia. According to the applicant's opinion, this document expressed the intention to form a state of predominantly Serb people with absolute exclusion of two other peoples and violation of their rights.[42] This intention was confirmed during the 1992–1995 war when systematic and planned ethnic cleansing of Bosniaks and Croats was carried out on the territory under the control of the Army of the Bosnian-Serb Republic, with numerous confirmed violations of international humanitarian law that culminated in genocide in Srebrenica in 1995.[43]

In addition to this, the applicant pointed out that 9 January was celebrated in the RS as a holiday related exclusively to the Serb people. The claim was substantiated by the fact that, in addition the secular ceremonies, religious ones were organized to celebrate the date, including the baptismal feast of the RS – Saint Archdeacon Stefan, which represented the clear identification of the entity with the Orthodox Christianity. Both active participation of the Orthodox priests in the secular ceremonies and organizing ceremonies of the SOC to celebrate the holiday made it known to members of other religious groups that this was exclusively a holiday of the dominant religious and ethnic group.[44]

At the request of the BiH Constitutional Court, the Venice Commission gave its opinion on the case in the capacity of *amicus curiae*. The Commission noted that the holiday of January 9 can be related to two events. The first is the day of Saint Stephen, the patron saint of Serbia and the RS entity of BiH, and the second is the adoption of the Declaration on the Proclamation of the Republic of the Serb People of BiH by the Assembly of the Serb People in BiH on 9 January 1992. In concluding on the discriminatory nature of the said holiday, the Commission put forward two arguments. First, although it is exclusively related to one constituent people, all legal entities are prohibited from working on that day, which forces members of other constituent peoples to celebrate it. Second, it is related to the unpleasant war events of the 1990s and arouses feelings of humiliation and discomfort among non-Serb citizens of RS.[45]

42 Constitutional Court of BiH, Case no. U 3/13, 26 November 2015, para. 12–13.

43 See United Nations – International Criminal Tribunal for the Former Yugoslavia (ICTY), *Trial Judgement Summary for Ratko Mladić*, Case No. IT-09–92-T, The Hague, 22 November 2017, accessed 16 April 2021, www.icty.org/x/cases/mladic/tjug/en/171122-summary-en.pdf. The full text of the judgment (5 volumes) is available at www.icty.org/en/cases/judgement-list#2017.

44 Constitutional Court of BiH, Case no. U 3/13, para. 45.

45 European Commission for Democracy Through Law (Venice Commission), *Amicus curiae* brief for the Constitutional Court of Bosnia and Herzegovina on the Compatibility with the Non-discrimination Principle of the Selection of the Republic Day of the Republika Srpska, adopted by the Venice commission at its plenary session (Venice, October 11–12, 2013), para. 37. The feelings of humiliation and discomfort were also emphasized in the letter which Cardinal Vinko Puljić, Catholic Archbishop and president of the Bishops' Conference

The Constitutional Court of BiH found that Art. 3. b) of the Law on Holidays of the RS "which stipulates to mark the Republic Day on January 9, establishes a privileged position of members of the Serb people in relation to members of the Bosniak and Croat people, Others and citizens of the Republika Srpska due to the fact that this date is part of the historical heritage of the Serb people only, as well as because of marking the baptismal feast of the Republika Srpska, which is connected to tradition and customs also only of the Serb people."[46] The Court also took a clear position that

> the established practice of marking the holiday as a function of exercising public authority on January 9, when the Day of the Republic is celebrated with the baptismal feast of the Republic of Srpska, regardless of whether it is a separate or unique celebration of the two events, which includes liturgy and breaking of the feast cake in the Orthodox church led by dignitaries of the Serb Orthodox Church, and the presence of the dignitaries of that Church in the rest of the celebration ceremony, they are not in accordance with the proclaimed principle of the separation of church and state.[47]

Despite the fact that the Bosnian Constitution stipulates that the constitutional courts' decisions "shall be final and binding",[48] both the RS government and the

---

of BiH, sent to Patriarch Irinej, the leader of the SOC, expressing his disagreement with the Patriarch's statements given during the celebration on 9 January 2016. Puljić noted that:

> the Republic of Srpska celebrates its entity holiday "Baptismal feast and the Day of the RS" on 9 January 2016, despite the ruling of the Constitutional Court of Bosnia and Herzegovina that the Day, whatever that means, is unconstitutional. You, as the supreme head of the Serb Orthodox Church, joined this manifestation, which is the cause of great disputes in BiH. After the Holy Hierarch's Liturgy in the Cathedral of Christ the Savior in Banja Luka, Patriarch Irinej, as the first spiritual leader of the Serb Orthodox Church, provoked incredulity, disgust and disappointment in many of our fellow citizens, especially Catholics, but also other believers.

Referring to the statement of the Patriarch given on the occasion of the January 9 celebration that RS was founded on "the truth of God, on the justice of God", Cardinal Puljić pointed out that no one has been convicted for serious war crimes by any court of the RS. On the contrary, he argued that the truth was constantly concealed and distorted and that perpetrators of war crimes, instead of their victims, were protected and assisted. That, Puljić continued, has nothing to do with truth and justice, least of all with the truth of God and His justice. He reminded that numerous war crimes were committed in the period 1992–1995 on behalf of the RS, which is why it was not "founded on the blood of the holy martyrs" but "on the bones of the holy martyrs". He also commented that, by linking the most terrible war crimes to the realization of Divine justice, Patriarch Irinej inflicted an additional insult – in a particularly painful way – on all the victims of the past war who had experienced various tortures and disenfranchisements. See Bishops' Conference of BiH, "Reaction of the Bishops' Conference of BiH to the statements of Patriarch Irinej," 15 February 2016, accessed 31 January 2021, www.ktabkbih.net/info.asp?id=63411.

46 Constitutional Court of BiH, U 3/13, 26 November 2015, para. 97.

47 Constitutional Court of BiH, U 3/13, 26 November 2015, para. 94.

48 Art. VI, para. 4., Constitution of BiH, accessed 17 April 2021, www.ustavnisud.ba/public/down/USTAV_BOSNE_I_HERCEGOVINE_engl.pdf.

opposition, with the exception of Bosniak and Croat representatives, refused to apply the decision. Instead, on 26 October 2016 the Assembly passed a distinct Law on the RS Day and separated it from the Law on the RS Holidays. January 9 was again set as the date, emphasizing that "Republic Day is marked and celebrated as a secular holiday", as well as that "the Government of the RS by its decision regulates the manner of marking and celebration".[49] The Constitutional Court of BiH decided on 28 March 2019 that the designation of January 9 as a national holiday in the 2016 Law on the RS Day was unconstitutional for the same reasons stipulated in its decision U 3/13. However, despite warnings from international representatives in BiH and the Constitutional Court, RS authorities continued to celebrate the unconstitutional holiday of January 9th in the presence of representatives of Serbia and the Embassy of the Russian Federation in BiH, as well as with involvement of the SOC patriarch.[50]

However, the celebration of RS Day through the religious ceremony of the dominant SOC is just the tip of the iceberg, given the fact that almost every city, municipality, government and public institution in this entity has its baptismal feast. For example, the entity Ministry of Interior marks November 21 as the Feast of Synaxis of the Archangels Michael and Gabriel. On the occasion of the 2019 celebration, Jefrem, the Bishop of Banja Luka, presented Dragan Lukač, the RS Minister of the Interior, with a high decoration of the SOC – the Order of the Holy King Milutin, while a memorial temple was consecrated at the Training Center of the Ministry.[51] The city authorities of Banja Luka, the capital of the RS, together with the representatives of the SOC, celebrate the feast of the Ascension of Jesus Christ on June 6 as the day of the city's baptismal feast. The celebration begins with the performance of the holy liturgy and is usually part of a wider public event called "Spring in Banja Luka".[52] The baptismal feast of the city of Zvornik is St. Petka Trnova, who is also considered the patron saint of the city. It is celebrated on August 8, which begins with the holy liturgy and continues with a procession through the city led by the icon of St. Petka Trnova. On that occasion, representatives of the city authorities and the SOC are visiting the monument to the fallen soldiers of the RS Army. The celebration is organized as part of a wider

49 Art. 2, para. (2) and Art. 3, Law on the RS Day, *Official Gazette of the RS*, 113/16.

50 Gojko Veselinović, "Dan Republike Srpske i ovaj put mimo Ustava," [Republika Srpska Day and This Time Against the Constitution] accessed 24 January 2021, www.slobodnaevropa.org/a/dan-rs-mimo-ustava/30366435.html; Predrag Zvijerac, "Uz neustavni Dan RS: Sva svjetovna i vjerska praznovanja u BiH," [With the Unconstitutional Day of RS: All Secular and Religious Celebrations in BiH] accessed 16 April 2021, www.slobodnaevropa.org/a/dan-republike-2021-srpske-praznici-bih/31038812.html.

51 Milorad Milojević, "Ko lomi pogaču za crkveno-državne praznike u Republici Srpskoj," [Who Breaks the Bread for Church-State Holidays in Republika Srpska] accessed 17 April 2021, www.slobodnaevropa.org/a/cijena-crkveno-drzavnih-praznika-u-rs/30287097.html.

52 Srna, "Liturgijom počelo obilježavanje krsne slave grada Banja Luke," [The Celebration of the Baptism of the City of Banja Luka Began with the Liturgy] accessed 24 January 2021, www.nezavisne.com/novosti/banjaluka/Liturgijom-pocelo-obiljezavanje-krsne-slave-grada-Banjaluka/542235.

event called "Summer in Zvornik".[53] The city of Doboj every year on August 19 celebrates the Orthodox holiday of Transfiguration of Jesus. Milorad Dodik, the Serb member of the Presidency of BiH, was declared the godfather of the 2019 celebration. On that occasion, the Orthodox bishop Fotije named the SOC as the "spiritual mother" of the RS.[54] Moreover, St. Vitus Day, the holiday of the SOC, is celebrated on June 28, as the baptismal feast of the 3rd Infantry Regiment of the Armed Forces of BiH, which inherits the identity and military heritage of the former Army of the RS.[55] A particularly problematic practice is the celebration of the feast of Saint Sava, the first archbishop of the SOC, as a school day in which non-Orthodox students are often forced to participate.[56] This practice not only contravenes the principle of state neutrality towards various religions, but also violates the right to freedom of belief of children and their parents.

There is no any legal basis for such identification of the RS authorities with the festivals of the entity's dominant church.[57] On the contrary, it stands in sharp contrast to the case law of the Constitutional Court of BiH[58] and the principle of equality of religious communities proclaimed in the Constitution of the RS entity[59] and the LFR.[60] The tradition dates back to the 1992–1995 war and is still part of RS political and public life, 25 years after the signing of the Dayton Peace Agreement. Sociologist Ivan Sijakovic claimed that such events show a close connection between religion and politics in the RS, which is reflected in the

53 "U prisustvu velikog broja Zvorničana i gostiju: Litijom i lomljenjem slavskog kolača obilježena slava grada Zvornika," [In the Presence of a Large Number of Zvornik Residents and Guests: The Baptismal Feast of the City of Zvornik Was Marked with a Litany and the Breaking of the Feast Cake] accessed 24 January 2021, http://infobirac.net/2019/08/08/u-prisustvu-velikog-broja-zvornicana-i-gostiju-litijom-i-lomljenjem-slavskog-kolaca-obiljezena-slava-grada-zvornika/.

54 N. Če., "Grad Doboj obilježio Krsnu slavu," [The City of Doboj Celebrated the Baptismal Feast] accessed 24 January 2021, https://avaz.ba/vijesti/bih/510471/grad-doboj-obiljezio-krsnu-slavu-kumovao-milorad-dodik.

55 "Proslavljen Vidovdan – krsna slava Vojske Republike Srpske i 3. pješadijskog (Republika Srpska) puka," [Vidovdan Is Celebrated – the Baptismal Feast of the Army of the Republika Srpska and the 3rd Infantry (Republic of Srpska) Regiment] accessed 31 January 2021, http://os.mod.gov.ba/o-oruzanim-snagama-bih/tradicija/3-pjesadijski-puk-os-bih/vijesti/default.aspx?id=16798&langTag=bs-BA.

56 See "U školama širom Srpske obilježen Savindan," [Savindan Was Celebrated in Schools Throughout Srpska] accessed 23 June 2021, https://lat.rtrs.tv/vijesti/vijest.php?id=367612; Gordana Katana, "Postaje li RS društvo u kojem nesrbi i 'nevjernici' nemaju izbora: Diskriminacija po svetosavlju," [Is the RS Becoming a Society in Which Non-Serbs and 'Non-Believers' Have No Choice: Discrimination Based on the Celebration of Saint Sava] accessed 23 June 2021, https://inforadar.ba/postaje-li-rs-drustvo-u-kojem-nesrbi-i-nevjernici-nemaju-izbora-diskriminacija-po-svetosavlju/.

57 See Constitutional Court of BiH, Case no. U 3/13, 26 November 2015, para. 50.

58 Constitutional Court of BiH, Case no. U 3/13, 26 November 2015; Case no. U 4/04, 31 March 2006; Case no. U 5/98, August 18–19, 2000.

59 Art. 28, para. 2, Constitution of the RS, *Official Gazette of the RS*, 21/92 – consolidated version, 28/94, 8/96, 13/96, 15/96, 16/96, 21/96, 21/02, 26/02, 30/02, 31/02, 69/02, 31/03, 98/03, 115/05, 117/05, 48/11.

60 Art. 14, Law on Freedom of Religion.

interference of both the SOC in politics and, conversely, politics in church affairs. According to his opinion, it can also be seen as "a kind of proving, separating, wanting it to be an indicator that you are different, not to tolerate anyone who is not like that and the like. Instead of finding ways to get closer, you are constantly inserting ways of discord".[61]

6 Conclusion

The state religion law in BiH provides a broad normative framework for the manifestation of religion in the public sphere. Apart from the fact that the right to wear or display religious symbols is implicitly covered by the general guarantee of freedom of religion in public, the right of religious communities to display their own symbols and signs is explicitly stated in the LFR.

In the post-war period, two issues concerning the presence of religious symbols in public sphere were widely discussed, namely the construction of large-scale crosses on the government-owned property around several Bosnian cities and the wearing of niqab in the public places. The first issue is clearly related to the internal political situation in BiH, which is torn between demands for the preservation of territorial integrity, civil society values and multiculturalism, on the one hand, and separatist ethno-national aspirations present in the Serb and Croat political corps, on the other hand. The second issue has shown how developments in Europe concerning religious freedom and the problematization of the "Muslim issue" are reflected in BiH where they are then placed in the domestic political context which is heavily burdened by interethnic tensions.

The issue of public recognition of religious holidays is not regulated at the state level, but at the level of entities and BD BiH, while labour and civil service law contain unharmonized provisions on the right of private and public employees to days off to celebrate religious holidays. It is noticeable that both religious symbolism and public recognition of the holidays of the dominant religious community are more present in RS than in FBiH and BD BiH. The celebration of secular holidays through religious ceremonies, with the active participation of the SOC, puts Orthodox Serbs in a privileged position in relation to other citizens of this entity.

Given that one of the political goals set by Radovan Karadžić, the first president of the RS,[62] was "state demarcation from the other two national communities",[63]

61 Milorad Milojević, "Ko lomi pogaču za crkveno-državne praznike u Republici Srpskoj," [Who Breaks the Bread for Church-State Holidays in Republika Srpska].

62 He was sentenced to life imprisonment by the decision of the Mechanism for International Criminal Courts (MICT), the successor of the ICTY. In a final decision, the Appeals Chamber upheld the findings of the first-instance verdict on Karadžić's responsibility for ethnic cleansing of Bosniaks and Croats in BiH, the Srebrenica genocide, years of terrorizing Sarajevo and taking the UN members hostage. See Stephanie van den Berg and Toby Sterling, "Ex-Bosnian Serb Wartime Leader Karadzic Sentenced to Life in Prison," accessed 17 April 2021, www.reuters.com/article/us-warcrimes-bosnia-karadzic-idUSKCN1R1003.

63 Decision on Strategic Goals of the Serb People in Bosnia and Herzegovina, *Official Gazette of the RS*, 22/93.

it can be reasonably concluded that religious symbolism of the SOC is used to cement ethnic divisions and the results of ethnic cleansing and genocide committed by the Army of the RS against non-Serbs in the territory of this entity in the period 1992–1995. In a series of decisions, the Constitutional Court of BiH established that these practices are not in line with the values of democratic and multicultural society and the principle of separation of state and religious communities. However, RS authorities persistently ignore these binding decisions of the country's highest court and continue the discriminatory practice of favouring religious symbols and SOC feasts.

9 Marriage and divorce

The interaction of state law and religious norms

1 Introduction

The relationship between religion, state law and the regulation of the private sphere has recently become very topical in academic debates in Europe.[1] The issue has been raised whether in the context of ever-increasing multiculturalization of European societies, the monopoly of state law over the regulation of the private sphere of marriage, family and inheritance is still justified? In other words, is the recognition of a particular form of legal pluralism that respects religious, customary, and cultural differences in society desirable or even necessary in national constitutional orders? The question of whether the right to freedom of religion or belief includes the application of religious and customary norms in the private sphere, that is, whether legal pluralism is compatible with the rule of law, equality and individual human rights, has also been considered at supranational, European level.[2]

Bosnia and Herzegovina (BiH or Bosnia) has a long history of multiculturalism which, *inter alia*, manifested through the coexistence of normative orders that originate from various religious traditions. Under the Ottoman state, the Habsburg monarchy and the Kingdom of Yugoslavia, this coexistence took the form of "juridical legal pluralism", using the terminology of J. Griffiths, that is, state recognition of the authority of more than one normative order in society. In contrast, with the adoption of the secular model in the mid-20th century, one can only speak of "empirical legal pluralism" manifested through the factual relevance

1 See e.g. Ayelet Shachar, *Multicultural Jurisdictions: Cultural Differences and Women's Rights* (Cambridge: Cambridge University Press, 2001); Ihsan Yilmaz, *Muslim Laws, Politics and Society in Modern Nation States: Dynamic Legal Pluralisms in England, Turkey and Pakistan* (Aldershot and Burlington: Ashgate Publishing, 2005); Rubya Mehdi, Hanne Peterson, Erik Reenberg Sand and Gordon R. Woodman, eds., *Law and Religion in Multicultural Societies* (Copenhagen: DJOF Publishing, 2008); Rex Ahdar and Nicholas Aroney, *Shari'a in the West* (New York: Oxford University Press, 2010); Andrea Buchler, *Islamic Law in Europe? Legal Pluralism and Its Limits in European Family Laws* (Surrey: Ashgate, 2011); Harun Karčić, *Šerijat i pravni pluralizam u Evropi: Primjeri koegzistencije religijskog i sekularnog prava na starom kontinentu* [Sharia and Legal Pluralism in Europe: Examples of Coexistence of Religious and Secular Law on the Old Continent] (Sarajevo: Centar za napredne studije, 2018).

2 *Refah Partisi (the Welfare Party) and Others v. Turkey* [GC], nos. 41340/98 and three others, ECHR 2003-II.

DOI: 10.4324/9780429266683-12

of norms of religious law for believers, without their administration through the state apparatus.

The aim of this chapter is to explore the interaction between religious norms and state law in the sphere of private law in BiH. Our research interest will be focused on marriage and divorce, as traditionally important issues of religious ordering. In particular, several research questions need to be answered, namely: What is the relevance of religious norms on marriage and divorce in BiH as a secular state? Which aspects of religious marital and divorce laws may be applied in parallel with state law, based on the right to freedom of religion or belief? To what extent has the state, through legislation, has already shown a willingness to accommodate religious norms? Are there internal mechanisms within religious communities for regulating the private sphere and applying religious norms on the formation and termination of marriage?

In order to answer these and related questions, it is necessary to analyse the relevant provisions of state religion and family laws and the case law of the Constitutional Court of BiH, as well as the applicable internal regulations of religious communities. It concludes, first, that there is a clear dividing line between the scope of state law and religious norms on marriage and divorce, and second, that systems of religious norms on marriage and divorce are applied informally, within the religious community in addition to state law.

2 Religion and the formation of marriage: a state law perspective

The constitutional law of BiH deals with marriage and the family as part of the guarantees of fundamental human rights, that is, the right to private and family life and the right to marry and to found a family.[3] In addition, the Constitution of the Republic of Srpska (RS) incorporates the basic principles of family law, including the special protection enjoyed by the "family, mother and child" and the principle that marital and family relations are governed by law.[4] These principles are further elaborated through the family laws of the two entities, that is, the FBiH and the RS, as well as the Brčko District of Bosnia and Herzegovina (BDBiH).

Although these laws are mostly secular, major religious traditions have influenced the content of at least some of their provisions. For example, marriage is

3 Art. II, para. 3.f) and j), Constitution of BiH, accessed 16 January 2021, www.ccbh.ba/public/down/USTAV_BOSNE_I_HERCEGOVINE_engl.pdf; Art. 13, Constitution of the RS, *Official Gazette of the RS*, 21/92. Amendments of Constitution of RS, *Official Gazette of the RS*, 28/94, 8/96, 13/96, 15/96, 16/96, 21/96, 21/02, 26/02, 30/02, 31/02, 69/02, 31/03, 98/03, 115/05, 117/05; Art. 13, para. 9, Statute of the BD BiH – Consolidated Text, *Official Gazette of the BDBiH*, 2/10. The Constitution of the FBiH guarantees, with slightly different terminology, the right to protection of family and children, Art. II, para. 1. j), *Official Gazette of FBiH*, 1/94, 13/97, 16/02, 22/02, 52/02, 63/03, 9/04, 20/04, 33/04, 71/05, 72/05, 88/08.

4 Art. 36, Constitution of the RS.

defined as "a legally regulated union of the life of a woman and a man",[5] which excludes the possibility of concluding same-sex marriages, as well as marriages whose validity is limited in time. A marriage does not produce any legal consequences if it is not concluded between two persons of the opposite sex,[6] and will be annulled if it is proved that it was not established with the aim of a community of life.[7] Further, the principle of monogamy of the marital union is adopted.[8] Marital barriers include blood kinship in the straight and lateral line up to the fourth degree and in-law kinship.[9]

A marriage, in order to produce legal effects, must be concluded in a civil form, which has been the norm since 1946 when the family law was secularized.[10] However, given the traditionally important influence of religion on marital issues, positive family laws recognize the right of a spouse to perform a religious wedding ceremony after entering into a civil marriage. The recognition of the right to religious marriage represents an expression of the constitutional right to freedom of religion. Yet the supremacy of state law over religious norms is emphasized through the criminalization of the solemnization of religious marriage if performed before civil marriage.[11]

The issue of recognizing the legal effects of religious marriage was raised during negotiations on bilateral agreements between the state and religious communities. Thus, the initial drafts agreements with the Holy See and the Islamic Community in Bosnia and Herzegovina (IC) included clauses on recognition of civil effects of religious marriage, however in both cases they were subsequently abandoned by the negotiating parties. As the main objection to the recognition of a religious marriage, the state raised its incompatibility with the positive family legislation.[12] On the other hand, Vukšić argued that the omission of recognition of church marriage may also be seen as a consequence of an expression of the accustomedness of the faithful to the cumulative conclusion of civil and religious

5 Art. 6, Family law of the FBiH, *Official Gazette of the FBiH*, 35/05, 31/14; Art. 4, para. 1), Family law of the RS, *Official Gazette of the RS*, 54/2002, 41/2008, 63/2014 and 56/2019; Art. 4, para. 1), Family law of the BD BiH, Official Gazette of BD BiH, 23/2007.

6 Art. 8. a), Family law of the FBiH; Art. 14 and 15, Family law of the RS; Art. 6, Family law of the BD BiH.

7 Art. 35, Family law of the FBiH.

8 Art. 10, Family law of the FBiH; Art. 31, Family law of the RS; Art. 21, Family law of the BD BiH.

9 Art. 12, para. 1, Family law of the FBiH; see also Art. 33, para. 1 and Art. 35, para. 1, Family law of the RS; Art. 23, 25, Family law of the BD BiH.

10 Art. 26, Constituton of the Federal People's Republic of Yugoslavia, accessed 20 April 2020, file:///C:/Users/Nedim/Downloads/aj_10_02_10_txt_ustav1946.pdf; Basic law on marriage – Consolidated text, *Official Gazette of the SFRY* (Socialist Federal Republic of Yugoslavia), 12/65; Family law of the Socialist Republic of Bosnia and Herzegovina, *Official Gazette of the SR BiH*, 21/79, 42/89.

11 Namely, an official of a religious community is prohibited from marrying persons before they enter into a civil marriage under the threat of a fine of up to 500 to 2000 BAM (Art. 383, para. 3), Family law of the FBiH).

12 See Office of Legislation of the CMBiH, Opinion on the Draft Basis for Concluding Agreement Between the Islamic Community in Bosnia and Herzegovina and Bosnia and Herzegovina: A Letter to the MHRR, no. 01–02–293/11, 24 May 2011.

marriage and the multi-confessional structure of Bosnian society. Besides, the obligation of church pastors to lead additional administration and communicate with the registrar's office was avoided as well as potential conflicts between state law and the "secret marriages" which the church law recognizes under certain circumstances.[13] Though he may be right, the more plausible explanation seems to be that religious communities have put this issue on the negotiating agenda as part of their broader negotiating strategy in which they were willing to accept a compromise on the issue to achieve more important goals in other domains.

Art. 9 of the European Convention on Human Rights (ECHR), as interpreted by the European Court of Human Rights (ECtHR), does not oblige Contracting States to recognize the civil consequences of a religious marriage. Such recognition, however, falls within the broader scope of the right to freedom of religion governed by the domestic law of the Contracting States. If the state recognizes a religious marriage, it is obliged to treat different religious denominations equally in this regard.[14] Therefore, non-recognition of religious marriage in domestic law cannot be qualified as a violation of BiH's obligations under the ECHR, but appears to be an anomaly in relation to improved standards of religious freedom in other areas.

In addition, prescribing civil marriage as the only legally relevant mode of establishing a marital union and assigning a second-class position to a religious marriage has no adequate historical or sociological justification in the Bosnian context. As mentioned earlier, religious marriage in BiH has a much longer tradition than civil marriage, which was introduced into the legal system in the conditions of anti-religious communist totalitarian ideology. Furthermore, statistics indicate a significant increase in interest in religious marriage since the 1990s.[15] Also, a comparative legal perspective shows that many European countries equate religious and civil marriage in terms of their legal effects,[16] including Croatia, the former Yugoslav republic.

The public interests of prescribing civil marriage consist in determining the fulfilment of all conditions for marriage, that is, that the future spouses enter into

13 Tomo Vukšić, "Značenje Temeljnog ugovora između Svete Stolice i BiH te dodatnoga protokola na njega," [The Meaning of the Basic Agreement Between the Holy See and BiH and the Additional Protocol to It] accessed 1 April 2020, www.bkbih.ba/info.php?id=220.

14 *Savez crkava "Riječ života" and Others v. Croatia*, no. 7798/08, § 91–93, 9 December 2010.

15 Mustafa Hasani and Nedim Begović, "Praksa šerijatskih vjenčanja u Islamskoj zajednici u Bosni i Hercegovini," [The Practice of 'Sharia Wedding' in the Islamic Community in Bosnia and Herzegovina] *Glasnik Rijaseta Islamske zajednice u Bosni i Hercegovini* LXIII, Sarajevo, no. 11–12 (2014): 1129. According to D. Sandi, today approximately 80% of civil marriages in the Republic of Serbia and the Bosnian entity Republic of Srpska are celebrated through a religious ceremony in the Serb Orthodox Church (SOC), which speaks to the importance of religious marriages (Dragomir Sando, "Shvaćanje crkvenog braka u Pravoslavnoj crkvi," [Understanding the Church Marriage in the Orthodox Church] in *Dvoje njih bit će jedno tijelo: Zbornik radova s okruglog stola o braku i bračnoj zajednici iz perspektive vjerskih zajednica i civilnog zakonodavstva*, ed. Pavo Jurišić (Sarajevo: Caritas of the Bishop Conference of BiH, 2009), 30.

16 The introduction of civil marriage in Europe began only at the end of the 16th century and in countries that had religious minorities to enable their members to marry in a religiously neutral form. With the French Revolution, a trend toward compulsory civil marriage began, with the aim of limiting the influence of the Church. See Büchler, *Islamic Law in Europe*, 110.

marriage of their own free will, that there are no marital impediments between them and that they are aware of the legal consequences of the marriage.[17] These interests could be effectively protected in the regime of legal recognition of religious marriage, provided that the following procedures are provided: (a) future spouses should obtain a state certificate confirming that they meet the legal requirements before entering into religious marriage, including minimum age, free will, and so on and (b) religious communities should regularly inform registry offices of religious marriages contracted by their members.

3 State and the formation of marriage: a religious law perspective

After considering the way in which state law regulated the influence of religion on marriage, it will be interesting to examine the opposite perspective, that is, how religion perceives civil marriage, as well as the importance of religious celebration of marital union in the context of the lack of its official recognition. Unlike the Catholic Church in Bosnia and Herzegovina (CC) and the SOC, the IC has no officially adopted regulations governing the application of Islamic marital law among its members. Instead, the IC bodies, responsible for interpreting Islamic law, refer to the scholarly works of classical and contemporary Islamic jurists, as well as codifications of Islamic family law. Another significant difference lies in the fact that the IC, unlike the two churches, does not manage its own courts that would aim to enforce religious law among the members of the Community. However, the underlying goal of the IC is to ensure the "correct understanding and living Islam" and that the community's members "live in conformity of Islamic norms".[18] This goal should be achieved through the interpretation of Islamic law, meaning providing expert advice in form of juristic opinions (*fatwas*), as well as encouraging Muslims to abide by them voluntary, rather than by coercive enforcement in the courts. In addition, the observance of Sharia was framed as a guiding principle for all activities of the community.[19]

In the organizational scheme of the IC, the authority to interpret Islamic norms through a fatwa is divided between *ra'is al-ʿulama*, the Council of Muftis and individual muftis. *Ra'is al-ʿulama*, as a head of the Islamic Community in Bosnia and Herzegovina, has the rank of Grand Mufti which gives him the authority to issue fatwas. In carrying out this task, he is assisted by a *fatwa-amin* who is entrusted with answering questions from members of the IC regarding the interpretation of Islamic norms.[20] A person with a higher Islamic education and specialization in the field of Islamic jurisprudence (*fiqh*) may be appointed to the position of *fatwa-amin*.[21] The muftis are authorities of the IC

17 Büchler, *Islamic Law in Europe?* 110.

18 Art. 6, Constitution of the IC – Consolidated Text, accessed 21 April 2020, https://staticdn.islamskazajednica.ba/images/stories/Ustavi/Ustav_IZ-e_precisceni_tekst_2014.pdf.

19 Art. 55, 57, Constitution of the IC.

20 Art. 61, Constitution of the IC.

21 "Fetva-i emin" [Fatwa-amin] accessed 21 April 2020, www.islamskazajednica.ba/fetva-i-emin.

in the area of their districts (*muftiluk*) which are established at the regional level and include several local branches (*majlis*).[22] Although it is their responsibility to issue fatwas, they rarely do so in an individual capacity.[23] The preferred way is to issue fatwas through the Council of Muftis whose role is, *inter alia*, to supervise the compliance of the activities of the IC with Sharia law, as well as to give authoritative interpretations of Islamic norms by providing answers to various questions and dilemmas facing by Muslims in their ordinary lives.[24]

The IC provides an opportunity to its members that, after concluding a civil marriage, they enter into a marriage in accordance with the provisions of Islamic law. The ceremony of concluding marriage before imam in the IC is commonly called a "Sharia wedding". Although the practice of double marriage ceremony has existed for more than seven decades, enhanced protection of religious freedom and the revival of Islamic identity in the post-1990s period have led to an increase of interest for the performance of Sharia weddings. In this context, one can also notice the increased interest in the Islamic qualification of civil marriage, the meaning and purpose of Sharia wedding and their mutual relationship.[25]

The IC's position is that a Sharia wedding may not be performed in mosques without a previously concluded civil marriage, namely in order to respect the state family law and ensure the possibility of exercising the legal rights of the spouses arising from the civil marriage.[26] As for religious qualification of a civil marriage, it is considered valid under Islamic law, provided that the couple, when concluding it, took care to meet all the conditions for marriage, including those provided by Islamic but not the state law (e.g. that there is no milk kinship among the spouses or that they both are Muslims, etc.).

"Assuming that all the Sharia conditions for the validity of a marriage are met, civil marriage itself marks the beginning of a marital relationship", it is stated in the *fatwa-amin*'s response. This interpretation is in line with the Islamic conception of marriage as a civil contract arising from the consent of the spouses and whose validity does not depend on its conclusion before a religious authority. Having said that, marriage is by no means devoid of its strong religious and spiritual meaning. The Qur'an describes it as a "firm covenant" that enables psycho-emotional stability by cultivating feelings of love and compassion among spouses

22 Art. 43, 44, 52, Constitution of the IC.

23 So far only two *fatwas* of the IC's muftis have been published on the official website of the IC, while the rest ones have been issued by the Council of Muftis (or former the Council for Fatwas) and *ra'is al-ʿulama* (see "Fetve i rezolucije," [Fatwas and Resolutions] accessed 21 April 2020, www.islamskazajednica.ba/fetve-i-rezolucije).

24 Art. 60, Constitution of the IC.

25 On the official website of the IC, one can notice a large number of questions addressed to the fatwa-emin directly related to the legal nature and importance of Sharia and civil marriages. See "Bračno pravo," [Matrimonial Law] *Dini islam – Pitanja i odgovori*, accessed 21 April 2020, www.islamskazajednica.ba/bracno-pravo.

26 "Šerijatsko vjenčanje prije građanskog," [Sharia Wedding Before Civil One] *Dini Islam – Pitanja i odgovori*, accessed 21 April 2020, www.rijaset.ba/index.php?option=com_content &view=article&id=8393:erijatsko-vjenanje-prije-graanskog&catid=142&Itemid=538.

and other family members. At the same time, it is the only legitimate basis for sexual relations and establishing a family unit.[27]

Given the aforementioned Islamic qualification of civil marriage, the question arises of the nature and meaning of Sharia wedding. According to *fatwa-amin*, a Sharia wedding in a given context takes on an exclusively religious, spiritual and customary meaning that is, "a Sharia wedding is then only a registration of a factual situation and a religious act that blesses the marriage in question. And that has its symbolic value and should be supported."[28] Apart from the fact that a Sharia wedding is a sign that all the conditions for marriage prescribed by the Islamic law have been met,[29] it is significant because it also includes the clause on dower (*mahr*) which is not recognized in the state law.

In the regulation of marriage and other matters of private law, the CC applies the provisions of the *Codex Iuris Canonici* proclaimed in 1983 by Pope John Paul II and binding on the Latin or Roman Catholic Church.[30] Church members who wish to marry are required to do so in the church, in front of a local pastor or priest, and in the presence of two witnesses.[31] Namely, according to its doctrine, only a marriage concluded between a baptized man and a baptized woman, in accordance with church laws, has the status of a sacrament whose two essential characteristics are unity and indissolubility.[32] The term "unity" implies that a Catholic is not allowed to enter into more than one marriage, neither simultaneously (in the form of polygamy or polyandry), nor successively (entering into a second marriage during a life of a spouse from previous marriage). The following concept of "insolubility" means that a marital relationship lasts a lifetime and can only be broken by the death of one of the spouses.[33] Therefore, concluding only a

27 See Enes Ljevaković, "Bračna zajednica: priprema, sklapanje, tradicija s islamskog aspekta," [Marriage Communion, Preparation, Formation and Tradition from Islamic Perspective] in *Dvoje njih bit će jedno tijelo: Zbornik radova s okruglog stola o braku i bračnoj zajednici iz perspektive vjerskih zajednica i civilnog zakonodavstva*, ed. Pavo Jurišić (Sarajevo: Caritas of the Bishop Conference of BiH, 2009), 35–36.

28 "O građanskom i šerijatskom vjenčanju," [On Civil and Sharia Wedding] *Dini islam – Pitanja i odgovori*, accessed 21 April 2020, www.rijaset.ba/index.php?option=com_content&view=article&id=5434:o-graanskom-i-erijatskom-vjenanju&catid=142&Itemid=538.

29 For instance, when a Muslim woman concludes civil marriage with a non-Muslim man, this marriage is not deemed valid from Islamic perspective. The same applies to other situations in which the couple entering into civil marriage disregard Islamic conditions for marriage.

30 Velimir Blažević, *Vodič kroz crkveno pravo za vjernike* [The Guide Through the Church Law for the Faithful] (Sarajevo: Svjetlo riječi, 2007), 19–20. Marriage is regulated within Part I – Title VII of the Codex. See *Codex Iuris Canonici Fontium Annotatione Auctus – Zakonik kanonskog prava s izvorima* (Zagreb: Glas koncila, 1996), 519–565.

31 Kan. 1108 § 1, *Codex Iuris Canonici.*

32 Kan. 1055, 1056, *Codex Iuris Canonici.*

33 Tomo Vukšić, "Bračna zajednica, priprava, tradicija, sklapanje s katoličkog aspekta," [Marriage Union, Preparation, Tradition, Formation from Catholic Perspective] in *Dvoje njih bit će jedno tijelo: Zbornik radova s okruglog stola o braku i bračnoj zajednici iz perspektive vjerskih zajednica i civilnog zakonodavstva*, ed. Pavo Jurišić (Sarajevo: Caritas of the Bishop Conference of BiH, 2009), 19–20.

civil marriage is contrary to canonical norms, with certain exceptions.[34] The form of marriage in the church consists of several elements, namely the presence of a man and a woman entering into marriage, a church official and two witnesses, and the performance of the prescribed wedding ceremony.[35]

The SOC applies its own *Marriage Rules*, which were first adopted in 1933 while the amended edition was published in 1994. Marriage is defined in these rules as

> a sacred secret according to which two persons of different sexes, in the manner prescribed by the church, are bound by a lifelong spiritual and physical connection, for the sake of a complete life community and the birth and upbringing of children.[36]

Marriage takes place in the Orthodox Church, in the presence of two persons of different sexes who enter into marriage, a priest and two witnesses, and with the performance of the prescribed wedding ceremony.[37] The ritual character of a church marriage is emphasized by the provision that the consensuality of the will of the spouses is not decisive for the origin of the marriage, but the priest's blessing of that will.[38] In order for someone to be able to get married in the SOC, it is necessary to prove with an appropriate document that he or she has previously entered into a civil marriage. However, civil marriage only is not enough from the perspective of the Orthodox marital law. In other words, a marriage in the sense of the canon law of the SOC is null and void if it was concluded without the participation of the Church, that is, as a civil marriage or without a proper church rite.[39] In fact, any "life together and lasting union of two persons of different sexes who are not bound by the secret of a church marriage" is treated as an extramarital affair.[40] Unlike the Roman Catholic Church, which allows only one church marriage, the SOC allows the conclusion of a maximum of four successive marriages.[41]

As for the Jewish Community of Bosnia and Herzegovina (JC), given the small number of its members and its unfavourable age structure, the number of Jewish marriages is almost negligible. Besides, the community even does not have a resident rabbi let alone a rabbinical court who could act as a mediator in marital and family disputes of its members.[42]

34 For example, the marriage of a Catholic with an unbaptized person may, with the approval of the local pastor and the fulfillment of other prescribed conditions, take the form of a civil marriage (kan. 1127, § 2).

35 Vukšić, "Bračna zajednica," 24.

36 § 1, *Bračna pravila Srpske pravoslavne crkve (BP)*, 2nd ed. (Beograd: The Holy Synod of Bishops, 1994), accessed 21 April 2020, www.rastko.rs/bogoslovlje/bracna-pravila/index.html.

37 § 2, *Bračna pravila Srpske pravoslavne crkve (BP)*.

38 § 36, *Bračna pravila Srpske pravoslavne crkve (BP)*.

39 § 11 par. 3), § 33 par. 1) i 3), § 34 par. 1), § 38 par. 2), Bračna pravila Srpske pravoslavne crkve.

40 § 126, *Bračna pravila Srpske pravoslavne crkve (BP)*.

41 Dimšo Perić, "Bračno pravo Srpske pravoslavne crkve," [Matrimonial Law of the Serb Orthodox Church] in *Uporedna religijska prava*, ed. Fikret Karčić (Sarajevo: Faculty of Islamic Studies in Sarajevo, 2005), 244.

42 According to data from 2012, a total of 1,089 members were members of the JC, of which 743 members in Sarajevo (Boris Kožemjakin, "Jewish Community of Bosnia and

4 Informal religious-only marriages

Informal religious-only marriages are marriages that are concluded according to religious rites or norms but are not legalized in the form of civil marriage. The discussion of religious-only marriages is particularly relevant, though not exclusively, to the Muslim context,[43] because of this conception of marriage in Islamic law as a civil contract whose validity is not conditioned by the participation of the state or religious authority in its conclusion.[44] In the scholarly literature, these informal or unregistered Muslim marriages are commonly termed as "ordinary (*'urfi*)" or *nikah*-only marriages.

In BiH, a certain number of Muslim marriages are concluded through a private religious ceremony, without their registration with the registrar's office. These marriages are also not reported to the IC and often, but not exclusively, are concluded within Salafi communities. Given that such marriages take place in the private sphere, it is not possible to assess the extent of this phenomenon, nor to gain a complete insight into the motivation for their conclusion. However, based on the analysis of the "Questions and Answers" section on the official website of the IC, it is possible to identify some of the reasons for engaging in *nikah*-only marriages.

It appears that a *nikah*-only marriage represents a strategy used by some young people who are still studying to ensure the legitimacy of intimate relationships in accordance with their religious beliefs, without taking on the financial obligations arising from a civil marriage. Parents usually do not support such relationships and young people seek religious justification for their secret weddings.[45] Furthermore, individuals consider informal marriage as a possible framework for marriage with persons below the statutory marriage age or for a polygamous marriage not recognized by state family law.[46] *Nikah*-only marriages can also be pragmatically used to keep child benefits, student scholarships, or government

---

Herzegovina," in *Religions in Bosnia and Herzegovina: Profile of Religious Communities and Churches* (Sarajevo: Interreligious Council in Bosnia and Herzegovina, 2012), 189; Eli Tauber, "Bračna zajednica, priprava, sklapanje, tradicija sa židovskog aspekta i pogled na mješovite brakove," [Marital Union, Preparation, Conclusion, Tradition from the Jewish Aspect and View on Mixed Marriages] in *Dvoje njih bit će jedno tijelo: Zbornik radova s okruglog stola o braku i bračnoj zajednici iz perspektive vjerskih zajednica i civilnog zakonodavstva*, ur. Pavo Jurišić (Sarajevo: Caritas Biskupske konferencije BiH, 2009), 54.

43 "Secret marriages" allowed in certain circumstances by the canon law of the Roman Catholic Church are an example of religious-only marriages in a Christian context. As for the SOC, the number of church marriages that are not accompanied by civil marriages, as argued by D. Sando, is not small. See Sando, "Shvaćanje crkvenog braka," 30.

44 For discussion on religious-only marriages in different Muslim-minority and Muslim-majority contexts see the special issue of *Oxford Journal of Law and Religion*, vol. 7, no. 3 (October 2018).

45 "Sklapanje tajnog braka," [Contracting a Secret Marriage] *Dini islami – Pitanja i odgovori*, accessed 21 April 2020, www.islamskazajednica.ba/bracno-pravo/24683-sklapanje tajnog-braka.

46 "Šerijatsko vjenčanje između osoba koje nisu punoljetne," [Sharia Wedding Between Minor Persons] *Dini islami – Pitanja i odgovori*, accessed 21 April 2020, www.islamska-zajednica.ba/bracno-pravo/18498-serijatsko-vjencanje-izmedu-osoba-koje-nisu-punoljetne; "Šerijatski stav o poligamiji u BiH," [Sharia Stance Toward Poligamy in BiH]

social assistance.[47] Reasons may also be to avoid a more complicated procedure when marrying a foreign national[48] or a lengthy and unfinished divorce procedure of one of the future spouses.[49] Apart from mundane reasons, the interest in concluding *nikah*-only marriage in some cases is expressed in the language of human rights. For example, a female Muslim have posed the following question: "Why do I not have the right to marry first under the Shari'a, according to Islamic regulations, the way I want to? ... Why do I have to experience that the politics of the institution interfere with my faith and my religious rights?"[50] Other noted reasons range from the husband's refusal or procrastination to enter into a civil marriage,[51] avoidance of a civil marriage due to unresolved housing or other existential issues,[52] to, simply, ignorance of the law.

While the IC consistently promotes the conclusion of marriage in accordance with state law and its own regulations, this is not always the case in fatwas published in media that are not under the control of the IC. As already noted, non-recognition of religious-only marriages in the state law and the consequent inability to exercise legal protection of the rights of spouses' rights in such a marriage, as well as various abuses of unregistered marriages are the main reasons why the IC does not approve these practices. In an answer the *fatwa-amin* states as follows:

> We have repeatedly stressed that a sharia wedding can be performed only after a civil wedding because the rights and obligations that a marriage entails can be claimed in court only if the marriage is concluded before the registrar. The second, alternative basis is cohabitation, to which some other, specific provisions and rules apply. Secret marriages, and such is a marriage that is hidden from other people, apart from the direct actors of the secret wedding, most often from the parents of the "contracting parties", carry more

Dini islami – Pitanja i odgovori, accessed 21 April 2020, www.islamskazajednica.ba/bracno-pravo/17770-serijatski-stav-o-poligamiji-u-bih.

47 "Šerijatsko sklapanje braka prije općinskog," [Sharia Wedding Before the Municipal One] *Dini islami – Pitanja i odgovori*, accessed 21 April 2020, www.islamskazajednica.ba/bracno-pravo/23464-serijatsko-sklapanje-braka-prije-opcinskog.

48 "Šerijatsko vjenčanje," [Sharia Wedding] *Dini islami – Pitanja i odgovori*, accessed 21 April 2020, www.islamskazajednica.ba/bracno-pravo/6233-erijastsko-vjenanje.

49 "Razvod pa vjenčanje," [Divorce and then Wedding] *Dini islami – Pitanja i odgovori*, accessed 21 April 2020, www.islamskazajednica.ba/bracno-pravo/4834-razvod-pa-vjenanje-; "Vjenčanje s osobom koja nije sudski razvedena," [Marrying a Person Who Is Not Civilly Divorced] accessed 22 April 2020, www.islamskazajednica.ba/bracno-pravo/18829-vjencanje-s-osobom-koja-nije-sudski-razvedena.

50 "Nemogućnost šerijatskog prije općinskog vjenčanja," [Impossibility of Sharia Wedding Before the Civil One] *islami – Pitanja i odgovori*, accessed 21 April 2020, www.islamskazajednica.ba/bracno-pravo/1900-nemogust-serijatskog-prije-opskog-vjenja.

51 "Odgađanje/neobavljanje građanskog vjenčanja," [Delaying/Non-concluding Civil Wedding] *Dini islami – Pitanja i odgovori*, accessed 21 April 2020, www.islamskazajednica.ba/bracno-pravo/15914-odgadanje-neobavljanje-gradanskog-vjencanja.

52 "Tajna šerijatska vjenčanja," [Secret Sharia Weddings] *Dini islami – Pitanja i odgovori*, accessed 21 April 2020, www.islamskazajednica.ba/bracno-pravo/10699-tajna-erijatska-vjenanja.

> unknowns, potential problems and complications, lies, deception, fraud, resorting to abortion in case of conception, the constant fear of disclosure and other consequences of an adventurous approach and understanding of the extremely serious and responsible institution of marriage and the family and as such cannot be acceptable and morally justified in Islam. Secret marriage generally reduces the goals of marriage to only one goal, and that is the satisfaction of bodily instincts by neglecting all other goals which are no less important than the one mentioned. The contracting parties, if they have pure intentions, have no justifiable reason not to perform both civil and Sharia wedding and thus announce their marriage, so that there are no doubts and dilemmas about the nature of the relationship between them. In this particular case, all actors in this illegal act bear their share of responsibility and should be held accountable accordingly. None of them has been fully amnestied. The Islamic Community does not take any responsibility for this and similar cases, as its procedures and instructions are clear.[53]

The Bosnian Constitutional Court confirmed that religious marriage alone had no effect in terms of state law, and that persons who entered into such a marriage could not exercise judicial protection of their marital property rights. The court's decision referred to an appellant who performed a Sharia wedding in front of the Prijedor Committee of the IC in the presence of several witnesses, but did not enter into a civil marriage. The appellant's husband undertook, when concluding a religious marriage, to pay her a dower (*mahr*) in the event of a divorce.[54] The marriage was later divorced, but the appellant's husband refused to pay the *mahr*, for which she filed a lawsuit in June 2000 with the Sanski Most Municipal Court. The Court's judgment of 21 June 2000 rejected her request on the grounds that "the marriage was concluded according to Sharia law and that, as such, it falls within the framework of Islamic regulations, and not the regulations of the Family Law/89) which applies to civil marriage and does not include *mahr*". Deciding on the appeal against the judgment of the first instance court, the Bihać Cantonal Court ruled that the state could not interfere in the application of religious law since "the marriage entered into by the appellant was not concluded under civil law". Last, the Constitutional Court rejected the appeal as unfounded, citing the argument that "the appellant did not acquire 'property' within the meaning of Art. 1 of Protocol no. 1 to the European Convention", as the positive law of BiH

53 "Tajno sklapanje šerijatskog braka," [Concluding Sharia Marriage in Secrecy] accessed 22 April 2020, www.islamskazajednica.ba/bracno-pravo/28621-2020-tajno-sklapanje-serijatskog-braka-2020.

54 In Sharia law, *mahr* is the material obligation of a husband to his wife arising from the act of marriage. In practice, it is common for a smaller portion of the *mahr* to be given as a gift immediately after the wedding, while the other part is paid only after the termination of marriage, by the husband's death or divorce. See Ibrahim Džananović, *Primjena šerijatskog porodičnog prava kroz praksu Vrhovnog šerijatskog suda u Sarajevu* [The Application of Sharia Family Law in the Case Law of the Supreme Sharia Court in Sarajevo] (Sarajevo: Faculty of Islamic Studies, 2004), 105, 111.

does not recognize the institute of *mahr*.[55] The court also found that there had been no violation of the appellant's right to respect for her private and family life under Art. 8 of the ECHR,[56] as evidenced by her ability to lead a family life based on religious marriage without state interference.

5 Religion and the termination of marriage

Like the vast majority of European countries,[57] BiH does not recognize the civil consequences of divorce or annulment of a marriage performed in accordance with religious norms. Also, it does not recognize any civil effects of religious norms that deal with the consequences of formation or termination of a religious marriage, in terms of personal or property rights and obligations of spouses prescribed by religious norms.[58]

The three major religious communities in BiH have quite different perceptions of civil divorce and its validity from a religious point of view. At one end of the spectrum is the IC which recognizes civil divorce and does not provide itself with any essential role in the termination of marriage of its members. This can be understood in the light of the previously mentioned fact that the IC does not have arbitration bodies or spiritual courts that would deal with marital disputes, annulment of marriage, or divorce. Therefore, civil divorce under the conditions of secular state law is considered to simultaneously terminate a marriage within the meaning of Islamic norms. Divorced spouses are only expected to notify the *majlis* in which they previously entered into a religious marriage of a civil divorce, so that it can be registered in the registry books of the IC.[59]

However, the system of divorce in Islamic law is quite complex and includes, in addition to judicial divorce (*tafriq qada'i*), the categories of unilateral divorce (*talaq*) and divorce with financial compensation (*khul'*). The right to *talaq*, as a rule, belongs to the husband only, given his obligations to pay the *mahr* and alimony for his wife and children. Nevertheless, there is a possibility for the spouses to agree on the transfer of that right to the wife (*tafwid al-talaq*). *Talaq* can be effected verbally or in writing, and its validity, according to the dominant interpretation, does not depend on the approval of a state body (e.g. a court). Accordingly, the *fatwa-amin* argues that verbally pronounced *talaq* produces divorce in

55 Constitutional Court of BiH, Case no. U 62/01, April 5–6, 2002. See also Nedim Begović, "Ustavni okvir i Zakon o slobodi vjere i pravnom položaju crkava i vjerskih zajednica u BiH: Normativna projekcija bosanskohercegovačkog sekularizma," [Constitutional Framework and Law on Freedom of Religion and Legal Status of Churches and Religious Communities: Normative Projection of Bosnian-Herzegovinian Secularism] in *Sekularnost i religija: BiH i* regija, eds. Edin Šarčević and Drago Bojić (Sarajevo: Fondacija Centar za javno pravo, 2015), 95–96.

56 Constitutional Court of BiH, Case no. U 62/01, para. 15–16.

57 For more details see Norman Doe, *Law and Religion in Europe: A Comparative Introduction* (Oxford: Oxford University Press, 2011), 222–224.

58 See the Constitutional court's decision in the aforementioned case no. U 62/01.

59 "Šerijatski razvod braka," [Sharia Divorce] *Dini islami – Pitanja i odgovori*, accessed 22 April 2020, www.islamskazajednica.ba/bracno-pravo/18903-serijatski-razvod-braka.

terms of religious norms, but requires the spouses to complete the divorce before a civil court.[60]

Khulʿ represents the type of divorce which is initiated on the part of the wife which, according to classical Islamic jurisprudential doctrine, requires the consent of the husband and the willingness of the wife to financially compensate the husband.[61] In this type of divorce as well, the IC insists that a civil divorce be conducted first, which is then registered with the *majlis* in which the divorced spouses previously performed their Sharia wedding.[62] However, in terms of religious norms, *khulʿ* divorce occurs from the moment of reaching an agreement between the spouses and not from the moment of issuing a court decision on the consensual divorce.[63] One of the negative consequences of entering into only a religious marriage is a situation in which the wife is in uncertainty regarding her marital status, which is referred to in the literature as "limping marriage". This situation occurs when a religious-only marriage *de facto* breaks down and the wife cannot get a religious divorce because her husband is absent, of unknown residence, or simply refuses to consent to the divorce. In such cases, the IC does not provide the possibility of religious divorce, and the only option left to a woman in a "limping marriage" is to file for divorce to the imam before whom she entered into a religious marriage, whether in BiH or abroad.[64]

Unlike the IC, the CC and the SOC deal with the dissolution of church marriages of their members in accordance with ecclesiastical norms. It should be noted that the jurisdiction of these ecclesiastical courts is voluntary. Within the CC, there are two courts, namely the Ecclesiastical Court of the Archdiocese of Vrhbosna, based in Sarajevo, whose jurisdiction extends to the Diocese of Banja Luka also, and the Diocesan Ecclesiastical Court in Mostar, whose jurisdiction encompasses the Diocese of Mostar-Duvno and the Diocese of Trebinje-Mrkan. Church courts also operate within the five SOC dioceses in BiH.

The SOC *Marriage Rules* allow for a fault divorce, in cases where one spouse commits adultery or endangers the life of the other spouse, or in cases of

60 "Razvod braka," [Divorce] *Dini islami – Pitanja i odgovori*, accessed 22 April 2020, www.islamskazajednica.ba/bracno-pravo/2675-razvod-braka; "Razvod riječima," [Verbal Divorce] accessed 22 April 2020, www.islamskazajednica.ba/bracno-pravo/3575-razvod-rijea.

61 Compensation usually consists of the wife giving up the *mahr* and claiming alimony from her husband. Some reformist family laws of majority Muslim jurisdictions have adopted an approach whereby a court can award a *khul*ʿ divorce at the request of the wife, regardless of the husband's lack of consent. See Nedim Begović, *Vjerska sloboda i muslimanske manjine u Evropi* [Religious Freedom and Muslim Minorities in Europe] (Sarajevo: El-Kalem, 2015), 220.

62 "Procedura prilikom razvoda braka i odustajanja od mehra," [Procedure for Divorce and Forgoing the *Mahr*] *Dini islami – Pitanja i odgovori*, accessed 22 April 2020, www.islamskazajednica.ba/bracno-pravo/23663-procedura-prilikom-razvoda-braka-i-odustajanje-od-mehra.

63 Begović, *Vjerska sloboda i muslimanske manjine u Evropi*, 216.

64 "Razvod samo šerijatski sklopljenog braka," [Divorce of Sharia-only Marriage] *Dini islami – Pitanja i odgovori*, accessed 22 April 2020, www.islamskazajednica.ba/bracno-pravo/8416-razvod-samo-erijatski-sklopljenog-braka; "Razvod braka bez pristanka muža," [Divorce Without the Consent of the Husband] *Dini islami – Pitanja i odgovori*, accessed April 22, www.islamskazajednica.ba/bracno-pravo/6831-razvod-braka-bez-pristanka-mua.

intentional abortion, malicious abandonment of the spouse, disappearance of the spouse, physical or mental illness, moral depravity, and apostasy from the Orthodox faith. Divorced spouses may remarry if there are no obstacles, prohibitions, or penalties in the divorce judgment of the ecclesiastical court.[65] In contrast, the CC does not allow divorce, but only separation from bad-and-board, temporary and permanent, as well as the possibility of annulment of marriage in certain circumstances.

6 Conclusion

Pursuant to the principle of separation of state and religion, the Constitutional Court of BiH has clearly demarcated the spheres of influence of state law and religious norms in the field of private law. Accordingly, religious norms on marriage and divorce can be applied as an expression of the right to freedom of religion or belief in both its individual and collective aspects, but they do not bring any civil consequences. Initiatives for full recognition of religious marriage in terms of its civil effects that emerged during the negotiations on the conclusion of bilateral agreements between the state and religious communities did not bear fruit.

Major religious communities in BiH have taken different views on the validity or non-validity of civil marriage and divorce from the perspective of their internal regulations. The IC considers a civil marriage to be valid, provided that the conditions prescribed by the Islamic law are met at the time of its conclusion. In contrast, the CC and the SOC consider that only a marriage concluded in the form of a church rite, in accordance with canonical rules, is legitimate from a religious point of view. Similarly, while the IC recognizes the validity of civil divorce and does not deal with the dissolution of marriages of its members, the CC and the SOC run their own courts that deal with the mentioned issues in relation to their members.

65 For more details on divorce in the SOC see Perić, "Bračno pravo Srpske pravoslavne crkve," 256–259.

Conclusion

Since the collapse of Communism, and especially following the end of the war, Bosnia and Herzegovina (BiH or Bosnia) made significant progress in building a new normative/institutional framework to regulate freedom of religion and state-religion relations. This framework is largely based on international religion law, including the relevant provisions of the European Convention on Human Rights (ECHR), which is enshrined in the 1995 Constitution of BiH and takes precedence over other domestic laws. The backbone of the new framework is the Law on Freedom of Religion, which was adopted by the Bosnian parliament in 2004 as a result of a joint domestic and international effort. In addition to the constitution of the state and two entities and the Law on Freedom of Religion, the structure of the state religion law consists of various bylaws, bilateral protocols agreed between the state and religious communities and a corpus of evolving case law.

The four religious communities with long historical duration in Bosnia, namely the Islamic Community (IC), the Serb Orthodox Community (SOC), the Catholic Church (CC), and the Jewish Community (JC), played an active role in remodelling legal arrangements for the religious sphere to accord with the changed political climate and expectations of alignment with the values of the liberal democratic state. New legislation managed to balance between the individual and collective aspects of the right to freedom of religion or belief, restoring religion a place in the public sphere, but nonetheless still according preferential treatment to traditional churches and religious communities.

In addition to encompassing a number of provisions protecting the inner sphere of religious and other belief (*forum internum*), the national religion law protects a broad array of individual and collective religion and belief manifestations (*forum externum*) that can be subsumed under the general forms of freedom to manifest religion or belief recognized by Art. 9 of the ECHR. The restriction of these manifestations must not be arbitrary but based on law, and necessary to protect public safety, order, health, morals, and the rights and freedoms of others. The emerging case law of the Constitutional Court of BiH on religious freedom generally follows the interpretative methodology developed by the ECtHR in determining whether interference with the right to freedom of religion or belief constitutes a violation of Art. 9 of the ECHR.

DOI: 10.4324/9780429266683-13

The advancement of religious freedom can be observed in several important areas. Unlike previous communist laws, which declared religion a private matter with a limited right to publicity and established strict state control over religious collectives, the current state religion law emphasizes the public dimension of religion as well as the autonomy of religious communities in their internal affairs. The dimension of publicity can best be demonstrated through the right of both individual believers and religious communities to publicly advocate for their beliefs and doctrines, to organize religious ceremonies and gatherings in public places, to establish and run their own, faith-based media, or to disseminate information and opinions through public media. Also, confessional religious education has been returned to the public education system with the obligation of the state to ensure its funding and equal status with other school subjects.

Religious communities enjoy autonomy, both in doctrinal and institutional aspects. They are therefore free to teach their doctrines provided they do not spread hatred and prejudice towards any other religious collectivity or their members or towards non-religious citizens, which is a requirement of particular importance in post-conflict Bosnian society. In addition, religious communities are guaranteed the freedom of worship and the inviolability of their places of worship. Regarding the latter aspect, religious communities enjoy autonomy in a variety of matters that can be broadly classified into three main categories, namely legislative, administrative, and judicial or quasi-judicial autonomy. Accordingly, religious organizations are free to adopt their internal regulatory instruments without the state approval or to abide by the known systems of religious law. Although the general principle is that state authorities will not enforce these religious norms, there are exceptions when their civil effects are recognized, for example in cases of determining the legal personality of a religious community body or the need to build a place of worship. The current independence of religious structures in terms of the election, appointment, and dismissal of their dignitaries and other religious officials represent a significant advance, especially when compared with the tight state control of religion under the communist regime. The new state religion law expanded the meaning of religious autonomy, allowing religious communities to enter some areas that were previously under the almost exclusive jurisdiction of the state, such as public education and media, health and social care, family counselling and mediation, and so forth. In some of these specific regulatory contexts, the protection of individual religious rights is also highly satisfactory. For example, the religious rights of military personnel are protected in accordance with best comparative practice, with the exception of disputed issues of accommodation of religiously motivated wearing of beards or headgear. Similarly, freedom to practice the faith and religious spiritual care is provided to prisoners at a satisfactory level.

Despite these achievements, there are still a number of challenges and unresolved issues in exercising an individual's right to freedom of religion or belief. In the first place, the issue of the accommodation of religion in the workplace has not yet been adequately addressed by either the legislation or the domestic courts. The current labour and civil service laws still reflect the concept which dominated under the former communist regime that religion is solely a private matter of the individual rather than advanced standards for protecting freedom of religion, both in the private and public spheres. None of the three areas of law that could potentially serve as a ground for protecting religion in the workplace – religion law, non-discrimination law, and employment law – contain an explicit duty (or right) to reasonable accommodation. Also, the domestic courts' case law has so far provided no clear guidance on whether the prohibition of discrimination implies this right. The Bosnian Constitutional Court has indirectly addressed this issue in two cases involving the accommodation of religious practice in the public employment sector, but it has yet to be resolved through the Court's doctrinal engagement or, alternatively, appropriate legislative accommodations.

The provisions of applicable laws governing the work of police, judicial and in part civil servants remain controversial, especially as they contain a general ban on the exercise of religious beliefs in the workplace. Therefore, it is necessary to find appropriate solutions that will balance the individual right to freedom of religion and the principles of neutrality and impartiality.

Another area in which the regulatory framework affecting religion and the practice of religious accommodation needs to be improved is the healthcare sector. In particular, to ensure equal treatment of patients in terms of protecting their religious rights, hospitals across the country need to harmonize their internal policies and practice of religious accommodation.

Unfortunately, two and a half decades after the end of the war, there are still attacks on religious buildings and believers who make up a minority in a particular entity or place. In addition, members of minority religions in the Bosnian entity of Republic of Srpska (RS) are exposed to discrimination and unfavourable treatment in public schools, where they are often forced to participate in school day celebrations filled with the content and symbolism of the majority church.

The Bosnian Constitution did not regulate the relationship between the state and religious communities, but included important guarantees of religious freedom and equality of persons of different religious affiliation. However, the Constitutional Court of BiH confirmed the secular organization of the state and ruled out the possibility of providing privileged status or treatment to a certain church or religious community. The Court took into account the multi-religious character of Bosnian society, post-war discriminatory practice against religious minorities in the territory of the RS, as well as the principle of separation enshrined in the 2004 Law on Freedom of Religion. Namely, the law prohibits the establishment of one religion as state or official and requires equal treatment of religious communities in the country.

The separation of state and religion does not preclude state control and cooperation with religious communities. The terms of state control mainly concern the awarding of legal personality to religious communities through their registration with the Bosnian Ministry of Justice. The 2004 Law on Freedom of Religion established a two-tier registration system, distinguishing between traditional religious communities, those that acquired legal status before the law was enacted, and new religious organizations that must meet a certain set of criteria to be recognized as a legal entity.

The separation of state and religion should not be interpreted in the sense of strict state neutrality. On the contrary, the paradigm of separate spheres is complemented by the concept of mutual cooperation in areas of common interest such as education, culture, and charity. The terms of this cooperation are regulated by bilateral agreements between the state and religious communities. Apart from the fact that these agreements concretize legislative provisions of religious freedom and delineate the boundaries between the sacred and profane authorities, they tend to reinforce the position of traditional religious hierarchies *vis-à-vis* various institutional and ideological alternatives that flourished in the era of religious freedom.

However, the implementation of the cooperationist system that BiH opted for in the post-war period has not yet been completed. It has been hampered on the level of practical politics which is particularly evident in the dispute over the Draft Basic Agreement between BiH and the Islamic Community as well as poor implementation of already signed agreements with the two major churches in the country. Undoubtedly, resolving the dispute over the signing of an agreement with the Islamic Community and removing obstacles to the further implementation of already agreed agreements remains crucial for the further development of state-religion relations in the country.

However, there are also other aspects of the relations between the state and religious communities that need to be reconsidered. In the first place, favouring the SOC in the RS entity, which closely resembles the status of an official or established church, remains an anomaly in relation to the adopted principles of separation of state and religion and equality of religious communities at the state level. This favouring is manifested in a variety of areas, from government funding and the display of the church symbols in public institutions, to the inclusion of church ceremonies in the celebration of public holidays or days of government and public institutions, both at the entity and local levels.

The next issue of state-religion relations that requires attention concerns state financial aid to religious communities. Given the decentralized organization of the state, this aid is granted from different levels of government, from the state, through the entities, to the level of cantons (in FBiH), cities, and municipalities. In order to ensure a non-discriminatory treatment of religious communities in terms of state financial aid, envisaged by the 2004 state religion law, it is necessary to work on the harmonization of criteria for awarding aid, as well greater transparency in the distribution of aid at certain levels of government. Also, the 2004 Law on Freedom of Religion created an obligation of state to regulate the health, pension and disability insurance of religious officials. However, so far there have been no concrete responses from the state to several initiatives launched by religious communities to ensure the implementation of the outlined provision.

While in most issues concerning the registration and recognition of a legal personality of religious collectivities, the Bosnian religion law is comparable to other national laws in Europe, some of its aspects raises dilemmas about their compliance with international human rights standards. This primarily applies to the prescribing of a relatively high numerical criterion for the registration of a religious community, as well as the lack of clear normative instructions on the legality of the work of religious groups that are not registered with the Ministry of Justice of BiH or operate under the laws on associations. The tension between the demands for the preservation of religious pluralism as a necessary feature of a democratic society, on the one hand, and the preference given to state-recognized traditional religious communities, on the other hand, is particularly noticeable in the state's attitude towards the operation of informal religious groups.

Given these findings of the legislative framework, as well as the evolving practice of domestic courts, it can be concluded that in post-war BiH, the development of a cooperation model can be traced, albeit burdened with various challenges. While the separation of religion and state remains crucial for the effective protection of religious freedom and equality in a multi-ethnic/multi-religious Bosnian society, their cooperation in social fields of common interest can be seen as acknowledging the country's high religiosity and learning from the unpleasant experiences of the communist past.

Bibliography

Ademović, Nedim, ed., *Doktrinarni i praktični aspekti odnosa između države, crkava/vjerskih zajednica i pojedinca* [*Doctrinal and Practical Aspects of the Relationship between the State, Churches/Religious Communities and the Individual*] (Sarajevo: European Academy for Applied Research and Education in BiH, 2012).

Advisory Committee on the Framework Convention for the Protection of National Minorities, *Third Opinion on Bosnia and Herzegovina Adopted on 7 March 2013*, www.coe.int/en/web/minorities/bosnia-and-herzegovina.

Agencija za statistiku Bosne i Hercegovine, "Analiza: Država Bosna i Hercegovina," [Analysis: State of Bosnia and Herzegovina] www.statistika.ba/.

Agency for Gender Equality of BiH, "Reakcija na postupanje VSTV," [Reaction to the HJPC's Actions] https://arsbih.gov.ba/reakcija-na-postupanje-vstv-bih/.

Ahdar, Rex and Aroney, Nicholas, *Shari'a in the West* (New York: Oxford University Press, 2010).

Alibašić, Ahmet, "History of Inter-Religious Dialogue in Bosnia and Herzegovina: From Force-Feeding to Sustainability?" *Interdisciplinary Journal for Religion and Transformation in Contemporary Society* 6, no. 2 (2020): 343–364.

Alibašić, Ahmet, "Notes from the Meeting of the *Riyasat*'s Commission for Negotiations with the CMBiH held on July 19, 2016."

Alibašić, Ahmet, ed., *Religija i sekularna država: Uloga i značaj religije u sekularnom društvu iz muslimanske, kršćanske i jevrejske perspektive sa fokusom na Jugoistočnu Evropu* [Religion and the Secular State: The Role and Significance of Religion in Secular Society from a Muslim, Christian and Jewish Perspective with a Focus on Southeast Europe] (Sarajevo: Konrad Adenauer Foundation–Representation in BiH, European Abrahamic Forum, and Interreligious Institute in BiH, 2007).

Alibašić, Ahmet, "Religious Education in Public Schools in Bosnia and Herzegovina: Towards a Model Supporting Coexistence and Mutual Understanding," file:///C:/Users/Nedim/Downloads/Religious_Education_in_Bosnian_Public_Sc.pdf.

Alibašić, Ahmet and Begović, Nedim, "Reframing the Relations Between State and Religion in Post – War Bosnia: Learning to Be Free!" *Journal of Balkan and Near Eastern Studies* 19, no. 1 (2017): 19–34.

Arnautović, Marija, "Pokrivene žene: Zabrana nikaba je kršenje ljudskih prava," [Veiled Women: Banning the Niqab Is a Violation of Human Rights] www.slobodnaevropa.org/a/nikab_sarajevo_zene_protest/2109951.html.

Augustinović, Marija, "Travnički muftija: Nelegalni vjerski objekti biće birga države," [Mufti of Travnik: Illegal places of worship shall be the state's concern] 2 February 2016, www.slobodnaevropa.org/a/travnicki-muftija-nelegalni-vjerski-objekti-bice-briga-drzave/27527745.html.

Bacquet, Sylvie, *Religious Symbols and the Intervention of the Law: Symbolic Functionality in Pluralist States* (London and New York: Taylor & Francis Limited, 2021).

BBC, "Bosnia Women Protest at Ban on Headcarf," www.bbc.com/news/world-europe-35518768.

Bećirović, Denis, *Islamska zajednica u Bosni i Hercegovini za vrijeme avnojevske Jugoslavije (1945–1953)* [Islamic Community in Bosnia and Herzegovina During Avnojevska Yugoslavia (1945–1953)] (Zagreb and Sarajevo: Bosniak National Community for the City of Zagreb and Zagreb County, the Islamic Community in Croatia and the Institute of History Sarajevo, 2012).

Begović, Nedim, "Bosnia and Herzegovina," in *Yearbook of Muslims in Europe*, ed. Oliver Scharbrodt (Leiden and Boston: Brill, 2019), vol. 10, 132–133.

Begović, Nedim, "Freedom of Religion or Belief: Bosnian Muslim Engagement with a Fundamental Human Right," *Context – Journal of Interdisciplinary Studies* 7, no. 1 (2020): 63–83.

Begović, Nedim, "Freedom of Religion in the Workplace: The European Court of Human Rights Decisions on Applications Made by Muslim Apellants," *Journal of Muslims in Europe* 10, no. 2 (2021): 168–188.

Begović, Nedim, *Vjerska sloboda i muslimanske manjine u Evropi* [Religious Freedom and Muslim Minorities in Europe] (Sarajevo: El-Kalem, 2015).

Begović, Nedim, "Vjerski simboli u javnoj sferi: uporednopravna perspektiva," [Religious Symbols in Public Sphere: A Comparative Legal Perspective] *Novi Muallim* 12, no. 45 (2011): 43–50.

Berry, Stephanie E., "Freedom of Religion and Religious Symbols: Same Right–Different Interpretation?" 2021, www.ejiltalk.org/freedom-of-religion-and-religious-symbols-same-right-different-interpretation/.

Bishops' Conference of BiH, "Reaction of the Bishops' Conference of BiH to the Statements of Patriarch Irinej," 15 February 2016, www.ktabkbih.net/info.asp?id=63411.

Blažević, Velimir, *Vodič kroz crkveno pravo za vjernike* [The Guide Through the Church Law for the Faithful] (Sarajevo: Svjetlo riječi, 2007).

BLIC, "A Judge in Sarajevo Was Reported for an Easter Egg on the Table," 6 February 2018, Accessed 11 February 2021, www.blic.rs/vesti/republika-srpska/sudiju-u-sarajevu-prijavili-zbog-vaskrsnjeg-jajeta-na-stolu/x19s6qb.

"Bosna se nastoji prikazati kao katolička zemlja u kojoj su Bošnjaci strani elemenat," [Bosnia is sought to be portrayed as a Catholic country in which Bosniaks are a foreign element] https://hamdocamo.wordpress.com/2017/04/05/bosna-se-nastoji-prikazati-kao-katolicka-zemlja-2/.

Büchler, Andrea, *Islamic Law in Europe? Legal Pluralism and Its Limits in European Family Laws* (Farnham: Ashgate, 2011).

Če, N., "Grad Doboj obilježio Krsnu slavu," [The City of Doboj Celebrated the Baptismal Feast] accessed 24 January 2021, https://avaz.ba/vijesti/bih/510471/grad-doboj-obiljezio-krsnu-slavu-kumovao-milorad-dodik.

Census of Population, Households and Dwellings in Bosnia and Herzegovina: Final Results (Sarajevo: Agency for Statistics of Bosnia and Herzegovina, 2016), www.popis.gov.ba/popis2013/doc/RezultatiPopisa_BS.pdf.

Club of MPs of the SNSD, Proposal of the Law on the Prohibition of Wearing Clothes That Prevent Identification of 9 April 2010, file:///C:/Users/Nedim/Downloads/Prijedlog%20zakona%20o%20zabrani%20no%C5%A1enja%20odje%C4%87e%20koja%20onemogu%C4%87ava%20identifikaciju.pdf.

Commission on Security and Cooperation in Europe, *Bosnia and Herzegovina's Draft Religion Law: Draft Text Fails to Meet OSCE Commitments on Religious Freedom* (Washington: Commission on Security and Cooperation in Europe, 2003).

Council of Ministers of Bosnia and Herzegovina (CMBiH), The Bill on Non-Working Days During Religious Holidays in BiH, no. 05–02–2513/13, 30 September 2013.

Curtit, Françoise and Fornerod, Anne, "State Support for Religions: European Regulation," in *Public Funding of Religions in Europe*, ed. Francis Messner (London and New York: Routledge, 2015), 3–22.

Cvitković, Ivan, "Sloboda podrazumijeva ne samo slobodu religije već i slobodu od religije," [Freedom Entails Not Only Freedom of Religion but also Freedom from Religion] *Diskursi* 3, no. 4 (2013): 11–27.

Dakin, B., "*The Islamic Community in Bosnia and Herzegovina v. The Republika Srpska*: Human Rights in a Multi-Ethnic Bosnia," *Harvard Human Rights Journal* (2002): 245–268.

Dedović, Salem, "Izgradnja križeva u Stocu je kamen smutnje," [The construction of crosses in Stolac is a stone of trouble] https://tuzlalive.ba/izgradnja-krizeva-u-stocu-je-kamen-smutnje/.

Demir, Elma, *Diskriminacija u oblasti rada u Bosni i Hercegovini*, [Discrimination in the Field of Work in Bosnia and Herzegovina] (Sarajevo: Association for Democratic Initiatives, 2015).

Dini islam – Pitanja i odgovori, "Bračno pravo," [Matrimonial Law] www.islamskazajednica.ba/bracno-pravo.

Dini islam – Pitanja i odgovori, "Nemogućnost šerijatskog prije općinskog vjenčanja," [Impossibility of Sharia Wedding Before Civil One] www.islamskazajednica.ba/bracno-pravo/1900-nemogust-serijatskog-prije-opskog-vjenja.

Dini islam – Pitanja i odgovori, "O građanskom i šerijatskom vjenčanju," [On Civil and Sharia Wedding] www.rijaset.ba/index.php?option=com_content&view=article&id=5434:o-graanskom-i-erijatskom-vjenanju&catid=142&Itemid=538.

Dini islai – Pitanja i odgovori, "Odgađanje/neobavljanje građanskog vjenčanja," [Delaying/Non-Concluding Civil Wedding] www.islamskazajednica.ba/bracno-pravo/15914-odgadanje-neobavljanje-gradanskog-vjencanja.

Dini islam – Pitanja i odgovori, "Procedura prilikom razvoda braka i odustajanja od mehra," [Procedure for Divorce and Forgoing the *Mahr*] www.islamskazajednica.ba/bracno-pravo/23663-procedura-prilikom-razvoda-braka-i-odustajanje-od-mehra.

Dini islam – Pitanja i odgovori, "Razvod braka," [Divorce] www.islamskazajednica.ba/bracno-pravo/2675-razvod-braka.

Dini islami – Pitanja i odgovori, "Razvod braka bez pristanka muža," [Divorce Without the Consent of the Husband] www.islamskazajednica.ba/bracno-pravo/6831-razvod-braka-bez-pristanka-mua.

Dini islam – Pitanja i odgovori, "Razvod pa vjenčanje," [Divorce and then Wedding] www.islamskazajednica.ba/bracno-pravo/4834-razvod-pa-vjenanje-.

Dini islam – Pitanja i odgovori, "Razvod riječima," [Verbal Divorce] www.islamskazajednica.ba/bracno-pravo/3575-razvod-rijea.

Dini islam – Pitanja i odgovori, "Razvod samo šerijatski sklopljenog braka," [Divorce of Sharia-only Marriage] www.islamskazajednica.ba/bracno-pravo/8416-razvod-samo-erijatski-sklopljenog-braka.

Dini islami – Pitanja i odgovori, "Sklapanje tajnog braka," [Contracting a Secret Marriage] www.islamskazajednica.ba/bracno-pravo/24683-sklapanje-tajnog-braka.

Dini islami – Pitanja i odgovori, "Šerijatski razvod braka," [Sharia Divorce] www.islamskazajednica.ba/bracno-pravo/18903-serijatski-razvod-braka.

Dini islam – Pitanja i odgovori, "Šerijatski stav o poligamiji u BiH," [Sharia Stance Toward Poligamy in BiH] www.islamskazajednica.ba/bracno-pravo/17770-serijatski-stav-o-poligamiji-u-bih.

Dini islami – Pitanja i odgovori, "Šerijatsko sklapanje braka prije općinskog," [Sharia Wedding Before the Municipal One] www.islamskazajednica.ba/bracno-pravo/23464-serijatsko-sklapanje-braka-prije-opcinskog.

Dini islam – Pitanja i odgovori, "Šerijatsko vjenčanje," [Sharia Wedding] www.islamskazajednica.ba/bracno-pravo/6233-erijastsko-vjenanje.

Dini islam – Pitanja i odgovori, "Šerijatsko vjenčanje između osoba koje nisu punoljetne," [Sharia Wedding Between Minor Persons] www.islamskazajednica.ba/bracno-pravo/18498-serijatsko-vjencanje-izmedu-osoba-koje-nisu-punoljetne.

Dini islam – Pitanja i odgovori, "Šerijatsko vjenčanje prije građanskog," [Shari'a Wedding Before Civil One].

Dini islam – Pitanja i odgovori, "Tajna šerijatska vjenčanja," [Secret Sharia Weddings] www.islamskazajednica.ba/bracno-pravo/10699-tajna-erijatska-vjenanja.

Dini islam – Pitanja i odgovori, "Tajno sklapanje šerijatskog braka," [Concluding Sharia Marriage in Secrecy] www.islamskazajednica.ba/bracno-pravo/28621-2020-tajno-sklapanje-serijatskog-braka-2020.

Dini islami – Pitanja i odgovori, "Vjenčanje s osobom koja nije sudski razvedena," [Marrying a Person Who Is Not Civilly Divorced] www.islamskazajednica.ba/bracno-pravo/18829-vjencanje-s-osobom-koja-nije-sudski-razvedena.

Dizdarević, V. Zija, "Zvona nad državom," [Bells Over the State] www.pcnen.com/portal/2007/08/21/zvona-nad-drzavom/.

Doe, Norman, *Law and Religion in Europe: A Comparative Introduction* (New York: Oxford University Press, 2011).

Durham, W. Cole, Jr. and Ferrari, Silvio, eds., *Laws on Religion and the State in Post-Communist Europe* (Leuven: Peeters, 2004).

Durham, W. Cole, Jr. and Scharffs, Brett G., *Law and Religion: National, International, and Comparative Perspectives* (New York: Aspen Publishers, 2010).

Džananović, Ibrahim, *Primjena šerijatskog porodičnog prava kroz praksu Vrhovnog šerijatskog suda u Sarajevu* [The Application of Sharia Family Law in the Case Law of the Supreme Sharia Court in Sarajevo] (Sarajevo: Faculty of Islamic Studies, 2004).

Editors of Encyclopaedia, "Millet," *Encyclopedia Britannica*, 7 September 2010, www.britannica.com/topic/millet-religious-group.

Elbasani, Arolda, "Governing Islam in Plural Societies: Religious Freedom, State Neutrality and Traditional Heritage," *Journal of Balkan and Near Eastern Studies* 19, no. 1 (2017): 4–18.

"Entity: FBiH," www.statistika.ba/?lang=en#link2.

"Entity: RS," www.statistika.ba/?lang=en#link3.

European Court of Human Rights – Research Division, *Overview of the Court's Case-Law on Freedom of Religion*, 2013, www.echr.coe.int/Documents/Research_report_religion_ENG.pdf.

Evans, Jonathan and Baronavski, Chris, "How Do European Countries Differ in Religious Commitment? Use Our Interactive Map to Find Out," 2018, accessed 1 May 2020, www.pewresearch.org/fact-tank/2018/12/05/how-do-european-countries-differ-in-religious-commitment/.

Federal Ministry of Culture and Sports, "Pregled korisnika sredstava po transferima – 2014. god," [Review of beneficiaries by transfers–2014] www.fmks.gov.ba/download/2014/pregledkorisnikasredstava/ministarstvo/004.pdf.

Ferrari, Silvio, "State-Supported Display of Religious Symbols in the Public Space," *Journal of Catholic Legal Studies* 52, no. 7 (2013): 11–12.

Ferrari, Silvio and Durham, W. Cole, Jr. eds., *Law and Religion in Post-Communist Europe* (Leuven: Peeters, 2003).

"Fetva-i emin," [Fatwa-amin] www.islamskazajednica.ba/fetva-i-emin.

Flere, Sergej, Lavrič, Miran and Djordjević, Dragoljub B., "Religious References in the Constitution of European Post-Communist Countries and Ethno-symbolism," *Journal of Church and State* 59, no. 3 (2017): 466–488.

Gavison, Ruth and Perez, Nahshon, "Days of Rest in Multicultural Societies: Private, Public, Separate?" In *Law and Religion in Theoretical and Historical Context*, eds. Peter Cane, Carolyn Evans and Zoë Robinson (Cambridge: Cambridge University Press, 2008),186–213.

Halimović, Dženana, "Prijedlog o zabrani nikaba podijelio političare u BiH," [The Proposal to Ban the Niqab Divided Politicians in BiH] 28 July 2010, www.slobodnaevropa.org/a/prijedlog_o_zabrani_nikaba_podijelio_politicare_u_bih/2112389.html.

Hanušić, Adrijana, *The Ombudsman in the System of Protection Against Discrimination in BiH: Situation Analysis and Characteristic Problems* (Sarajevo: Analitika – Center for Social Research, 2012).

Hasani, Mustafa and Begović, Nedim, "Praksa šerijatskih vjenčanja u Islamskoj zajednici u Bosni i Hercegovini," [The Practice of 'Sharia Wedding' in the Islamic Community in Bosnia and Herzegovina] *Glasnik Rijaseta Islamske zajednice u Bosni i Hercegovini* LXIII, no. 11–12 (2014): 1124–1137.

"HDZ u mukama: Federalna inspekcija naredila uklanjanje križeva u Stocu," [HDZ in Agony: Federal Inspection Orders Removal of Crosses in Stolac] www.zasrebrenicu.ba/hdz-u-mukama-federalna-inspekcija-naredila-uklanjanje-krizeva-u-stocu.za.

HJPC, Memorandum, "Wearing Religious Marks in Judicial Institutions – Analysis," published on 19 February 2016, https://translate.google.com/translate?hl=bs&prev=_t&sl=bs&tl=en&u=www.pravosudje.ba/vstv/faces/vijesti.jsp%3Fid%3D59614.

Hogić, Nedim, *Pravosudni sistem u Bosni i Hercegovini* [Judicial System in Bosnia and Herzegovina] (Sarajevo: Foundation for the Development of Media and Civil Society "Mediacentar," 2014).

Howard, Erica, *Law and the Wearing of Religious Symbols in Europe* (London: Routledge, 2019).

Howard, Erica, *Law and the Wearing of Religious Symbols: European Bans on the Wearing of Religious Symbols in Education* (Abingdon: Routledge, 2012).

Ibišević, H., "Previranja u Starokatoličkoj crkvi kod Živinica prijete da prerastu u međunarodni skandal," [The turmoil in the Old Catholic Church near Živinice threatens to grow into an international scandal] http://tip.ba/2014/06/17/previranja-u-starokatolickoj-crkvi-kod-zivinica-prijete-da-prerastu-u-medunarodni-skandal/.

Imamović, Mustafa, *Historija Bošnjaka* [History of Bosniaks] (Sarajevo: Bošnjačka zajednica kulture, 1997).

Institution of the Human Rights Ombudsman of Bosnia and Herzegovina, *2017 Annual Report on the Results of the Activities of the Institution of the Human Rights Ombudsman of Bosnia and Herzegovina* (Banja Luka, 2018), www.ombudsmen.gov.ba/documents/obmudsmen_doc2018030810344228eng.pdf.

Institution of the Human Rights Ombudsman of Bosnia and Herzegovina, *2018 Annual Report on the Results of the Activities of the Institution of the Human Rights*

Ombudsman of Bosnia and Herzegovina (Banja Luka, 2019), www.ombudsmen.gov.ba/documents/obmudsmen_doc2019030109434379eng.pdf.

Institution of Human Rights Ombudsman of Bosnia and Herzegovina, *2019 Annual Report on the Results of the Activities of the Institution of the Human Rights Ombudsman of Bosnia and Herzegovina* (Banja Luka, 2020), www.ombudsmen.gov.ba/documents/obmudsmen_doc2020051813152592eng.pdf.

Interreligious Council in Bosnia and Herzegovina, "O nama," [About Us] https://mrv.ba/o-nama-2/.

IRC, "Osuda napada na Riječansku džamiju u Zvorniku," [Condemnation of the attack on the Riječanska mosque in Zvornik] https://avaz.ba/vijesti/bih/505172/osuda-napada-na-rijecansku-dzamiju-u-zvorniku.

Jurišić, Pavo, ed., *Dvoje njih bit će jedno tijelo: Zbornik radova s okruglog stola o braku i bračnoj zajednici iz perspektive vjerskih zajednica i civilnog zakonodavstva* [The two of them will be one body: Proceedings of the round table on marriage and marital union from the perspective of religious communities and civil legislation] (Sarajevo: Caritas of the Bishop Conference of BiH, 2009).

Jusić, Muhamed, "Bosnia and Herzegovina," in *Yearbook of Muslims in Europe*, ed. Oliver Scharbrodt (Leiden: Brill, 2018), vol. 9, 121–141.

Jusić, Muhamed, Smajić, Aid and Fazlović, Muhamed, "Bosnia and Herzegovina," in *Yearbook of Muslims in Europe*, ed. Oliver Scharbrodt (Leiden: Brill, 2017), vol. 8, 119–142.

Karčić, Fikret, "Zašto ne treba zakonom zabraniti nikab," [Why Shouldn't the Niqab Be Banned by Law] www.islamskazajednica.ba/aktuelno-arhiva/9294-zato-ne-treba-zakonom-zabraniti-nikab.

Karčić, Fikret, *Historija šerijatskog prava* [History of Sharia law] (Sarajevo: Fakultet islamskih nauka, 2005).

Karčić, Fikret, *The Other European Muslims: A Bosnian Experience* (Sarajevo: Center for Advanced Studies, 2015).

Karčić, Fikret, *Religija i pravo: Kratak uvod* [Religion and Law: A Short Introduction] (Sarajevo: Center for Advanced Studies, 2011).

Karčić, Fikret, "Vakufi i reprivatizacija," [Waqfs and reprivatization] *Gazette of the Riyasat of the Islamic Community in the SFRY*, no. 3 (1991): 267–272.

Karčić, Harun, *Šerijat i pravni pluralizam u Evropi: Primjeri koegzistencije religijskog i sekularnog prava na starom kontinentu* [Sharia and Legal Pluralism in Europe: Examples of Coexistence of Religious and Secular Law on the Old Continent] (Sarajevo: Centar za napredne studije, 2018).

Katana, Gordana, "Postaje li RS društvo u kojem nesrbi i 'nevjernici' nemaju izbora: Diskriminacija po svetosavlju," [Is the RS becoming a society in which non-Serbs and 'non-believers' have no choice: Discrimination based on the celebration of Saint Sava] https://inforadar.ba/postaje-li-rs-drustvo-u-kojem-nesrbi-i-nevjernici-nemaju-izbora-diskriminacija-po-svetosavlju/.

Katayoun, Alidadi, *Religion, Equality and Employment in Europe: The Case for Reasonable Accommodation* (Oxford and Portland: Hart, 2017).

Kovačević, Emir, "Za ili protiv vjerskih obilježja u pravosudnim institucijama u BiH," [For or Against Religious Symbols in Judicial Institutions in BiH] *Sveske za javno pravo* 7, no. 24 (2016): 29–32.

Koženjakin, Boris, "Jewish Community of Bosnia and Herzegovina," in *Religions in Bosnia and Herzegovina: Profile of Religious Communities and Churches* (Sarajevo: Interreligious Council in Bosnia and Herzegovina, 2012), 177–217.

Kuburić, Zorica and Moe, Christian, *Religion and Pluralism in Education: Comparative Approaches in the Western Balkans* (Novi Sad: CEIR and Kotor Network, 2006).

Kulenović, Nedim, *Court as a Policy-Maker? The Role and Effects of the Constitutional Court of Bosnia and Herzegovina in Democratic Transition and Consolidation* (Sarajevo: Analitika – Center for Social Research, 2016).

Kurtović, Amila, "Zabrane nošenja vjerskih obilježja na radnom mjestu," [Prohibitions on wearing religious symbols in the workplace] (Sarajevo: Analitika – Center for Social Research, 2018).

Lapandić, Nermin, "Pravo vojnih lica na slobodu vjere u oružanim snagama Bosne i Hercegovine," [The Right of Military Personnel to Freedom of Religion in the Armed Forces of Bosnia and Herzegovina] *Context* 1, no. 2 (2014): 55–74.

Lenhof, Lance S., "Freedom of Religious Association: The Right of Religious Organizations to Obtain Legal Entity Status Under the European Convention," *BYU Law Review*, no. 2 (2005): 561–609.

Lindholm, Tore, Durham, W. Cole, Jr. and Tahzib-Lie, Bahia G., eds., *Facilitating Freedom of Religion or Belief: A Deskbook* (Leiden: Martinus Nijhoff Publishers, 2004).

M. Er., "Poslije nekoliko mjeseci skrivanja dokumenta: Pogledajte Ugovor Islamske zajednice i BiH," [After a few months of hiding the document: See the agreement of Islamic Community and BiH] www.klix.ba/vijesti/bih/poslije-nekoliko-mjeseci-skrivanja-dokumenta-pogledajte-ugovor-islamske-zajednice-i-bih/151108064.

Malcolm, Noel, *Bosna: Kratka povijest* [Bosnia: A Short History] (Sarajevo: Buybook, 2011).

Marasović, Silvija, Klarić, Mirko and Balić, Ante, "Crkveni porez kao oblik financiranja djelatnosti vjerskih zajednica," [Church Tax as a Form of Financing the Activities of Religious Communities] *Zbornik radova Pravnog fakulteta u Splitu* 44, no. 3–4 (2007): 573–596.

McCrudden, Christopher and Prechal, Sacha, *The Concepts of Equality and Non-Discrimination in Europe: A Practical Approach* (European Network of Legal Experts in the Field of Gender Equality, 2009).

Mehdi, Rubya, Peterson, Hanne, Sand, Erik Reenberg and Woodman, Gordon R. eds., *Law and Religion in Multicultural Societies* (Copenhagen: DJOF Publishing, 2008).

Messner, Francis, ed., *Public Funding of Religions in Europe* (London and New York: Routledge, 2015).

Miličević, Neđo, "Sloboda vjere i vjeroispovijedanja," in *Godišnjak Pravnog fakulteta u Sarajevu* (Sarajevo: Pravni fakultet, 2004), 252–271.

Milojević, Milorad, "Ko lomi pogaču za crkveno-državne praznike u Republici Srpskoj," [Who Breaks the Bread for Church-State Holidays in Republika Srpska] (Sarajevo: Radio slobodna Evropa, 2019), www.slobodnaevropa.org/a/cijena-crkveno-drzavnih-praznika-u-rs/30287097.html.

Moravčíková, Michaela and Valová, Eleónora, eds., *Financing Churches and Religious Communities in the 21st Century* (Bratislava: Institute for State-Church Relations, 2010).

Muratagić, Jasmin, "Implikacije zaključka Visokog sudskog i tužilačkog vijeća BiH o zabrani isticanja vjerskih obilježja u pravosudnim institucijama," [Implications of the Conclusion of the High Judicial and Prosecutorial Council of BiH on the Prohibition of Display of Religious Insignia in the Judicial Institutions] http://fcjp.ba/templates/ja_avian_ii_d/images/green/Jasmin_Muratagic3.pdf.

Murdoch, Jim, *Protecting the Right to Freedom of Thought, Conscience and Religion Under the European Convention on Human Rights* (Strasbourg: Council of Europe, 2012).

Mušinović, E., "O navodnom uvođenju šerijata u BiH: Kako su regulisana prava na hadž, džumu i odijevanje," [Alleged Introduction of Sharia in BiH: How the Rights to Observe Hajj, Jumua and Dress Were Regulated] www.klix.ba/vijesti/bih/o-navodnom-uvodjenju-serijata-u-bih-kako-su-regulisana-prava-na-hadz-dzumu-i-odijevanje/151009046.

Obrenović, Mladen, "Finansiranje vjerskih zajednica: od državne kase do prodaje vina, sira ...," [Funding of Religious Communities: From the State Treasury to the Sale of Wine, Cheese ...] https://balkans.aljazeera.net/teme/2017/12/17/finansiranje-vjerskih-zajednica-od-drzavne-kase-do-prodaje-vina-sira.

Office of Mufti of Mostar, "Izgradnja križeva u Stocu upitna: Reagovalo Muftijstvo mostarsko, građani potpisuju peticiju," [The Construction of Crosses in Stolac Is Questionable: The Office of Mufti of Mostar Reacted, Citizens Sign a Petition] https://okanal.oslobodjenje.ba/okanal/vijesti/izgradnja-krizeva-u-stocu-upitna-regovalo-muftijstvo-mostarsko-gradjani-potpisuju-peticiju-7843.

Office of Parliamentary Military Commissioner of Bosnia and Herzegovina, Report on the Work of the Parliamentary Military Commissioner of Bosnia and Herzegovina for 2013, 2 February 2014, file:///C:/Users/Nedim/Downloads/Izvjestaj%20o%20radu%20Parl.vojnog%20pov.%20za%202013.-B.pdf.

Organization for Security and Co-operation in Europe (OSCE), Office for Democratic Institutions and Human Rights (ODIHR) and Venice Commission, *Guidelines on the Legal Personality of Religious or Belief Communities* (Warsaw: OSCE Office for Democratic Institutions and Human Rights (ODIHR), 2014), www.osce.org/odihr/139046?download=true.

Panel of Experts on Freedom of Religion or Belief of the Office for Democratic Institutions and Human Rights (ODIHR) of the Organization for Security and Co-operation in Europe (OSCE) in consultation with the European Commission for Democracy through Law (the Venice Commission) of the Council of Europe, *Guidelines for Review of Legislation Pertaining to Religion or Belief*, June 18–19, 2004.

Parolin, Pietro, "Temeljni ugovor između Svete Stolice i Bosne i Hercegovine u odnosu prema pravoslavnoj i muslimanskoj zajednici," [Basic Agreement Between the Holy See and Bosnia and Herzegovina in Relation to the Orthodox and Muslim Community] www.ktabkbih.net/info.asp?id=20630.

Perić, Dimšo, "Bračno pravo Srpske pravoslavne crkve," [Matrimonial Law of the Serbian Orthodox Church] In *Uporedna religijska prava*, ed. Fikret Karčić (Sarajevo: Faculty of Islamic Studies in Sarajevo, 2005), 237–265.

"Proslavljen Vidovdan – krsna slava Vojske Republike Srpske i 3. pješadijskog (Republika Srpska) puka," [Vidovdan Is Celebrated – the Baptismal Feast of the Army of the Republika Srpska and the 3rd Infantry (Republic of Srpska) Regiment] http://os.mod.gov.ba/o-oruzanim-snagama-bih/tradicija/3-pjesadijski-puk-os-bih/vijesti/default.aspx?id=16798&langTag=bs-BA.

Račius, Egdūnas, *Islam in Post-communist Eastern Europe: Between Churchification and Securitization* (Leiden and Boston: Brill, 2020).

Redaction, "Brojne reakcije javnosti zbog zabrane nošenja vjerskih obilježja," [Numerous Reactions from the Public Due to the Ban on Wearing Religious Symbols] www.diskriminacija.ba/vijesti/brojne-reakcije-javnosti-zbog-zabrane-no%C5%A1enja-vjerskih-obilje%C5%BEja.

"Religion 2013," www.statistika.ba/?show=8#link3.

RTRS, "U školama širom Srpske obilježen Savindan," [Savindan Was Celebrated in Schools throughout Srpska] https://lat.rtrs.tv/vijesti/vijest.php?id=367612.

RTRS, "Ugovor sa IZ – BiH se udaljava od sekularne države," [Agreement with the IC – BiH Is Moving Away from a Secular State] www.frontal.ba/novost/81161/ugovor-sa-iz-bih-se-udaljava-od-sekularne-drzave.

RTRS, "Uzbuna u Srpskoj: Sarajevo želi šerijatske propise na nivou BiH," [Alert in Srpska: Sarajevo Wants Sharia Regulations at the BiH Level] www.kurir.rs/region/bosna-i-hercegovina/uzbuna-u-srpskoj-sarajevo-zeli-serijatske- propise-na-nivou-bih-clanak-1958623.

Russo, Charles J., "Religion and Education in Bosnia: Integration Not Segregation?" *BYU Law Review*, no. 3 (2000): 945–966.

S. A., "Haos u Stocu: "Nećete graditi nelegalne križeve po Starom gradu!" [Chaos in Stolac: "You Will Not Build Illegal Crosses in the Old Town] https://novi.ba/clanak/17334/12.

S. H., "Čović i Ivanić zvanično odbili podržati ugovor države s Islamskom zajednicom u BiH," [Čović and Ivanić Officially Refused to Support the State's Agreement with the Islamic Community in BiH] www.klix.ba/vijesti/bih/covic-i-ivanic-zvanicno-odbili-podrzati-ugovor-drzave-s-islamskom-zajednicom-u-bih/180419073.

S. H., "Vlada u Sarajevu naredila: Jelovnike u javnim ustanovama prilagoditi vjerskim običajima," [The Government in Sarajevo Has Ordered: Menus in Public Institutions to Be Adjusted to Religious Customs] www.google.com/search?q=google+translate&oq=goo&aqs=chrome.1.69i60j69i59j0j69i59j69i57j69i60l3.1395j0j9&sourceid=chrome&ie=UTF-8.

Šarčević, Edin and Bojić, Drago, eds., *Sekularnost i religija: BiH i regija* [Secularity and Religion: BiH and Region] (Sarajevo: Fondacija Centar za javno pravo, 2015).

Sarkissian, Anni, "Religious Reestablishment in Post-Communist Polities," *Journal of Church and State* 51, no. 3 (2009): 472–501.

Simons, Greg and Westerlund, David, eds., *Religion, Politics and Nation-Building in Post-Communist Countries* (London and New York: Routledge, 2015).

Shachar, Ayelet, *Multicultural Jurisdictions: Cultural Differences and Women's Rights* (Cambridge: Cambridge University Press, 2001).

Skoko, Božo and Lučka, Dejan, *Povjerenje u medije i medijske slobode* [Trust in the Media and Media Freedoms] (Sarajevo: Friedrich-Ebert-Stiftung, 2017).

Srna, "Liturgijom počelo obilježavanje krsne slave grada Banja Luke," [The Celebration of the Baptism of the City of Banja Luka Began with the Liturgy] www.nezavisne.com/novosti/banjaluka/Liturgijom-pocelo-obiljezavanje-krsne-slave-grada-Banjaluka/542235

Stanisz, Piotr, Zawiślak, Michal and Ordon, Marta, eds., *Presence of the Cross in Public Spaces: Experiences of Selected European Countries* (Newcastle upon Tyne: Cambridge Scholars Publishing, 2016).

"Stočani na nogama zbog izgradnje križeva oko grada: Falsificiranje historije i kulturocid," [The Citizens of Stolac Are Protesting Against the Construction of Crosses Around the City: Falsification of History and Culturicide] www.klix.ba/vijesti/bih/stocani-na-nogama-zbog-izgradnje-krizeva-oko-grada-falsificiranje-historije-i-kulturocid/200128185.

"Stolac: Ne rušiti na Križevcu križa," [Stolac: Do Not Demolish the Cross on Križevac!] the Letter of Bishop Ratko Perić to Ramiz Mehmedagić, Minister of Spatial Planning of the FBiH of 17 July 2004, www.md-tm.ba/clanci/stolac-ne-rusiti-na-krizevcu-kriza.

Šurlan, Svjetlana, "Milionsku pomoć Srbije Vlada Republike Srpske podijelila crkvama," [The Government of the Republika Srpska Distributed Serbia's Million-Dollar Aid to Churches] www.capital.ba/milionsku-pomoc-donacija-srbije-vlada-republike-srpske-podijelila-crkvama-video/.

Temperman, Jeroen, ed., *The Lautsi Papers: Multidisciplinary Reflections on Religious Symbols in the Public School Classroom* (Leiden-Boston: Martinus Nijhoff Publishers, 2012).

Temperman, Jeroen, *State-Religion Relationships and Human Rights Law: Towards a Right to Religiously Neutral Governance* (Leiden and Boston: Martinus Nijhoff Publishers, 2010).

Temperman, Jeroen, Gunn, T. Jeremy and Evans, Malcolm D. eds., *The European Court of Human Rights and the Freedom of Religion or Belief: The 25 Years Since Kokkinakis* (Leiden: Brill, 2019).

Terzić, Sevima Sali, "Manifestacija vjerskih uvjerenja u pravosuđu: legitimno ograničavanje ili diskriminacija," [Manifestation of Religious Beliefs in the Judiciary: Legitimate Restriction or Discrimination] *Sveske za javno pravo* 7, no. 24 (2016): 8–21.

"U prisustvu velikog broja Zvorničana i gostiju: Litijom i lomljenjem slavskog kolača obilježena slava grada Zvornika," [In the Presence of a Large Number of Zvornik Residents and Guests: The Baptismal Feast of the City of Zvornik Was Marked with a Litany and the Breaking of the Feast Cake] http://infobirac.net/2019/08/08/u-prisustvu-velikog-broja-zvornicana-i-gostiju-litijom-i-lomljenjem-slavskog-kolaca-obiljezena-slava-grada-zvornika/.

UN Human Rights Committee (HRC), *CCPR General Comment No. 22: Article 18 (Freedom of Thought, Conscience or Religion)*, 30 July 1993, CCPR/C/21/Rev.1/Add.4, www.refworld.org/docid/453883fb22.html.

United Nations General Assembly: Human Rights Council, *Report of the Special Rapporteur on Freedom of Religion or Belief, Heiner Bielefeldt*, 22 December 2011, file:///C:/Users/User/Downloads/A-HRC-19–60_en.pdf.

U.S. Department of State – Bureau of Democracy, Human Rights, and Labor, *2016 Report on International Religious Freedom: Bosnia and Herzegovina*, https://d2v9ipibika81v.cloudfront.net/uploads/sites/270/2017/08/2016 International-Religious-Freedom-Report-BiH.pdf.

U.S. Department of State, Bureau of Democracy, Human Rights and Labor, *International Religious Freedom Report 2005, Bosnia and Herzegovina*, https://2009-2017.state.gov/j/drl/rls/irf/2005/51544.htm.

U.S. Department of State – Office of International Religious Freedom, *2020 Report on International Religious Freedom: Bosnia and Herzegovina*, https://ba.usembassy.gov/wp-content/uploads/sites/270/BOSNIA-AND-HERZEGOVINA-2020-INTERNATIONAL-RELIGIOUS-FREEDOM-REPORT.pdf.

U.S. Department of State – Office of International Religious Freedom, *2019 Report on International Religious Freedom: Bosnia and Herzegovina*, www.state.gov/reports/2019-report-on-international-religious-freedom/bosnia-and-herzegovina/.

"U školama širom Srpske obilježen Savindan," [Savindan Was Celebrated in Schools Throughout Srpska] https://lat.rtrs.tv/vijesti/vijest.php?id=367612.

Ulić, Jelena i Brajušković, Sandra, *Pregled nacionalnih sistema ustavnopravnih odnosa između države i crkve i uređenje imovinskih pitanja u nekoliko zemalja EU* [An Overview of National Systems of Constitutional Relations Between the State and the Church and the Regulation of Property Issues in Several EU Countries] (Podgorica: Istraživački centar Skupštine Crne Gore, 2019).

"Ustavnopravna komisija: Bez podrške zabrani nošenja odjeće koja onemogućava identifikaciju," [Constitutional and Legal Commission: No Support for a Ban on Wearing Clothing That Prevents Identification] https://vijesti.ba/clanak/12007/ustavnopravna-komisija-bez-podrske-zabrani-nosenja-odjece-koja-onemogucava-identifikaciju.

Van den Berg, Stephanie and Sterling, Toby, "Ex-Bosnian Serb Wartime Leader Karadzic Sentenced to Life in Prison," www.reuters.com/article/us-warcrimes-bosnia-karadzic-idUSKCN1R1003.

Vehabović, Faris, Izmirlija, Midhat and Kadribašić, Adnan, *Komentar Zakona o zabrani diskriminacije sa objašnjenjima i pregledom prakse u uporednom pravu* [Commentary on the Law on prohibition of discrimination with explanations and review of practice in comparative law] (Sarajevo: Center for Human Rights of University of Sarajevo, 2010).

Veselinović, Gojko, "Dan Republike Srpske i ovaj put mimo Ustava," [Republika Srpska Day and This Time Against the Constitution] www.slobodnaevropa.org/a/dan-rs-mimo-ustava/30366435.html.

Vukšić, Tomo, ed., *Crkva i država u Bosni i Hercegovini: Zakoni, podzakonski akti, ugovori i komentari* [Church and State in Bosnia and Herzegovina: Laws, By-laws, Agreements and Comments] (Sarajevo: Bishops Conference of Bosnia and Herzegovina, 2007).

Vukšić, Tomo, "Značenje Temeljnog ugovora između Svete Stolice i BiH te Dodatnog protokola na njega," [The Meaning of Basic Agreement Between the Holy See and Bosnia and Herzegovina and Additional Protocol on it] www.kuvn.org/upload/file/Temeljni%20ugovor.pdf.

Yeager, D., "The Human Rights Chamber for Bosnia and Herzegovina: A Case Study in Transitional Justice," *International Legal Perspectives* 14 (2004): 44–53.

Yilmaz Ihsan, *Muslim Laws, Politics and Society in Modern Nation States: Dynamic Legal Pluralisms in England, Turkey and Pakistan* (Aldershot and Burlington: Ashgate Publishing, 2005).

Zrinščak, Siniša, "Church, State and Society in Post-Communist Europe," in *Religion and the State: A Comparative Sociology*, eds. Jack Barbalet, Adam Possamai and Bryan S. Turner (London and New York: Athem Press, 2011), 157–182.

Zvijerac, Predrag, "Uz neustavni Dan RS: Sva svjetovna i vjerska praznovanja u BiH," [With the Unconstitutional Day of RS: All Secular and Religious Celebrations in BiH] www.slobodnaevropa.org/a/dan-republike-2021-srpske-praznici-bih/31038812.html.

Letters and interviews

Alibašić, Ahmet, e-mail Correspondence with Semiha Borovac, Minister of Human Rights and Refugees of BiH, 28 September 2014.

Alibašić, Ahmet, Member of the Negotiating Team, e-mail Correspondence with Amila Kahrović-Posavljak, Journalist of Magazine *BH Dani*, 21 October 2013.

Bosnian-Podrinje Canton of Goražde–Public Relations Service, Information no. 18-49-161-3/19, 15 August 2019.

Cabinet of the *ra'is al-ʿulama* of the IC, Conclusion of the Agreement Between Bosnia and Herzegovina and the Islamic Community in Bosnia and Herzegovina: A Letter to the PBiH, no. 01/R-09/10, 6 January 2010.

Čamdžić, Elvir, Employee of the PBiH, e-mail Correspondence with Mensur Karadža, Member of the Negotiation Team and Rifat Fetić, Chief of Staff of the *ra'is al-ʿulama* of the IC, 8 June 2017.

Central Bosnia Canton Travnik–Ministry of Health and Social Policy, Information no. 03–37–436/19–3, 3 October 2019.

Complaint to the Institution of the Ombudsman for Human Rights of BiH, no. Ž-BR-04–26/17, 30 January 2017.

Federal Ministry of Culture and Sport, Decision on Access to Information, no. 01/02–1–4677/19, 19 July 2019.

Federal Ministry of Health, Information no. 01–37–4342/19, 25 July 2019.

Foča University Hospital, Information no. a-1185/2, 23 July 2019.

Herceg-Bosna Canton–Ministry of Labor, Health, Social Welfare and Refugees, Information no. 09-01-49-46/18, 30 October 2018.

Herzegovina-Neretva Canton – Ministry of Health, Labor and Social Welfare, Information no. 06-02-39-1532/19, 23 July 2019.

HJPC, Letter no. 08-02-1-3163-1/2015, 21 October 2015.

HJPC, Letter no. 03-09-6-2008-2/2019, 5 June 2019.

Institution of Ombudsman for Human Rights of BiH, Response, no. Ž-SA-05–229/14, 3 March 2014.

Institution of Ombudsman for Human Rights of Bosnia and Herzegovina, Response no. Ž-SA-05–229/14, 3 March 2014.

Interview with Dr Ahmet Alibašić, Member of the Negotiating Team, Sarajevo, 30 June 2019.

Interview with Muhedin Garanović, Head of the Accounting and Finance Department of the Directorate for Economic and Financial Affairs of the *Riyasat* of the IC, Sarajevo, 29 October 2019.

Interview with Slavka Alagić, chief of Department for Registers of the MJ, Sarajevo, 21 August 2019.

MCA, Basic Agreement Between Bosnia and Herzegovina and the Islamic Community in Bosnia and Herzeogivna – Opinion: A Letter to the MHRR, no. br. 04-14-1-2394-EM/13, 11 June 2014.

MHRR, Appointment of a Negotiating Team on Behalf of the Islamic Community in Bosnia and Herzegovina: A Letter to the IC, no. 07-07-4546 1/11, 14 November 2011.

MHRR, Draft Agreement Between the Holy See and BiH on the Pastoral Care of Catholic Believers, Members of the Armed Forces of BiH: A Letter to the CMBiH, no. 01–38–7238/09, 12 December 2009.

MHRR, Information no. UP-I-05-07-7-25-3/19, 26 July 2019.

MHRR, Proposal of Basis for Negotiations with the Islamic Community in Bosnia and Herzegovina for Conclusion of the Basic Agreement Between Bosnia and Herzegovina and the Islamic Community in Bosnia and Herzegovina: A Letter to the CMBiH, 22 August 2011.

MHRR, Proposal for Regulating the Procedure of Concluding the Basic Agreement Between Bosnia and Herzegovina and the Islamic Community in Bosnia and Herzegovina: A Letter to the CMBiH, Document Not Numbered or Dated.

Ministry for Human Rights and Refugees – Department for Human Rights, Response to the Request for Information on the Issue of the Free Manifestation of Religion, 11 March 2014.

Ministry of Justice of the RS, Information no. 08.030/240–123/19, 3 October 2019.

MJ, Letter no. 09-02-4-5353/15, 27 May 2015.

MJ, Opinion on the Basic Agreement Between Bosnia and Herzegovina and the Islamic Community in Bosnia and Herzegovina: A Letter to the MHRR, no. 08-02-4-4320/14, 4 June 2014.

Municipality of Center Sarajevo, Decision on Access to information, no. 10–49–1355/19, 30 July 2019.

Municipality of Srebrenica – Department for Social Affairs and Public Services, Response to a Request for Access to Information, no. 06–1525/19, 22 July 2019.

Office of Legislation of the CMBiH, Opinion on the Draft Basis for Concluding Agreement Between the Islamic Community in Bosnia and Herzegovina and Bosnia and Herzegovina: A Letter to the MHRR, no. 01–02–293/11, 24 May 2011.

Republic Secretariat for Religions, Response to a Request for Access to Information, e-mail Sent to E. Kovačević on 8 October 2019.

Riyasat of the IC, Letter to the HJPC, no. 05–03–1476/16, 3 March 2016.

University Clinical Center of Republika Srpska, Information no. 01–10216–2/19, 8 August 2019.

University Clinical Hospital Mostar, Information no. 5393/19, 8 August 2019.

University of Tuzla, Notice: A Letter to the Institution of Ombudsman for Human Rights of BiH, no. 01–4813/17–1, 6 September 2017.

Zenica Penitentiary, Information: A Letter to the Institution of the Human Rights Ombudsman of BiH, no. 01–12–2344/15, 13 March 2015.

Zenica Penitentiary, Letter no. 01–12–2154/19, 20 August 2019.

Index

www.ingramcontent.com/pod-product-compliance
Lightning Source LLC
LaVergne TN
LVHW011134300926
849160LV00008B/644
9781032171302